P9-BJP-281

3 2301 00013930 7

The Vanishing People

ALSO BY KATHARINE BRIGGS

British Folktales

An Encyclopedia of Fairies:
Hobgoblins, Brownies, Bogies, and
Other Supernatural Creatures

The Vanishing People

Fairy Lore and Legends

Katharine Briggs

Illustrations by Mary I. French

PANTHEON BOOKS, NEW YORK

Library of Congress Cataloging in Publication Data
Briggs, Katharine Mary.
The Vanishing People.
Bibliography: pp. 203–6
Includes indexes.
  1. Fairies.   2. Fairy tales—History and
criticism.   I. Title.
GR549.B75 1978   398.2′1   78-53523
ISBN 0-394-50248-5

TO KATHARINE LAW AND CAROL DUFF

This is the first book written entirely at Southolme, so it is fitting that it should be dedicated to them, whose kindness and enthusiasm made it possible.

CONTENTS ❧❧❧❧❧❧❧❧❧❧❧❧❧❧❧

PREFACE ᏁᏁᏁᏁᏁᏁᏁᏁᏁᏁᏁᏁᏁ

THE VANISHING PEOPLE would seem to be an appropriate descriptive name for the fairies of tradition for two reasons. The first is that they are generally supposed to be visible, to those people who are able to see them, between one eye-blink and the next. Seventy years ago, in my childhood, one was often told not to fix one's eyes, presumably because this was interpreted as an effort to watch the fairies. An Irishman who had captured a Lepracaun could keep hold of him only so long as he did not glance aside for an instant. The fairies, if they wished, could made themselves visible to all but the most insensitive mortals and they also became visible to those who stepped into fairy territory or were in possession of a four-leafed clover. As we shall see, those who had anointed their eyes with fairy ointment could see them constantly, whether they had made themselves visible or not, but, as a rule, the fairies were supposed to have the power of appearing or vanishing at will. The other reason is that from the fourteenth century the fairies were supposed to have left the country, either recently or some time ago. Chaucer's Wife of Bath puts their departure 'manye hundred yeres ago', in King Arthur's time; 'But now can no man see none elves mo.'

In the seventeenth century Bishop Corbet puts them back into pre-Reformation England:

But since of late Elizabeth
    And later James came in,
They never danced on any heath
    As when the time have been.

Yet they still lingered on.

In the nineteenth century Hugh Miller recorded the final departure of the fairies from Scotland, a miserable and rather squalid cavalcade, the last of whom said, 'The People of Peace shall never more be seen in Scotland'. In Oxfordshire A. J. Evans, writing in *The Folk-Lore Journal*, told how an old man called Will Hughes had seen them dancing near the Rollright Stones and disappearing into a hole close to the King Stone. This was supposed to be their final disappearance from England, but even in the Midlands, now, in the twentieth century, with all its commitment to modern science and its own supersitions of extrasensory perceptions, of flying saucers and Loch Ness monsters, people still claim, rather diffidently, that they have encountered the fairies. As for Ireland and the

Highlands of Scotland they do not even pretend to think that they have gone, though it is often said that fewer people now believe in them. Truly it seems that they are always vanishing and always popping back again.

In this short study of fairy beliefs, I have dealt almost entirely with the traditions of Great Britain and Ireland, but we are an admixture of races here and it would be parochial and even misleading to confine ourselves to these islands alone, without a glance at the 'creatures of a middle nature between man and angels' who have exercised the imagination of our neighbours. In the first chapter which deals with a theme deeply rooted in Man's psychological experience, I have touched on the legends and beliefs about the supernatural passage of time which are to be found in other cultures. These have been only superficially touched on, however, and in other chapters I have contracted my scope to those supernatural creatures which may be thought to have blood relationship to the British fairies.

When we are disentangling oral traditions we are bound to find great variations in the names given and in the beliefs held about them. These occur not only individually and regionally but even sometimes in the same individual. Many people find no intellectual discomfort in holding two different, and even contrary beliefs, at the same time. They have possibly received information from different sources in their childhood and it has never occurred to them to try to reconcile them. Many of the differences are regional. For instance, the words *Pixies*, *Piskies* and *Pigsies* are used for almost indistinguishable creatures. The first is most commonly used in Somerset, the second in Cornwall and the last in Devon, but even this is not invariable. Theological differences sometimes entered into fairylore. For instance, the word *Hobgoblin* may puzzle many people. *Goblins* are generally taken to be evil and malicious spirits, hostile to mankind. *Hobs* and *lobs* are on the whole friendly towards men and ready to be kind to those who treat them civilly. The prefix *Hob* suggests a helpful spirit. Thus *Hobthrust* is a North Country Brownie and *Hobgoblins* are the great class of spirits who perform helpful labours for the country people. To most of the Puritans, however, all fairies were evil creatures, servants of the Devil, and Bunyan's 'Hobgoblin nor foul Fiend' has made a deep impression on our vocabulary. The early Christian missionaries, with whole tribes and nations to convert, extended a good deal of toleration to the more harmless pagan practices and beliefs. Some they Christianized successfully, but a good deal of undigested matter remained in the faith of the common people into late medieval times, which to the reformers appeared pure heathendom. We find this duality surviving in the fairy beliefs. Those who are bewildered by the profusion of fairy names will find a glossary of them in the appendix, which will help them to disentangle regional variations in the names from differences of character and function.

Readers who are interested in the international aspect of the fairy may find the lists of Type and Index Numbers at the end of the book useful and suggestive. If they consult the two books cited they will gain a very fair notion of the scope and range of the beliefs. They will find plenty to go upon.

K. M. Briggs

CHAPTER 1 – THE SUPERNATURAL PASSAGE OF TIME IN FAIRYLAND

LL THROUGH the world, wherever the idea of Fairyland or of a supernatural country was evolved, it was accompanied by a strong feeling of the relativity of time. This may well have been founded on the experiences of a dream or of a state of trance. It is common in a dream to pass through long and varied experiences in the mortal time occupied between, let us say, beginning to fall out of bed and landing with a bump on the floor. In a state of trance, on the other hand, the mental processes can be so retarded that one train of thought is slowly pursued for several hours. Both these psychological experiences are reproduced in legends of visits to fairyland or to the Other World. The latter is the most frequent, but the first is also found.

Hartland, who devotes two chapters of his book, *The Science of Fairy Tales* to 'The Supernatural Lapse of Time in Fairyland', gives several examples of this *multum in parvo* effect.[1] Many of them are illustrations of religious or philosophic concepts rather than tales of fairyland. We have, for instance, Mohammed's journey into Paradise on the back of the beast Alborac, in which he passed through all the Seven Heavens and had a long conversation with Allah Himself deep in the Seventh, and yet the whole experience took only the tenth part of a night. There is also the experience of a Brahmin who fell into a meditation on the state of the departed, in the course of which his spirit left him and entered into the body of a new-born child. This child grew up as a cobbler, travelled into another country, where he was chosen as king and reigned prosperously until his former low caste became known, when his subjects fell into despair and many of them fled the country while he himself committed suicide. His spirit then re-entered his former body which it had only left for a few minutes of mortal time, though the actuality of his experiences as a cobbler was demonstrated by the arrival of some fugitives from the country which he had formerly ruled. On the same basic theme Hartland also gives a legend of a real fairyland which he draws from Sikes' *British Goblins*. A young lad from Pembrokeshire joined a fairy ring, and when the dance was over he was led into a most beautiful country in which there was a glittering palace set in the midst of an exquisite garden, where he was told he might live as long as he liked if he observed one prohibition. In the centre of the garden there was a well where many gold and silver fish swam, and he was strictly forbidden to drink from the water of that well. The longing to do so grew on him, until one day he dipped his cupped hands into the water. As he touched it a shriek rang through the garden, and he found himself among his father's sheep on the cold hillside. All the days and weeks as the temptation grew on him had taken barely an hour of earthly time.

These stories are much rarer, however, than those in which a year and a day has appeared to be no more than a half-hour's dance, or two months of happiness have taken two hundred years of mortal time. These tales have a worldwide distribution and are told of various supernatural states other than Fairyland. A medieval Christian legend is that in which a monk is entranced listening to the singing of a snow-white bird, and stands there, rapt into heavenly places and invisible to the inhabitants of the passing world until he returns to it, sometimes after three hundred years of listening. The best-known version of the story is that told by Longfellow in *The Golden Legend*,[2] but there are versions of it scattered all over Europe. An early one from Germany is told by Hartland of the Abbey of Afflinghem. In the time of Fulgentius, who was Abbot at the end of the eleventh century, a strange monk knocked at the gate and said that he had left it that morning after matins to walk in the forest. His story was that during matins they sang the ninetieth psalm, and when they came to the verse, 'A thousand years in thy sight are but as yesterday', he fell into a deep meditation, and sat until all the brethren had left the chapel. As he was still sitting in the choir a little bird flew in, and sang such heavenly strains that his soul was rapt, and he followed the bird into the forest that surrounded the monastery. He stood listening to the bird until it flew away, and then returned to the monastery, but found everything strangely different. Fulgentius asked him who had been king and abbot when he left the chapel that morning, and found that both had died more than three hundred years before. Hartland does not tell us whether the monk crumbled into dust as soon as he tasted the first mouthful of human food, as happens in many of these stories, in one, for instance, told in Transylvania. Both these legends are quoted by Hartland from Thorpe's *Northern Mythology*.[3] Not all these legends, however, are from Christian sources. In the second branch of *The Mabinogion*,[4] 'Branwen Daughter of Llyr', when the poor remnant of the great host which Bran the Blessed had led over to Ireland to avenge the cruel indignities inflicted on Branwen were carrying his head back to London to be buried under the White Mount, they paused to feast in Harlech. They were detained there for seven years by the singing of the three magical birds of Rhiannon, which made them forget all their sorrows and losses. Bran was credited with having introduced Christianity into Wales, but it is generally accepted that Rhiannon, Pryderi and the other heroes and heroines of the

Four Branches of the Mabinogi belonged to the primitive deities of Wales as the Dananns did of Ireland.

In the stories which I have just mentioned it was singing, visions, dreams which stretched time into another dimension, but journeys into another world or realm are still more likely to do so. Urashima Taro, one of the most widespread and best-known of the Japanese folktales, dating from as early as the eighth century, might well be a tale of a mermaiden from Ireland or Brittany. The emphasis on filial piety, however, makes it seem specially oriental. Perhaps the variant of the tale best known in England is that published during the First World War in *Edmund Dulac's Fairy Book*[5]. In this version Urashima Taro, the devout son of an aging mother, who has avoided matrimony because he did not earn enough to keep three, was summoned by a turtle who came three times to his hook, to the Kingdom under the Water to meet a beautiful sea-maiden with whom he spent several days in great happiness. He began, however, to be anxious about his mother, and begged to return to get food for her. His bride was loth to part with him, but sent him to shore with a casket, which she told him not to open. He recognised the beach, but beyond it everything was changed. The hut in which he and his mother had lived was gone, and he saw no one that he knew. At length in despair he opened the casket. A mist came out of it, his face changed, his back bent, his limbs failed him, and in a few moments he crumbled into dust. Two hundred years had passed since he left the land, and they had been released out of the casket. The version recorded in *Folktales of Japan*[6] has a happier though a rather indeterminate ending. According to this the sea-princess gave Urashima a three-tiered jewel box and told him that he might open it in case of necessity. He found himself in a changed land, as in the older version, and went into a house where an old man was weaving straw. He asked him if he had ever heard of Urashima Taro. 'My grandfather used to tell me a story of a fisherman of that name', the old man replied, 'who was carried into the depths of the sea by the Dragon King. But he never came back again'.

'And what happened to his Mother?' asked Urashima Taro.

'Oh, she died long ago,' said the old man, and Urashima left him, and found the ruins of his former home, with nothing remaining except the stone wash-basin and the garden steps. He sat down in reverie, and at last he opened the three-tiered box. In the first tray there was a crane's feather, from the second only a puff of smoke came out, in the third there was a mirror, and looking into it Urashima saw old age coming over his face, but as he looked the crane's feather curled round his neck and he changed into a crane. He flew up and circled round his mother's grave. As he flew his sea-princess came out of the sea in the form of a turtle and watched his flight. Some say this is the origin of the Crane and Turtle Dance at Ise.

One of the earliest stories about a visit to Fairyland is told in *De Nugis Curialium*[7] by Walter Map, contemporary and friend of Giraldus Cambrensis. It is about an ancient British king, Herla, who reigned on the Border of Wales. So many points of interest are raised in this story, one of our earliest fairy-tales, that it is worth reproducing it in full.

About King Herla:

That there was but one court similar to this of ours we learn from old stories. These tell us that Herla, the king of the very ancient Britons, was led into a compact by another, seemingly a pigmy in the lowness of his stature, which did not exceed that of an ape. As the story hath it, this dwarf drew near, sitting on a huge goat—just such a man as Pan is pictured, with glowing face, enormous head, and a red beard so long that it touched his breast (which was brightly adorned with a dappled fawn skin), a hairy belly, and thighs which degenerated into goat-feet. Herla spake to him with no one by. Quoth the pigmy: 'I, the king of many kings and chiefs and of a people numerous beyond all count, willingly, sent from them to thee, and though I am to thee unknown, yet I glory in the fame which hath raised thee high above other kings, since thou art the best and the nearest to me in place and blood, and art moreover worthy of having me grace with high honour thy wedding as guest, when the King of the French giveth his daughter to thee—an arrangement concluded without thy knowledge, and lo, his messengers come this very day. Let there be an abiding compact between us, that I shall attend thy wedding, and thou mine a year later to the day.' With these words he turned his back with more than a tiger's swiftness and vanished from the king's sight. Then the king, returning in amazement, received the ambassadors and accepted their terms. As he was sitting in high state at the wedding feast, the pigmy entered before the first course with so great a multitude of his fellows that the tables were filled and more had to find places without than within, in the pigmy's own pavilions which were pitched in a moment. From these tents servants sprang forth with vases made of precious stones, perfect in form and fashioned with inimitable art, and they filled the palace, and pavilions with gold and crystal vessels, nor did they serve any food or drink in silver or in wood. They were present wherever they were wanted, and offered nothing from royal or other stores, but a bountiful entertainment only from their own, and thus, from the supplies brought with them, they outstripped the desires and requests of all.

Everything which Herla had prepared was left untouched. His servants sat in idleness, for they were not called upon and hence rendered no service. The pigmies were everywhere, winning everybody's thanks, aflame with the glory of their garments and gems, like the sun and moon before other stars, a burden to no one in word or deed, never in the way and never out of the way. Their king, in the midst of the ministrations of his servants, thus addressed King Herla: 'O best of kings, the Lord is my witness that, according to our compact, I am present at thy wedding. But if anything that thou cravest besides what thou seest here can be asked of me, I shall willingly supply it; but if not, thou must not put off thy requital of this high honour when I shall ask for it. Without pausing for an answer to these words he suddenly returned to his pavilion and departed with his men about the time of cock-crow. But just a year later he suddenly appeared to Herla, and sought from him the discharge of his compact. Herla assented, and having provided himself with the wherewithal for the discharge of his debt, followed where he was led. He and his guide entered a cavern in a very lofty cliff, and after a space of darkness they passed into light, seemingly not of sun or of moon but many lamps, to the home of the pigmies—a mansion in every way glorious, like the palace of the sun in Ovid's description. Having celebrated there the marriage, and having discharged fittingly his debt to the pigmy, Herla, with the sanction of his host, withdrew laden with gifts and with presents of horses, dogs, hawks, and all things befitting venery and falconry. The pigmy conducted his guests to the darkness and at parting gave to them a small bloodhound, to be carried in arms, strictly forbidding any one of Herla's whole company to dismount until the dog should leap forward from his bearer. Then, having said farewell, he returned to his country. When Herla in a short time was restored to sunlight and to his kingdom, he accosted an old shepherd and asked for news of his queen by name. Then the shepherd, regarding him with wonder, thus replied: 'My lord, I scarce understand thy language, since I am a Saxon and thou a Briton. But I have never heard of the name of that queen, save that men tell of one so called, a queen of the very ancient Britons, and wife of King Herla, who is reported in legends to have disappeared with a pigmy into this cliff and to have been seen nevermore on earth. The Saxons, having driven out the natives, have possessed this kingdom for full two hundred years.' The king, who had deemed his stay to be of three days only, could scarcely sit his horse for wonder. Some of his fellows, forsooth, heedless of the pigmy's warnings, dismounted before the descent of the dog, and were immediately changed to dust. But the king, understanding the reason for this change, prohibited, by threat of like death, any one to touch the earth before the descent of the dog. But the dog never descended.

Hence the story hath it that King Herla, in endless wandering, maketh mad marches with his army without stay or rest. Many have seen that army, as they declare. But finally, in the first year of the coronation of our King Henry, it ceased, so men say, to visit our kingdom frequently as in the past. And then it was seen by many Welsh sinking into the river Wye at Hereford. But from that hour that wild march ceased.

One may note here that it is said two hundred years since the Saxons conquered the Britons and that King Herla had been one of the early Kings of Britain and had disappeared long before that time, and therefore one may plausibly conjecture that the three days of revelry had actually taken three hundred years. Loose though the time connection may be, there generally seems to be some correspondence between mortal and fairy time. A day may occupy a month, a year, a hundred years, yet there is some interaction between them in time, and particularly in season. Terrible though the result of the pigmy king's visit was to Herla and his queen, it seems to have been undertaken in a spirit of good-fellowship, and it is possible that when King Herla and his Ride disappeared finally into the River Wye they may well joined the Pigmy King in his subterranean kingdom.

The Rout of Herla, or Harlequin, was known in Brittany as well as in England, and was one of the earlier of those Wild Hunts of which the first leader was Woden, though he was succeeded by Gabriel's Ratchets, the Devil and his Dandy Dogs, Dando's Dogs, the Seven Whistlers and others. An early account of one of those Rides is given in the Anglo-Saxon Chronicle in 1127 and is quoted by Brian Branston in *The Lost Gods of England*[8]: 'Let no one be surprised at what we are about to relate, for it was common gossip up and down the countryside that after February 6th many people both saw and heard a whole pack of huntsmen in full cry. They straddled black horses and black bucks while their hounds were pitch black with staring hideous eyes.'

This was no doubt a direct descendant of Woden, the first rider about whom we have any information, who continued in post-Christian times in Scandinavia; hunting not the lost souls of men but the little, harmless woodwives. Later, as is usual in folklore, the devil took over Woden's function, and was succeeded by the angel Gabriel, and by notorious local characters; but of all these Herla is the only one who rode as a victim of the supernatural passage of time in Fairyland.

Wales is particularly full of stories about the return of victims detained among the fairies. The one most commonly told is that of 'Llewellyn and Rhys', which first appeared in Crofton Croker's *Fairy Legends and Traditions of the South of Ireland*, vol. III.[9] It was told to him by Davidd Shone, who claimed to be an eyewitness of Rhys's rescue.

Llewellyn and Rhys were two farm labourers living at Llwyn y Ffynas, who had been carrying lime for their master, and returned home at night driving their ponies before them. Rhys put his foot on a fairy-ring, heard the sound of music and dancing and disappeared through the deep dusk, calling out to his companion to drive the ponies home, as he would follow him. Llewellyn called and waited, but saw and heard nothing, and at length went home, thinking that Rhys had made an excuse to slip off to the alehouse. The next day Rhys had not returned, and as time went on Llewellyn began to be suspected of having made away with him. He was arrested, but held without trial in case Rhys should turn up again. Nearly a year had passed when a farmer who was an authority on fairy lore suggested that on the anniversary of the night when Rhys disappeared Llewellyn might be taken, with witnesses, to the spot. This was agreed to, and the company, of whom Davidd Shone was one, were led by Llewellyn to the place where he had lost Rhys. 'This should be the very place,' he said; 'and listen, I hear music.' No-one else heard it until Llewellyn suggested that one of the company should put a foot on his. Davidd Shone did so, and, sure enough, he heard entrancingly sweet dance music. One after another the witnesses touched Llewellyn's foot with theirs on the edge of the fairy ring. They not only heard the music but saw numberless little creatures of the size of children of three or four whirling round in a circle with Rhys amongst them. Llewellyn, without stepping further into the circle, reached out, and catching hold of Rhys's smock plucked him by force out of the ring. He seemed quite dazed. 'Where are the horses?' he said.

'Horses indeed!' said Llewellyn angrily. 'Where have you been all this year long? Come back with me and clear my name from murder.'

'Yes, I'll come back as soon as I've finished this dance. I've only been five minutes at it.'

'Five minutes indeed!' said Llewellyn. 'Come back with me now.'

They took him back by force, and could hardly get him to believe that a whole year had passed while he was dancing. Poor Rhys pined and drooped after this. He soon took to his bed and faded away. It is seldom that captives in Fairyland recover from the experience.

It is more common in the Welsh legends for those who have returned from a prolonged visit to Fairyland to crumble into dust like Urashima

Taro. An impressive version of that tale is told by Wirt Sikes in *British Gobleins*.[10] Its hero is Taffy ap Sion, a shoemaker's son living near Pencader in Carmarthenshire. One day he happened to put his foot in a fairy circle on the hillside, and joined the dancers there, for a few minutes, as it seemed to him. In the pace of the dancing he shot out of the circle and found himself at once in a changed scene. The rough mountainside had been cultivated, and where his father's cottage had been there stood a fine stone house. Taffy took it for a fairy enchantment, and set out along the path that he knew by heart. Presently he ran into a formidable thorn hedge, too old and sturdy to be raised by glamour. He climbed over it and came into a neat farm-yard, where a large dog, a complete stranger to him, ran at him, barking fiercely. A farmer came out to call the dog in, and was concerned at Taffy's wan looks and tattered clothing. He could make nothing of Taffy's story, but said that the house had been built by his great-grandfather and repaired by his grandfather, and that he himself had added a wing to it three years before. He did not even know the name of Sion Evan y Crydd, Taffy's father, but suggested that they should go to a very old woman, Catti Shon of Pencader, who knew all the traditions of the district, and would probably be able to disentangle the story, though it was already plain to the farmer that his strange guest must have been inveigled into Fairyland. They set out in single file along the narrow track, and as they went down the farmer heard the footsteps behind growing lighter and lighter, and turned just in time to see the stranger crumble, and fall to the ground, a thimbleful of black ashes. Shaken though he was he went down to see Catti, and learned from her that her grandfather had known Shon y Cryyd of Glanrhyd whose young son had disappeared one morning and had never been heard of again, so that it was thought he had been taken by the fairies. The mere touch of mortal ground had not called down the weight of years on Taffy, he had violated no explicit taboo, but when he had told his story and his problem had been solved he accepted the limitations of mortality.

In these two stories, and many like them in Wales and elsewhere, the victim is not tempted into an underground nor submarine kingdom, nor transported to a magic island, but remains entranced and invisible as days and seasons pass on a small piece of mortal earth, made invisible by glamour. It is, however, more common for the visitors to Fairyland to have entered a different realm, as King Herla did.

Grant Stewart, in *The Popular Superstitions and Festive Amusements of the Highlanders of Scotland*,[11] tells a tale very like that of Rhys and Llewellyn. MacGillivray, a tenant of Cairngorm, had newly removed with his two sons to the forest of Glenavon, known to be haunted by both ghosts and fairies. The two sons went out late one night to look for some sheep that had strayed. In the course of their search they passed a 'shian', or fairy hill, and in the darkness it looked like a turret with the door open and light streaming out of every crevice. As they came nearer they heard the most beautiful dance music, and the elder brother, Rory MacGillivray, who was an enthusiast for dancing, determined to go inside. Donald, the younger, was more prudent, and begged his brother not to go in, but Rory broke away from him and disappeared into the shian. Donald dared not follow him, but he climbed up to one of the windows and saw Rory jigging and reeling with the best of them. He called out to his brother, moving from window to window, and begged him in the most affecting terms he could think of to come out from that evil and perilous place, but Rory seemed to hear nothing, and at last Donald returned home and told his father what had happened. Every means that could be thought of was taken for his recovery, but without success, and at last a Wise Man said to Donald: 'Only you can rescue him. Return to the shian a year and a day from the time you lost him, fasten a rowan cross to your clothing and enter boldly, and in the Name of the Highest, claim your brother. If he will not come, carry him out by force; they will have no power to prevent you.'

Donald was no hero, and was filled with dread, but the entreaties of his father, his love for his brother and his faith in the rowan cross prevailed with him. When the time came he entered the shian with trembling feet, saw his brother in the middle of a Highland Fling, caught him by the collar and commanded him, in the words dictated by the Wise Man, to come out with him directly. Rory was willing to come, but only asked to be allowed to finish the reel that he was dancing. He had only, he said, been in the place for half-an-hour. Even when he had been dragged forcibly from the shian he could not believe that a year had passed while he danced, and was only convinced when he saw the new-born calves grown into stirks and the babes-in-arms walking.

There was no rescue for the two fiddlers in Grant Stewart's next story:[12] they played out their appointed time. There were two famous fiddlers living in Strathspey in the sixteenth century or thereabouts who decided to go one Christmas time to Inverness to hire themselves out for any festivities that were on foot. They arrived at the town, secured lodgings and sent round the bellman to announce their arrival, their accomplishments, a list of the reels, strathspeys and jigs in their repertoire, with their charges for a day, a night or an hour. In a short time a gentleman, very wizened and old but with elegant manners and address, called on them and engaged them to play at a great gathering that very night to which he himself would conduct them. He did not cavil at their charges, and indeed promised to double them; so they set out in high spirits; but when they reached their destination they were dismayed, for it was not like any of the castles they knew, but a great, rough tower, more like a fairy Tomhan than any human habitation that they knew. However, their guide reassured them, and once they were inside all their uneasiness vanished, for they had never seen a more gorgeous place, nor a more beautiful and elegant assembly of guests. They played all night without fatigue, for they were entranced by the dancing and their refreshments. In the morning their guide paid them generously and thanked them, and they only wished the night had been longer. But when they went out of the castle the whole scene was changed. The great tower was a low hill out of which they crept, and when they made their way to the town it was all different, and the inhabitants who thronged the streets, more numerous than ever, were dressed in strange, fantastic clothes the like of which they had never seen, who in their turn stared at the two oddities dressed in ancient rags. At length they began to suspect that these were men who had been carried away by the fairies, and this was confirmed by an old man who hobbled up, and who, after he had questioned them, said: 'I know who you are, you are the two men my great-grandfather lodged, who, as it was supposed, were decoyed by Thomas Rymer into Tomnafurich. Sore did your friends lament you, but a hundred years have passed since then, and your very names are forgot.'

The two fiddlers believed, and were glad to have come out alive from that sinister place. As they were speaking the bells began to ring out, for it was the Sabbath, and the fiddlers thought it right to go to church to give thanks for their delivery. So they went directly to the kirk, and sat in a pew waiting for the congregation. When all were in the Minister went up to the desk, and at the first words of holy scripture the two old fiddlers crumbled into dust.

The Irish traditions of the supernatural passage of time in Fairyland are among the most poetic of all. Everyone knows something of the story of Oisin,[13] or Ossian as he is called in the Highlands of Scotland. He was the great poet and singer of the Fianna Finn, the son of Fionn mac Cumhal and Sadth, a woman of the Sidh who was pursued by the Dark Druid, Fear Doirche, who had turned her into a deer. Fionn rescued and wedded her, but the Dark Druid stole her away in his absence, and she was lost to Fionn for ever. However, one day when he was hunting a terrible clamour arose among the dogs, and he found his two special hounds, Bran and Sceolan, protecting a lovely little boy from the onslaught of the rest of the pack. Fionn caught him up in his arms. 'Oisin, my little fawn!' he exclaimed, for he knew him at once for his son and Sadth's. It was no wonder, with the fairy blood in his vains, that Oisin became a great singer, and he was a great warrior too, for he lived through the best days of the Fianna Finn, and survived the great battle of Garbha, where his son Osgar, the next to him in prowess, was killed: but not long after that the fairy Princess Niamh of the Golden Locks invited him to go with her to Tir Nan Og, the Land of the Ever-Young across the sea, and he went, and none of the Fianna Finn ever saw him again.

Many years later, after the Fianna were dead and almost forgotten, he came back, riding on the great white horse which had been sent to fetch him into Tir Nan Og. To him it only seemed that he had been away for a few months, and he wished to see Fionn and the Fianna Finn again to tell them that all was more than well with him. Niamh was very loth to let him go, but in the end she gave him the white horse to ride and earnestly begged him not to touch the earth of Ireland with his foot, or he would never get back to the Land of Tir Nan Og. He promised, and rode lightly away over the waves. The sea was the same as ever, but when he got to the coast of Ireland everything was changed. The forests had shrunk, the rivers were narrower and deeper, the hills seemed small. He rode to the great stronghold of Tara, and there was nothing left but a green, rounded hill. There was no voice, no face that he knew anywere. Half broken-hearted he turned his horse's head to go back to Niamh of the Golden Locks. As he rode he passed a group of the little, stunted men he had noticed before. They were struggling with all their might to lift a great stone trough that they had found in the earth, but in vain. Oisin had compassion on their weakness and their courage, and he drew rein for a moment to help them. They looked with amazement at the great golden warrior towering above them. Without dismounting, he bent down from the saddle and lifted the stone trough with one hand; but as he raised it the saddle-girth slipped and he fell to the ground. The white charger reared and galloped away towards the sea with thundering hoofs. Where the golden warrior had fallen, there lay an old, old man with the weight of hundreds of years on him. But Oisin did not crumble into dust. He lived on, and told the new race of the old, heroic days of the Fianna Finn, and won the love of St Patrick; for many hundreds of years had passed, and Christianity had come into the land, so that it was full of the sound of church bells. But Oisin had no desire for a Heaven where there was no hunting or fighting, however full it might be of sweet music, and he never ceased to lament the passing of the Heroic Age.

The story of Bran son of Febal[14] is on the same pattern as that of Oisin, but it has a happier ending, at least for the fairy lovers. Bran, the son of Febal, was once summoned by Mannanon, son of Lir, to view one of his islands, Emhaim, the Isle of Women. This was the way in which he was summoned. He was walking one day near his own dun when he heard a sound of music in the air which was so sweet that he sat down to listen to it, and was lulled asleep. When he awoke he found himself holding a silver branch in his hand covered with white apple-blossom. He carried it back with him to his dun. When he was in the middle of his company suddenly a woman in strange clothing stood before him and began to sing. She sang about the Isle of Emhaim, where there was no winter or want or care and where the golden horses of Mannanon pranced upon the beach, and games and play went on forever without weariness. She invited Bran to seek out that Island and visit the lady of it. When she had finished she turned to go, and the silver branch leapt out of Bran's hand to hers, and she carried it away with her. Next morning Bran went down to the shore and prepared a fleet of curraghs to row out over the sea, searching for the Isle of Emhaim. On the way Mannanon passed them, driving his golden chariot over the waves, and he invited them to go to Emhaim and pointed out the way. They passed many islands as they travelled, but came in the end to the Isle of Women, where the Chief Woman drew them ashore and welcomed them; and she and Bran lived together in great delight. When they had been there for what seemed a year, though in that winterless land it was not easy to tell, some of Bran's company began to yearn for Ireland, and Nechtan, son of Coluinn, was specially urgent to return, if only for an hour. The Chief Woman, Bran's lover, was most unwilling to let them go; but Bran promised that they would only stay for a short time and immediately return. Then she warned them, as Niamh had warned Oisin, that they must only speak to their friends from the boat and must not touch the soil of Ireland, for if they did they would never return to Emhaim. Bran promised again, and they rowed away and reached the coast of Ireland at a place called Scrub Bruin. People gathered on the shore, and Bran hailed them and asked if there were any there who knew Bran son of Febal. They answered that no such man was alive now in Ireland, but that in the stories told by their oldest men there were mentions of how one Bran son of Febal sailed away hundreds of years ago to look for the Isle of Women. When Nechtan heard that he leapt out of his curragh like one frantic and waded towards the land. When he touched the soil of Ireland his years came on him, and he fell into a pile of dust. Bran was warned by his fate. He stayed for a little time telling of what happened to him, then he and companions turned their little fleet and rowed back again to the timeless joys of the Isle of Emhaim.

This tale is told delightfully in Lady Gregory's *Gods and Fighting Men*, and a full study of it is to be found in Alfred Nutt's *Voyage of Bran*, accompanying

Kuno Meyer's translation of the original tale from the Ancient Irish.

The supernatural bride in an Italian folk-story was more prudent than either Niamh or Bran's bride, for she accompanied her husband on his return to the mortal world. Hartland cites the tale from Comparetti, and an English translation of it by H. C. Coote is to be found in *The Folk-Lore Records*,II.[15] It begins as a variant of the Swan Maiden tale. The hero sets out to seek Fortune and finds her in the form of a beautiful maiden bathing in a pool. He steals her clothes, and with them her *Book of Command* by means of which he is able to force her to wed him. One day, however, when he is out, his mother gives her the book, and she immediately returns to The Island of Happiness which is her home. Her husband goes out to seek her, and after many adventures he finds her and lives with her in great happiness for what seems to him two months. After that time he becomes anxious to see his mother again. His wife tries to dissuade him, but when she sees that nothing will content him but to go she gives him a great white horse, and mounts behind him. They ride over the sea to Italy, but here, as in the other stories, he finds a changed scene, for the two months have been two hundred years. They meet some fellow-travellers on their journey as they ride towards his old home. The first is a lean old woman, dragging a cartful of shoes behind her which she has worn out on her travels. She is very weak, and as she reaches them she stumbles and falls to the ground. The hero would have jumped down to lift her up, but Fortune calls out—'Beware! That is Death!' and he refrains. Next they meet an old lord, richly clothed but riding a leg-weary horse, which founders and falls just as they meet. Again the hero would have leapt down to help, but Fortune cries out, 'Beware, that is the Devil!' So they leave him with his foundered horse and ride on until they reach her husband's old home, which was changed beyond recognition. Search as they may they can find no one who had so much as heard his mother's name, so in the end he consents to turn his horse's head and ride back with his wife to the island of Happiness, to live with her forever.

In Rip Van Winkle,[16] Washington Irving's literary version of the supernatural lapse of time, the twenty years were passed in a sleep which followed the drinking of the fairy wine, always a forbidden thing. Hartland is doubtful whether Irving was re-telling an authentic legend of the Catskill Mountains or whether, as he suspects, he had converted a very similar story from Otmar's *Traditions of the Harz*, where the haunted mountain was the Kyffhauser. If this was so Hendrik Hudson and his crew must have sprung from Washington Irving's imagination. It will, of course, be remembered that the supernatural company visited by Rip Van Winkle were not fairies but the dead. However, the association between the fairies and the dead is often very close in folk tradition.

In this story Rip Van Winkle reached what seemed rather more than his natural age in his twenty years sleep, but there was no question of his crumbling into dust, in fact he lived out the later part of his life in much more comfortable circumstances than when he had been under the domination of his shrewish wife.

A possible explanation of the crumbling bodies could be that the victims had long been dead and that their 'vital spirits', as they were called, returned in an illusory body that crumbled as soon as they were touched by reality. Something like this was said by that strange woman, Isobel Gowdie, who made an extraordinary confession of her activities as a witch and of what happened to the victims of elf-shot.[17]

'I haid a little horse, and wold say, "HORSE AND HATTOCK, IN THE DIVILLIS NAME!" And than ve vold flie away quhair ve vold, be ewin as strawes wold flie wpon an hieway. We will flie lyk strawes quhan we pleas; wild-strawes and corne-strawes will be horses to ws, and ve put thaim betwixt our foot, and say, "HORSE AND HATTOCK, IN THE DEVELLIS name!" An quhan any sies thes strawes in a whirlewind, and doe not then sanctifie them selves, we may shoot them dead at owr pleasour. Any that ar shot be vs, their sowell will goe to Hevin, bot their bodies remains with ws and will flie as horsis to ws, als small as strawes.'

These strange, mad outpourings at least throw some light on the fairy beliefs held by the peasantry of Scotland in the seventeenth century.

The last word on the subject may have been said quite lately in 'The Noon-Tide Ghost', a story sent in 1929 to Ruth L. Tongue by a correspondent who took it down from an old farmer in the Luccombe, the Porlock area of Exmoor. It is to be found in *Forgotten Tales of the English Counties*.[18]

'Tis a old ancient tale they do tell about farm (i.e. the storyteller's farm).

There were a queer old chap kept kept a-hanging round village. Folk did see 'en to owl-light and night-time, some did zay he shined like a spunky—as you d' call a Jacky-my-Lanthorn—but some volks 'ill tell 'ee anything. He come in noontime too but all was afraid to speak to 'en for all his clothes was of a strange fashion.

Then one noon he come to view outside our varm door and the granny couldn't abear his sorrow, she ups and speaks to 'en as priest d' say she should. 'In the name of the Lord why troublest thou me?' she say and a-called out, 'Yew poor unhappy soul, come tell I.'

And the old grey ghost he zay, 'Where be my mill then? And my son's cottage by the oak coppices? There be a gurt stone mill by river and no cottage and only one gurt aged old oak.' Then the granny she see the rights of it. 'Be church still there?'

'They've a-got a new stone one since I went to market s'morning, and I did promise Bet I 'oodn't stay late. Where be my dear old wife?'

The granny she see how 'twas but she kept her peace and only say, 'Who did 'ee meet on the road?'

'A queer sort of chap and we got to wagering games and old merriment, and he d'want me to stay longer, but I gainsayed 'en, Bet 'ood be a-waiting. Where be my dear wife?'

And then, they d'say, there were a light, and a wind that smelled sweet as a primrose bank and a voice like a throstle in song said, 'Come whoame now, my dear, yew don't belong down there no more. Come on whoame.' And the sad old ghost he give a beautivul smile and he went clean away.

It is clear what happened to this old man at any rate. He had died some time before, but his ghost was earthbound by the desire for his old home, and was released, as it often is in ghost stories, by the unburdening of his trouble to a sympathetic listener.

CHAPTER 2 – THE ORIGINS OF FAIRY BELIEFS AND BELIEFS ABOUT FAIRY ORIGINS

HE QUESTION of fairy beliefs divides itself into two parts. In the first place we have the folklorists' researches into the reason why all over the world people have believed in a race of creatures, either superhuman or slightly sub-human, who are neither gods nor, strictly speaking, ghosts and who have much in common with humanity, but who differ from men in their powers, properties and attributes; and there are secondly the opinions held of the fairies by those people who believe in them. It will be seen that those investigating start from a different premise and rely upon different methods.

Let us begin with the folklorists. Folklore is the study of traditional practices, customs, beliefs and arts. These last include music, drama, poetry, narrative, both fictional and legendary, and traditional crafts with the mystique and customs attached to them.

In this book I am dealing with a restricted area, that of belief and narrative, though sometimes, songs and dances are said to be learned from the fairies and they are also said to be able to teach special crafts.

One of the most recent examinations of fairy beliefs is to be found in *Hereditas*,[1] a collection of essays and studies presented to Professor Séamus Ó Duilearga, formerly the Honorary Director of the Irish Folklore Commission, and published in 1975. It is 'Some Notes on Fairies and the Fairy Faith' by the famous folklorist, Reidar Th. Christiansen, and contains an interesting comparison between the Scandinavian fairy faith and that held, or formerly held, in Ireland. Ireland is one of the bastions of the fairy faith, and though the young people are now rather sceptical, there are still many believers among the elderly. Christiansen gives an example as recent as 1959 when the course of a road had to be altered because its projected route cut through a fairy palace.[2] A new road was being built at Toorglas in County Mayo and the road-builders went on strike rather than destroy a fairy palace on its route. The head of the Commission went down to try to settle the matter and was told by the local farmers that they themselves did not believe in the Little People but that the breach of tabu was causing so much uneasiness in the neighbourhood that it would be wiser to re-route the road. This was accordingly done. Here it was no matter of airy whim, but a serious belief, held quite recently.

Professor Christiansen was specially qualified to compare and contrast the fairy beliefs of Scandinavia and Ireland but he was also much struck with the widespread beliefs about supernatural creatures of the fairy type, not only in Europe but through the whole world, so strikingly similar in many ways that he felt himself forced to admit that they originated in the human situation. His theory was that the fairy beliefs answered the questions of the untimely death of young people, of mysterious epidemics among cattle, of climatic disasters, of both wasting diseases and strokes, of infantile paralysis and of the birth of mongol and otherwise deficient children. Considering therefore that this is a universal belief, he does not make a minute general analysis of the origins of the fairy faith in Scandinavia or in Ireland. He does, however, suggest once that the idea of the small size of the fairies may have arisen from observation of the dimensions of the prehistoric earth dwellings which were popularly supposed to be the home of the fairies.[3]

Professor Christiansen assumes that the small size of the fairies was part of the universal fairy belief, though in earlier times there is good evidence for life-sized fairies, as for instance, those who were fairy brides to mortals, and these full-size fairies still persist. The 'seers' interviewed by Evans Wentz in *Fairy Faith in Celtic Countries*[3] (1911) seem all to have thought of the Sidh as of mortal or more than mortal size. In the testimony of one Irish mystic put into the form of a dialogue the informant is asked (p. 62):

'You speak of the opalescent being as great beings; what stature do you assign to them, and to the shining beings?'

'The opalescent beings seem to be about fourteen feet in stature, though I do not know why I attribute to them such definite height, since I had nothing to compare them with; but I have always considered them as much taller than our race. The shining beings seem to be about our own stature or just a little taller. Peasant and other Irish seers do not usually speak of the Sidhe as being little but as being tall: an old schoolmaster in the West of Ireland described them to me from his own visions as tall beautiful people, and he used some Gaelic words, which I took as meaning that they were shining with every colour.'

A confirmation of this opinion was given by Michael Reddy of Rosses Point, a sailor. He said (p. 68):[4]

'I saw the gentry on the strand at Lower Rosses Point about forty years ago. I first saw them like an officer pointing at me what seemed a sword; and when I got on the Greenlands I saw a great company of gentry, like soldiers, in red, laughing and shouting. Their leader was a big man, and they were ordinary human size.'[5]

On the whole, however, Reidar Christiansen is justified in speaking of the fairies as small, or very small. He has slightly simplified the conception, but the whole subject is such a complex one that it is difficult to compress it into a small space, and in this article he is dealing with current beliefs.

Something of the same simplification is to be found in his treatment of the second aspect of our subject, the beliefs about fairy origins, and here again we may believe that Christiansen is dealing with the up-to-date aspect of the subject. Many of the folk theories of the fairy origins have a theological Christian background, and that highlighted by Professor Christiansen is the one common to Ireland and the Scottish Highlands—the fairies as fallen angels. A vivid and detailed account of this is given by Alexander Carmichael in *Carmina Gadelica* and repeated in *The Fairy Faith in Celtic Countries*.[6] According to this some of the angels seduced by Satan were not prominent in his councils, but might rather be counted his dupes. When Michael hurled the hosts of Satan out of Heaven they were followed by an almost endless stream of these comparatively innocent victims of his unholy eloquence. The Shining Host of Heaven was thinning rapidly, and the Son, seeing the danger, cried out: 'Father, Father, the City is being emptied!' God raised his hand; the gates of Heaven closed, the seduced angels stopped bewildered and recollected themselves, and those who were already descending stopped in their tracks, some in the sky, some in the sea, some on mountains and in woods, some further on their way towards Hell, in bowels of the earth, and the foremost angels, wholly committed to evil, in the burning lake. This origin makes the final position of the Sidh at the Day of Judgement a very perilous one. In Scotland Kirk, the author of *The Secret Commonwealth*,[7] describes their destiny as 'pendulous' until the Day of Judgement, but according to Christiansen the general verdict in Ireland is that they are damned souls. He mentions several Irish anecdotes in which a human is anxiously questioned by some of the Sidh as to their final destination. The human, pitying them, asks the question of a Saint, or of the priest during the elevation of the Host when he cannot lie. Always the answer is unfavourable, and when this is reported to the Sidh they break out into terrible lamentations. A similar story is told by J. F. Campbell of Islay in his *Popular Tales of the West Highlands*.[8] The Scandinavian assessment of the fairy fate is more charitable, but as Christiansen points out, their supposed origin is different, and allows more possibility for hope. There are variants of this legend, but the most commonly told is of the hidden children of Eve. After the Fall Adam and Eve settled down to domesticity and were the parents of a large number of children, so many that Eve was ashamed of them. One day God, walking through the world, called on Eve and asked her to present her children to Him. Eve sent half of them to hide and brought out those she thought most presentable; but God was not deceived. 'Let those who were hidden from me,' He said, 'be hidden from all Mankind.' This was the beginning of the Huldre, 'the Hidden people'. A different story is that the Huldre were the offspring of Adam and his first wife, Lilith, about whom there was much apochryphal information. At any rate in the Scandinavian beliefs the fairies were half-human in origin and were not creatures of another order as the angels were, good or bad.

An earlier investigator of fairy beliefs, though still of this century, was Evans Wentz, from whose book, *The Fairy Faith in Celtic Countries*, I have already quoted.

In 1908 Evans Wentz, an American of Celtic descent, who had worked for some years under John Rhys, the Oxford Professor of Celtic Studies, set out on an exploration of the Celtic area—Ireland, the Highlands of Scotland, Wales, Cornwall, the Isle of Man and Brittany. He began by consulting the leading folklore experts of each region, Douglas Hyde in Ireland, Alexander Carmichael in the Scottish Highlands, John Rhys of Wales, Henry Jenner of Cornwall, Sophia Morrison of the Isle of Man and Professor Anatole le Bras of Brittany; then he travelled through all the regions, for the most part on foot like J. F. Campbell and Alexander Carmichael, visiting and living in peasant cottages and collecting material from people of all classes of society. It was no doubt a help to him in his researches that he was himself a believer in fairies, so that though he researched as a folklorist he encountered believers without a trace of scepticism or condescension, and was therefore given access to experiences and beliefs that would have been withheld from a more sophisticated investigator. Most of these point, as do many of Lady Wilde's[9] stories, to a strong connection between the fairies and the dead. Christiansen still found traces of this, but believed that the fairies were the captors and guardians of the dead rather than the dead themselves. The recently dead are certainly often described as being among the fairies, but the dead of the ancient tribes of Ireland are also thought of as *The Gentry*. John Boglin, for instance, of Kilmessan, near Tara, who was about sixty years when he gave his evidence, reported this of the fairy tribes.

'There is said to be a whole tribe of little red men living in Glen Odder, between Ringleston and Tara; and in long evenings in June they have been heard. There are other breeds or castes of fairies; and it seems to me, when I recall our ancient traditions, that some of these fairies are of the Fir Bolgs, some of the Tuatha de Danaan, and some of the Milesians. All of them have been seen round the western slope of Tara, dressed in ancient Irish costumes. Unlike the little red men, these fairy races are warlike and given to making invasions.'[10]

Later on in giving his evidence, John Boglin said:

The Fairies are the Dead—'According to the local belief, fairies are the spirits of the departed. Tradition says that Hugh O'Neil in the sixteenth century, after his march to the south, encamped his army on the *Rath* or *Fort* of Ringlestown, to be assisted by the spirits of the mighty dead who dwelt within this rath. And it is believed that Gerald Fitzgerald has been seen coming out of the Hill of Mollyellen, down in County Louth, leading his horse and dressed in the old Irish costume, with heartplate, spear and war outfit.'[11]

In Scotland, which was next visited by Evans Wentz, the evil fairies, *The Host* or *Sluagh*, were thought of as the dead, and the fairies or *Shee* are spirits who were decoyed out of their natural allegiance by *The Proud Angel*. In a footnote to one piece of evidence, taken from *Carmina Gadelica*, (p. 108), Alexander Carmichael explains the difference.

Sluagh. 'hosts', the spirit-world. The 'hosts' are the spirits of mortals who have died . . . According to one informant, the spirits fly about in great clouds, up and down the face of the earth like starlings, and come back to the scenes of their earthly transgressions. No soul of them is without the clouds of earth, dimming the brightness of the works of God, nor can any win heaven, till satisfaction is made for the sins of earth.[12]

In Man again, the same belief of 'The Proud Angel' is held, though there are traces of the fairies as the descendants of the ancient gods, particularly Mannanon, son of Lir, a belief we also find in Ireland. In Wales the origin is more vaguely given in such sayings as 'The old folk thought them a kind of spirit from a spirit world'. In Cornwall the connection between the pixies and the dead seems to be closer, at least among the country people. On p. 172, for instance, we have:

Nature of Piskies—'I always understood the piskies to be little people. A great deal was said about ghosts in this place. Whether or not piskies are the same as ghosts, I cannot tell, but I fancy the old folk thought they were.'[13]

The same opinion of their *Fées*, Corrigans and Lutins as fallen angels as we find about the fairy people in Ireland and Scotland, seems to be held in Brittany, though in parts of Southern Brittany they appear to be more beneficent, and some tradition of god-like attributes hangs about them.[14]

There will be occasion to return to the evidence collected by Evans Wentz later in this book, but I have here given a short summary of his account of the beliefs about fairy origins held by his informants.

Varying theories have been set forth from time to time by students of folklore. One of the most clear-cut is the suggestion made by David MacRitchie that the fairy beliefs sprang from the memory of an earlier race of rather dwarfish people, pre-Neolithic dwellers in caves or earthworks, who used flints arrows, had much knowledge of the hidden paths in their country and were credited with power over weather and other magical skills. The chief works of David MacRitchie which uphold this thesis are *The Testimony of Tradition* (1890) and *Fians, Fairies and Picts* (1893). In these he equates the Picts with the Fians and Fairies. Passages in J. F. Campbell's *Popular Tales of the West Highlands* first suggested the theory to him, and some of Campbell's tales could be plausibly ascribed to the existence of a conquered race, lurking in woods and mounds and hanging round farms, doing casual service for gifts of food, but distrustful of their conquerors' clothing as a badge of servitude. Indeed the whole pattern of the Brownie stories could be explained along these lines. Another tale which is particularly apt as a proof of MacRitchie's theory is 'The Isle of Sanntraigh', in volume II of *The Popular Tales*.[15] It is not very widely known and is worth giving in its entirety.

There was a herd's wife in the Island of Sanntraigh, and she had a kettle. A woman of peace (fairy) would come every day to seek the kettle. She would not say a word when she came, but she would catch hold of the kettle. When she would catch the kettle, the woman of the house would say:

> A smith is able to make
> Cold iron hot with coal.
> The due of a kettle is bones,
> And to bring it back again.

The woman of peace would come back every day with the kettle and flesh and bones in it. On a day that was there, the housewife was for going over the ferry to Baile a Chaisteil, and she said to her man, 'If thou wilt say to the woman of peace as I say, I will go to Baile Castle.' 'Oo! I will say it. Surely it's I that will say it.' He was spinning a heather rope to be set on the house. He saw a woman coming and a shadow from her feet, and he took fear of her. He shut the door. He stopped his work. When she came to the door she did not find the door open, and he did not open it for her. She went above a hole that was in the house. The kettle have two jumps, and at the third leap it went out at the ridge of the house. The night came, and the kettle came not. The wife came back over the ferry, and she did not see a bit of the kettle within, and she asked, 'Where was the kettle?' 'Well then I don't care where it is,' said the man; 'I never took such a fright as I took at it. I shut the door, and she did not come any more with it.' 'Good-for-nothing wretch, what didst thou do? There are two that will be ill off—thyself and I.' 'She will come tomorrow with it.' 'She will not come.'

She hasted herself and she went away. She reached the knoll, and there was no man within. It was after dinner, and they were out in the mouth of the night. She went in. She saw the kettle, and she lifted it with her. It was heavy for her with the remnants that they left in it. When the old carle that was within saw her going out, he said,

> Silent wife, silent wife,
> That come on us from the land of chase,
> Thou man on the surface of the 'Bruth',
> Loose the black, and slip the Fierce.

The two dogs were let loose; and she was not long away when she heard the clatter of the dogs coming. She kept the remnant that was in the kettle, so that if she could get it with her, well, and if the dogs should come that she might throw it at them. She perceived the dogs coming. She put her hand in the kettle. She took the board out of it, and she threw at them a quarter of what was in it. They noticed it there for a while. She perceived them again, and she threw another piece at them when they closed upon her. She went away walking as well as she might; when she came near the farm, she threw the mouth of the pot downwards, and there she left them all that was in it. The dogs of the town struck (up) a barking when they saw the dogs of peace stopping. The woman of peace never came more to seek the kettle.

One can see how well this could apply to the members of a lurking conquered tribe and to the newly settled conquerors. Each one, as we can see, was formidable and uncanny to the other. It is noticeable that cold iron is mentioned in the Sanntraigh woman's incantation to the visiting fairy. MacRitchie's contention would be that to the Neolithic people wrought iron would be uncanny. The 'people of peace' would have no kettle, but they had conquered their fear enough to be desirous of the use of a kettle which they could not manufacture. The fairy wife was uncanny to the man of Sanntraigh, but his wife, rushing silently into the bruth, was uncanny to its inhabitants also. The only supernatural event was the leaping up of the kettle, and it could be suggested that the fairy wife could have hooked it up, and that the incident had been slightly magnified by the husband.

Campbell, interested as he was in the folktales, often had a naturalistic explanation at hand and was sceptical about transformation and enchantments, as for instance in the introduction to volume I (CXV), where he says:

'The ancient Gauls wore helmets which represented beasts. The king's sons, when they came home to their dwellings, put off *Cochal*, the husk, and became men; and when they go out they resume the *Cochal*, and become animals of various kinds. May this not mean that they put on their armour?'[16]

He is even more explicit later:

'This class of stories is so widely spread, so matter-of-fact, hangs so well together, and is so implicitly believed all over the United Kingdom, that I am persuaded of the former existence of a race of men in these islands who were smaller in stature than the Celts; who used stone arrows, lived in conical mounds like the Lapps, knew some mechanical arts, pilfered goods and stole children; and were perhaps contemporary with some species of wild cattle, horses and great auks, which frequented marshy ground, and are now remembered as water-bulls and water-horses, and boories, and such like impossible creatures.'[17]

It would be hard to quarrel with MacRitchie's conclusions if he had been content to apply them to some of the fairy traditions, but he stretches his theory to cover the whole body of the fairy belief everywhere and this is asking too much of it. Archaeological evidence is also lacking for the small size of the Picts; the bodies found in the tombs which were traditionally supposed to be the homes of the fairies were of average human size.

John Rhys in his *Celtic Folklore* sometimes seems to take the same view as MacRitchie, particularly in one chapter on, 'Race in Folklore and Myth', where he traces the fairies from the Picts or from earlier races, relying on such primitive practices as their habit of reckoning in fives instead of tens and on the impression sometimes created that they were a race of women ignorant of paternity. This is a view founded on a casual study of the traditions, and Rhys actually believed in the multiple origin of the fairy faith. He says, for instance:

'I should hesitate to do anything so rash as to pronounce the fairies to be all of one and the same origin; they may well be of several. For instance, there may be the representatives of the ghosts of departed men and women, regarded as one's ancestors; but there can hardly be any doubt that others, and those possibly not the least interesting have originated in the demons and divinities—not all of ancestral origin—with which the weird fancy of our remote forefathers peopled lades and streams, bays and creeks and estuaries.'[18]

The distinction between the feared and venerated spirits of ancestors, nature spirits and the remnants of ancient mythology is very hard to draw, but there seems little doubt that the gods of Ireland, for example, were the originals of the Irish fairies, though some folklorists and archaeologists believe that the gods were descended from the spirits of dead ancestors. The matter is discussed by O'Curry and dealt with at some length by Wood-Martin in *Elder Faiths of Ireland: Pre-Christian Traditions*.[19] There seems no doubt that the children of the Goddess Don were the Dana O'Sidh and there, conquered by the invading Milesians, took to the hollow hills and became the *Daoine Sidh* or 'Deeny Shee'. The Fianna Finn and their contemporaries fought, loved and mated with these Daoine Sidh. Originally of human or more than human size, they dwindled through successive generations from the small size of humans to the size of three-years children, and sometimes to midgets.

Some of them retained a godlike status in the legends. An example is Mannanon, Son of Lir, a sea-god to whom the Isle of Man specially belonged, but who presided over Tir Nan Og, the Land of the Ever-Young, to which Niamh of the Golden Locks took her lover, Oisin. Mermaids and the river and tree spirits, which remain in tradition often as souls of the dead, may once have been minor gods.

The Scandinavian elves were from very early days a part of the Norse mythology. In the times of the Aesir and Vanir they were part of the pattern of the world, as the nymphs, satyrs and fauns, the naiads and tritons were part of the classical cosmology. The elves of Scandinavian mythology were of two kinds, 'the light elves' and 'the dark elves'. Dr H. R. Ellis Davidson in *Scandinavian Mythology* mentions the possibility that the *light elves* might once have been the same as the *fair giants* and the *dark elves* have been the hostile giants with whom the others were at war, and that the elves, as they passed into folklore became a homelier, smaller people. She also suggests some connection between the elves and the dead. In the passage *Elves and land-spirits* she says:

There seems to be some link between the elves and the dead within the earth, who still benefit men and who may be born again into the world through their descendants. The early King Olaf, thought to be reborn in the person of the Christian King Olaf the Holy, was called 'Elf of Geirstad', and sacrifices were said to be made to him and also to elves dwelling in mounds. Another race of beings linked closely with the earth were the land-spirits, said to follow 'lucky' men and to give help with hunting and fishing. They were believed to dwell in hills, stones and rivers, and they sometimes appeared in animal form or as little men and women. It was said to be forbidden to bring ships into harbour with menacing figure-heads, because they might frighten the land-spirits.[20] According to the later Scandinavian mythology the light elves, under the dominion of Freyr, one of the Vanir, and the god of vegetation, had already something of the same character as the elves in Elizabethan England, small, tricksy, flower-loving creatures, though in earlier times they had been more various and more beautiful. Their home was Alfheim, one of the nine realms of the world in Scandinavian cosmology. The Saxon elves seem to have been larger and more formidable. There are spells against elfshot in the Anglo-Saxon Charm-books. In Scotland down to the seventeenth century the elves were full-sized and Fairyland was called Elfame.

The French *Fées* had a mythological origin also, for they derived from the Fata. In Hesiod's *Theogony* there are three Fates only, the daughters of Night named Clotho, Lachesis, and Atropos. Clotho spun the thread of each individual life, Lachesis took it from her and twisted it into various shapes, Atropos, with her inexorable shears, snapped it short at the appointed time.[21] Out of these three half-goddesses the Fata developed in post-classical times, who became the *Hadas* in Spain and *Fées* in France. In medieval times they visited the house where a child was born, with gifts of good and evil fortune, as they came to Oberon's birth in the Romance of *Huon of Bordeaux*, and in the sophisticated fairy tales of Perrault and his successors they became fairy godmothers and were not afraid to visit Christian baptisms. In the medieval Arthurian romances they came into England as fays, and 'fai-ery', a state of enchantment, came to be used for those who cast the spell. It will be seen that there was a respectable ancestry here for those who claimed that the fairies were sprung from minor godlings.

Lewis Spence, in *British Fairy Origins*,[22] makes a fair and detailed examination of the various theories about the origin of fairy beliefs, as spirits of the dead, deified ancestors, elementals or nature spirits, the memory of aboriginal races, diminished gods or totemic forms. He mentions but dismisses the theory that they may be a blend of all these, and in the end concludes that the weight of evidence makes it likely that the fairies are sprung from the feared and venerated dead. Many aspects of the fairy beliefs may be plausibly accounted for by this hypothesis: for instance the small size of the fairies, for in primitive times the soul was commonly thought of as a miniature form of the man which came out of his mouth in sleep or trance and had to return to the body before he could become conscious. A very good case may be made out for this theory, not least from the opinions of many of the believers, as in the Cornish story of 'The Fairy Dwelling on Selena Moor' in Bottrell's *Traditions and Hearthside Stories of Cornwall*,[23] where the whole position is neatly and logically laid down—the fairies are the spirits of the heathen dead, not good enough for

Heaven nor bad enough for Hell, who recruit themselves from time to time by seizing such humans as are rash enough to eat their food, and they are gradually dwindling by exercising their power of shape-shifting. They can take the form of birds or beasts, but every time that they resume their proper shape they are a little smaller than they were before. As time goes on they gradually lose their power of enjoyment and suffering so that in the end they live on the memory of feelings they once had. It is a curiously convincing picture, and the whole situation is worked out with a thoroughness unusual in folk tradition. There are other aspects of the fairy belief, however, which are better fitted by other hypotheses: the MacRitchie theory is a convincing explanation of some tales and traditions; psychic experiences and extrasensory perception cannot be entirely dismissed and a body of beliefs so diverse and uncoordinated as fairy lore seems to call for something less rigid than a single formula.

CHAPTER 3 – THE TROOPING FAIRIES

N NEARLY ALL the countries where fairy beliefs are to be found some at least of the fairy people are supposed to gregarious, riding in procession, hunting, holding court and feasting, and above all dancing. This is perhaps particularly true of the British Isles, though in France, Italy, Scandinavia and Germany there are the same tales of dancing, revelry, and processions. In the British Isles the Trooping Fairies may be of mortal size through various stages down to creatures so small that a heather bell may make a cap for one of them. They may be evil, dealing death or sickness to every man and creature they pass on their way, like the *Sluagh* of the Highlands; they may steal unchurched wives from child-bed, or snatch away unchristened babies leaving animated stocks or sickly children of their own in their place, or they may be harmless and even beneficial—fertility spirits watching over the growth of flowers or bringing good luck to herds or children. They may be closely connected with the dead or associated with witches in their revels. The fairy wives were generally stolen away by humans from among a company of dancing fairies as in the early folk-tale of Wild Edric,[1] who broke into a fairy house in the Forest of Clun and stole the most beautiful from a dance of fairies. They were married with the usual traditional imposition of a taboo. After many happy years the taboo was violated, and he lost his wife for ever and pined away searching for her. After his death, however, he and his wife led a Fairy Rade through the Welsh Borders, the sight of which was said to portend disaster, and this tradition lasted for six hundred years.

Often the fairy wives were Seal Maidens or Swan Maidens, captured by the theft of their transforming skins. In Wales the fairy wives came from the bottom of a lake and entered into a willing contract with a prohibition attached to it.[2] Almost invariably this taboo would be broken and the wives would disappear, as the Seal Maidens would be lost if they could find their stolen seal-skins. The Welsh Maidens were not generally captured from a troop, but they seemed sometimes to emerge from their lakes in company, hunting with their fairy hounds or otherwise disporting themselves. The Swan Maidens—who were very widely dispersed in Europe, and indeed through the world—were generally first seen in bevies, like the Seal Maidens, though in some versions of the tale the maiden is solitary. Often the Swan-Maiden theme is to be found in tales of the *Nix Nought Nothing*[3] and in this variant the swans are generally sisters, the daughters of the magician or ogre who has the hero in his power. There is not so much of the fairy revelry in this tale, it is the Seal Maidens rather than those in bird form which sport and play in bevies, but there are many versions of it through the world with birds of various kinds taking the place of the swans—doves, guinea-fowl, partridges, pea-hens. In these islands the tale is to be found in Ireland, Scotland or Wales, and in Europe there are Dutch, Finnish, Greek, Pomeranian, Hungarian, Rumanian, Russian and Spanish variants, as well as some from the *Arabian Nights*, from India and from the Red Indians of America. Unlike the Lake Fairies of Wales and the Seal Maidens, the Swan Maiden Wives did not always leave their husbands, and if they did, were generally recovered again.

A story nearly as widespread as this is the tale of the two humps, in which a hump-backed man accidentally overhears the fairies dancing and singing. An Irish version is given by Crofton Croker in *Fairy Legends and Traditions of the South of Ireland*[4] and tells how a little hunchback nicknamed Lusmore, who found walking difficult, was resting one dark night on his way home by the ruined prehistoric fort of Knock-Grafton when he heard the sweetest music coming from inside. Hundreds of little voices were singing over and over again '*Da Luan, Da Mort!*' (Monday, Tuesday!). He listened, enraptured at first, but after a time began to feel that though the melody was beautiful the words were monotonous. So in a moment's pause in the music he piped up very harmoniously, '*Agus da Cadin!*' (And Wednesday too!). There was a startled silence for a moment, and then the voices took up the refrain with Lusmore's addition; '*Da Luan, Da Mort! Da Luan Da Mort! Da Luan Da Mort! Agus da Cadin!*' A door burst open in the fort and light streamed out. Lusmore found himself twirling like a leaf in the wind into a great, beautiful hall, brightly lit and gaily decorated 'Aren't you the grand fellow!' the fairies cried, 'to give us a fine new ending to our song!' He was set up in state above the musicians, and servants waited on him as if he had been the first in the land. The song with its new addition went on with the sweetest harmony; but presently Lusmore noticed that a group of the graver fairies were consulting together earnestly and he began to be a little uneasy, for it is well known that fairies are tricky and he was afraid that he might have done something to offend them. But presently all fell silent and one little fellow stepped up to him and said:

> 'Lusmore! Lusmore!
> Doubt not nor deplore,
> For the hump which you bore
> On your back is no more.
> Look down on the floor,
> And view it, Lusmore!'

And as he spoke Lusmore's hump slid off his shoulders, and lay, a great lump, on the floor. Lusmore cautiously raised his head, for, poor fellow, it had been almost down to his knees before. He felt so light and straight that he thought he might bump the high ceiling above him He burst out into laughter, and all the fairies around him laughed and clapped their hands, and danced and sang more merrily than ever and Lusmore watched them in such joy as he had never known, till the motion and the beauty overcame him and he fell sound asleep. When he waked it was full day and the birds were singing all round him. When he had said his prayers he felt behind his back, and there was no hump there. He jumped up from the ground, a sprightly, merry fellow, as straight as an arrow, and in a new suit of clothes as well, for the old ones would fit him no longer and the fairies had dressed him from top to toe. He went skipping and dancing home, and the neighbours who met him on the way could hardly believe he was the same man.

The story of Lusmore's healing spread far and wide, and one day an old woman arrived all the way from Waterford to ask how it happened that he was cured, for a friend of hers had a hump-backed son who almost dead with the weight he had to carry. Lusmore, who had always been a good-natured little fellow, told her the whole story, and she went back delighted to tell her friend all about it, and the two women hired a cart and brought Jack Madden, the little hunchback, to the moat of Knockgrafton and left him there, just as it was falling dark. Jack Madden had always been a peevish, ill-tempered little fellow, but was keen enough to be cured now, and he thought he'd maybe get a fine suit, for he was always keener on what he could get that what he could give. The two women went away, and it wasn't long before the music struck up, sweeter than ever for they had Lusmore's refrain to round it out. There was no pause however, for where the pause had been the refrain fitted in. After hearing it seven times Jack Madden could wait no longer, and yelled out, all against the time and the tune, 'Augus da Cadin, Augus da Hena'.

The mound opened again, the light streamed out and Jack Madden was whisked into the Hall, with the fairies screaming and roaring around him, 'Who spoiled our tune? Who spoiled our tune?'. Then the leader stepped up to him and said:

> 'Jack Madden! Jack Madden!
> Your words came so bad in
> The tune we feel glad in;
> This castle you're had in
> That your life we may sadden;
> Here's two lumps for Jack Madden.'

With that twenty of the strongest fairies brought out Lusmore's old hump and set it on the top of Jack Madden's where it stuck fast as if it had been nailed there. Then they kicked him out into the moat, where the two women found him in the morning, more dead than alive, indeed it is said that the poor little fellow did not live much longer after he had been taken home.

In other versions of this tale the fairies are offended by more than breach of rhythm. In the Spanish version[5] the fairies mention the three first days of the week in their song, 'Lunes y Martes y Miercoles tres' which are added to by Pepito the hunchback 'Jueves y Viernes y Sabado seis'. This is received with delight, but Cirillo, the second hunchback, cuts into the tune with 'y Domingo Siete' and the mention of Sunday violates a fairy taboo, so that all the reward he gets is Petito's hump. The Breton version, given by Keightley, strikes a more sombre note. In it the Korred's song and revelry is a joyless performance from which they can only escape when a mortal teaches them a song ending 'And now the week is ended'. They are delighted when their song is continued, but when the second participant ends with 'Ha Disadarn, ha Disul' (And Saturday and Sunday) and insists that there is no more they become furious with frustration and punish him instead of rewarding him.[6]

In the English and German variations of the tale a hunchback who has pleased the fairies has his hump removed, and it is fastened on the back of an intruder who has displeased them, but we miss the pleasant episode of the new addition to the fairy song. There are many more stories of the dances of the fairies, but these will serve as an example.

We find many examples of the Fairy Rades, too, sinister or pleasing. The early story of Wild Edric's Ride has already been mentioned as well as the Highland *Sluagh* and the Devil's Dandy Dogs. A grotesquely sinister account of the Fairy Rade is given by Alexander Montgomery in *The Flouting of Polwart*, written when the Scottish witch-fever was at its height.

> In the hinder end harvest, on a hallow even,
> Quhen our good neighboures doth ryd, if I reid rycht,
> Sum bukled on a buinvaud, and some one a bene,
> Ay trottand in trowpes from the twylychte;
> Some saidland a sho aipe all graithed into greine
> Some hobland one ane hempstalk, hovand to the heicht.
> The King of phairie, and his Court, with the elph queine,
> With mony elrich Incubus was ridand that nycht.[7]

Hallowe'en was the time in Celtic areas when fairies, witches, and ghosts were supposed to dance together.

Here we have presumably, man-sized fairies, very near to devils if not identical with them; but even at that time there were gentler fairies, like the Fairy Queen who, passing on her Hallowe'en Rade, paused to disenchant the knight who had been transformed into an 'ugly worm' by the witch Alison Gross in Child's Ballad No. 35.

> But as it fell out last Hallow-even,
> When the seely court was riding by,
> The queen lighted down on a gowany bank,
> Not far frae the tree where I wont to lie.
>
> She took me up in her milk-white han
> An she's stroaked me three times o'er her knee;
> She chang'd me again to my ain proper shape,
> An I nae mair maun toddle about the tree.[8]

After some two hundred years the fairies had dwindled in Scottish Lowlands, as elsewhere, and were more leniently regarded, though it is only fair to say that this account comes from Cromek's *Nithsdale and Galloway Song*, and Cromek generally makes the best of the fairies. This description of the Fairy Rade was given by an old woman and remembered from her youth.

In the night afore Roodmass I had trysted with a neebor lass a Scots mile frae hame to talk anent buying braws i' the fair. We had nae sutten lang aneath the haw-buss till we heard the loud laugh of fowk riding, wi' the jingling o' bridles, and the clanking o' hoofs. We banged up, thinking they wad ride owre us. We kent nae but it was drunken fowk ridin' to the fair i' the forenight. We glowred roun' and roun', and sune saw it was the Fairie-fowks Rade. We cowred down till they passed by. A beam o' light was dancing owre them mair bonnie than moonshine: they were a' wee wee fowk wi' green scarfs on, but ane that rade foremost, and that ane was a good deal larger that the lave wi' bonnie lang hair, bun' about wi' a strap whilk glinted like stars. They rade on braw wee white naigs, wi' unco lang swooping tails, an' manes hung wi' whustles that the win' played on. This an' their tongue when they sang was like the soun' o' a far awa psalm. Marion an' me was in a brade lea fiel', where they came by us; a high hedge o' haw-trees keepit them frae gaun through Johnnie Corrie's corn, but they lap a' owre it like sparrows, and gallopt into a green know beyont it. We gaed i' the morning to look at the treddit corn; but the fient a hoof mark was there, nor a blade broken.[9]

Even smaller fairies were described in Cornwall in Hunt's *Popular Romances of the West of England*[10] as going out to revel on The Gump near St

Just Fairy Court with a great company, with its bodyguard of Spriggans followed by an uncountable multitude of tiny, beautiful people. They were so small that the high table with the throne of the Prince and Princess and its wealth of gold plate could have been covered by the Miser's hat who tried to capture them. Equally small but more homely hordes of fairies go out on foraging expeditions, like those frightened away by the Hampshire farmer in Keightley's story, 'The Fairy Thieves'. One ear of corn was a heavy load for each of them, but they came in such a swarm that the corn spread out in the granary was rapidly diminishing when the farmer found them at work.[11]

In Ireland some of the revelling fairies are small but there is a Fairy Rade of mortal size led by Finvara, the King of the Dead and his queen, Oonagh. These fairies may all be the Dead, at least the host is largely recruited by them, and mortals who ventured to cross their course on Hallowe'en Night were in danger of being captured by them. Often Finvara's hosts attend a kind of fair, with revelry and dancing and all kinds of goods displayed for sale.[12]

A less fatal one, though not without danger, was long supposed to be held in Somerset at Blackdown, near Pittminster. The earliest account we have of it was given by Bovet in *Pandaemonium, or The Devil's Cloyster* (1684).

> The place near which they most ordinarily showed themselves was on the side of a hill, named black-down, between the parishes of Pittminster and Chestonford, not many miles from Tanton. Those that have had occasion to travel that way have frequently seen them there, appearing like men and women, of a stature generally near the smaller size of men. Their habits used to be of red, blue, or green, according to the old way of country garb, with high crowned hats. One time, about fifty years since, a person living at Comb St. Nicholas, a parish lying on one side of that hill, near Chard, was riding towards his home that way, and saw, just before him, on the side of the hill, a great company of people, that seemed to him like country folks assembled as at a fair. There were all sorts of commodities, to his appearance, as at our ordinary fairs; pewterers, shoemakers, pedlars, with all kind of trinkets, fruit, and drinking-booths. He could not remember anything which he had usually seen at fairs but what he saw there. It was once in his thoughts that it might be some fair for Chestonford, there being a considerable one at some time of the year; but then again he considered that it was not the season for it. He was under very great surprise, and admired what the meaning of what he saw should be. At length it came into his mind what he had heard concerning the Fairies on the side of

that hill, and it being near the road he was to take, he resolved to ride in amongst them, and see what they were. Accordingly he put on his horse that way, and, though he saw them perfectly all along as he came, yet when he was upon the place where all this had appeared to him, he could discern nothing at all, only seemed to be crowded and thrust, as when one passes through a throng of people. All the rest became invisible to him until he came to a little distance, and then it appeared to him again as at first. He found himself in pain, and so hastened home; where, being arrived, lameness seized him all on one side, which continued on him as he lived, which was many years; for he was living in Comb, and gave an account to any that inquired of this accident for more than twenty years afterwards; and this relation I had from a person of known honour, who had it from the man himself.

There were some whose names I have now forgot, but they then lived at a gentleman's house, named Comb Farm, near the place before specified: both the man, his wife, and divers of the neighbours, assured me they had, at many times, seen this fair-keeping in the summer-time, as they came from Tanton-market, but that they durst not adventure in amongst them; for that every one that had done so had received great damage by it.[13]

The curious feature of this account is that the fairies were only visible from a distance and were invisible, though still tangible, when one ventured among them. The later accounts of the Fairy Fair which were preserved in tradition till the middle of the century, did not dwell on this aspect of the tale. Ruth Tongue collected two different versions of the tale which were published in *Somerset Folklore* in which mortals visited the fair. In the second a farmer, courteous to the fairies and on good terms with them, brought a pewter mug which took his fancy and which had turned into solid silver by the morning,[14] and in the first a rude, covetous fellow tried to steal a cup from one of the stalls with disastrous results. This is in the direct line of fairy tradition.[15]

Fairies that were indubitably the dead are to be found in a delightful medieval poem, 'The Romance of King Orfeo' reproduced in W. C. Hazlitt's *Fairy Tales Legends and Romances Illustrating Shakespeare*.[16] It is a retelling of the classical Legend of Orpheus and Eurydice in which Pluto appears as the King of the Feyrey, who bore Dame Meroudys away from the midst of the armed guards set round her by King Orfeo, as Midir carried Etain away from her human husband in the Irish legend. Orfeo, after wandering for years through the wilderness in search of his wife, comes to the edge of the fairy realm and sees a great troop of fairy knights out hunting, but loses them. Shortly afterwards a bevy of fairy ladies pass him out hawking, with Meroudys among them. She and Orfeo recognise each other, but do not speak, and Meroudys is borne away by her companions. Orfeo, however, manages to follow them and by his boldness and great skill as a harper wins his wife back with the full consent of the Fairy King. There is no violated taboo and no looking back, so they both come home again and live together in great happiness. Some aspects of this fairyland are grim and sinister, with the bodies of those who had died violent deaths standing all round the royal palace, but it is plain that even in that grisly place they had their recreations. It was not from a hunting, however, but from a solemn Hallows E'en Rade that Young Tamlane was rescued by Burd Janet, his mortal sweetheart.

All these fairies, riding or hunting, touched the ground of middle earth as they rode, but other trooping fairies travelled by levitation as the *Sluagh* did, either by a potent word or by straddling a bean-stick or piece of ragwort, or by wearing a magical cap. There are many stories of mortals who join fairy expeditions, many of which end in a cellar where the fairies royster and drink. One of these is to be found in Hunt's *Popular Romances*. It was on the night of Pickrous Day—a time of celebrations to the tinners—and John Sturtridge had just left a party at the inn and was making his way home across Tregardon Down when he came across a band of piskies and found himself going round and round quite mazed, though he would have said he knew every inch of the way on the darkest night. He went this way and that, with tittering voices all round him. Suddenly they piped up clearly, however, 'Ho and away for Par Beach!' In desperation John cried out the same, and felt himself caught up and flying through the air, and in less than a minute he landed on Par Beach. They danced there for a while, and then struck up with: 'Ho and away for Squire Tremain's cellar!' John repeated the shout, and found himself as quick as thought in Squire Tremain's cellar, surrounded by great casks of wine on which the fairies were already busy. John followed their example and drank to such good purpose that when they raised the cry for home he was already fast asleep. The butler found him next morning stumbling among the casks with a big silver tankard in his hand and quite unable to explain how he got there. They brought him before the judge and his story was so lame that he was sentenced to be hanged. Poor John was in despair, but when the day of the hanging came and he was already on the scaffold a little woman of commanding appearance came pushing her way through the crowd, and when she got near him she cried aloud in a shrill clear voice 'Ho and away for France!' and he shot off the scaffold into the air and disappeared.

It seems true to say that, though the fairies usually resent uninvited guests at their revels, they generally rescue anyone who gets into trouble by joining them on these excursions.[17] There are many stories of their supernatural levitation. A Scottish one is that given by Walter Scott in *Border Minstrelsy* about the visit by the Laird of Duffus to the King of France's cellar, and the fairy cup he brought back from it. Here his own eloquence was sufficient to secure his release. In Hereford tradition there was a boy who needed help as urgently as John Sturtridge. It is to be found in E. M. Leather's *Folk-Lore of Herefordshire*.[18] The fairies here flew by means of a white cap. A boy lost his way going home through a forest and wandered in the darkness until he lay down quite exhausted and fell asleep for a few hours. He waked to find a bear lying beside him with its head on his bundle of clothes. He was terrified at first, but the bear was so tame that he followed it, and it led towards the light shining from a little hut. A little woman opened the door to him and invited him kindly into the house. There was another little woman sitting by the fire. They gave him something to eat and drink and said he would have to share their bed because there was no other. They all went to sleep, but at twelve o'clock the two old women leapt up and each put on a white cap which was hanging on the bedpost. Then one said, 'Here's off' and the other said, 'Here's after!' and one after the other they flew out of the door. The boy was afraid to be alone and he saw another cap hanging on the bedpost, so he put it on and said 'Here's after' as the second little woman had done. At once his feet left the ground, and he shot after them, and found himself in the middle of a fairy ring. They all danced merrily for a time, and then one said, 'Here's off to a gentleman's house!' and the others cried, 'Here's after!', and so did the boy. They landed on the top of a tall chimney, and the first said, 'Here's down the chimney!', and the others said 'Here's after!' and down they all went to the kitchen. Then it was, 'Here's to the cellar!' and 'Here's after!' and they found themselves in a great cellar, where they began to collect bottles of wine and put them in their pouches. They opened one and gave it to the boy, and he emptied the whole bottle and fell fast asleep. When he awakened it was day and they had all gone. The boy went timidly up to the kitchen where the servants caught hold of him and took him to the master. There had been losses of wine lately, and the boy could give no explanation that satisfied anybody, so he was taken to the judge and sentenced to be hanged. He was standing terrified on the scaffold when he saw a little woman in a white cap making her way through the throng. She had another white cap in her hand, and she begged the judge to let him be hanged with the white cap on his head. The judge agreed, and the little woman said 'I'm off!' and the boy called out, 'I'm after', and in a moment they were back in the little hut in the forest.

The old woman took the cap off his head and explained to the boy that they were angry with him for taking one of their caps without leave, so they left him to take the consequences, and he must promise never to do such a thing again. So she gave him something to eat and told him the shortest way to go home.

These were kindly fairies; sometimes mortals find themselves snatched up against their will, as happened to The Poor Man of Peatlaw who inadvertently fell asleep in the middle of a fairy ring and found himself dragged at top speed through the air, and before he well knew what had happened he was landed in the middle of the populous town of Glasgow. His coat had been left on the Hill of Peatlaw in Selkirkshire and his blue bonnet was found sticking on the top of the steeple of Lanark Kirk. He was lucky enough to come across a carter who knew him, and carried him back to Selkirk more slowly that he had come, and he was luckier still to have suffered no physical harm.[19] According to the anonymous 'Discourse on Devils and Spirits' inserted in the 1660 edition of Scot's *Discovery of Witchcraft:*

> And many such have been taken away by the sayd Spirits, for a fortnight or month together, being carryed by them in chariots through the Air, over Hills, and Dales, Rocks and Precipices, till at last they have been found lying in some Meddow or Mountain bereaved of their sences, and commonly of one of their Members to boot.

In Ireland the Cluricans and other small trooping fairies will take a willing human from time to time to join in a faction fight or add his human strength to a hurling match. Sometimes they have reason to be sorry that they have done so, as the fairies had who took Jamie Freel to steal a young lady to be a fairy's bride when he rescued her by a blessing and took her home to be a bride to him in the end.[20]

There are solitary fairies as we shall see, but on the whole, whether they bless mortals, or blight them, whether they go out to dance harmlessly in their rings or to steal mothers, children, or food, they like to travel in flocks. Even that notorious solitary the Brownie is sometimes reputed, like the Phynodoree of Man, to be an exile from the Fairy Court and to desire his fine new clothes so that he may prank it again among the revellers.

These trooping fairies, even more than the solitary ones, have always been reported from very early times to have lately left the country or to be rapidly dwindling. Even as early as the first year of Henry the Second's reign King Herla and his rout were said to have been seen, according to Walter Map, disappearing into the River Wye near Hereford, and since that time they had ceased their wanderings. Chaucer's Wife of Bath at the beginning of her Tale, makes no doubt that the elves have gone.

> In th'olde days of the king Arthour,
> Of which that Britons speken greet honour,
> Al was this land fulfild of fayerye,
> The elf-queen, with hir joly companye,
> Daunced ful ofte in many a grene mede;
> This was the olde opinion, as I rede.
> I speke of manye hundred yeres ago;
> But now can no man see none elves mo.

She goes on to ascribe this to the great charity of limitours and friars and ends with shrewd irony:

> Women may go saufly up and doun,
> In every bush, or under every tree;
> There is noon other incubus but he.[21]

In the sixteenth century Reginald Scot had no doubt that the fairies had ceased to be believed in, however credulous people might be about witches, and in the seventeenth we have Bishop Corbet's delightful 'Farewell Rewards and Fairies' on the same theme. A little later in the century Aubrey records a tale of how the fairies were driven away by the peal of bells in Inkberrow Church. They were heard lamenting: 'Neither sleep, neither lie, Inkberrow's ting-tang hangs so high'. Yet in the beginning of the ninetenth century Hugh Miller in *Old Red Sandstone* gives a detailed account of the final departure of the fairies from Scotland, a sad and squalid cavalcade.

> On a Sabbath morning . . . the inmates of this little hamlet had all gone to church, all except a herd-boy, and a little girl, his sister, who were lounging beside one of the cottages; when, just as the shadow of the garden-dial had fallen on the line of noon, they saw a long cavalcade ascending out of the ravine through the wooded hollow. It winded among the knolls and bushes; and, turning round the northern gable of the cottage beside which the sole spectators of the scene were stationed, began to ascend the eminence toward the south. The horses were shaggy, diminutive things, speckled dun and grey; the riders, stunted, misgrown, ugly creatures, attired in antique jerkins of plaid, long grey cloaks, and little red caps, from under which their wild uncombed locks shot out over their cheeks and foreheads. The boy and his sister stood gazing in utter dismay and astonishment, as rider after rider, each one more uncouth and dwarfish than the one that had preceded it, passed the cottage, and disappeared among the brushwood which at that

period covered the hill, until at length the entire route, except the last rider, who lingered a few yards behind the others, had gone by. 'What are ye, little mannie? and where are ye going?' inquired the boy, his curiosity getting the better of his fears and his prudence. 'Not of the race of Adam,' said the creature, turning for a moment in his saddle: 'the People of Peace shall never more be seen in Scotland.'[22]

And again at the beginning of this century Ruth Tongue found a Somerset tradition of a family of Pixies driven away by the newly-hung bells of Withypool Church.[23]

It was said to be the church bells that drove the Trolls from Denmark in the story of 'Toller's Neighbours' to be found in Thorpe's *Yule-Tide Stories*.[24] This was the tale of a young couple newly settled in a lonely place considered as ill-omened, who were visited by a tiny man with a hunchback, a long white beard, a red cap on his head and a leather apron tied around him, whom he recognised at once as a Troll. The Troll had come as an Ambassador of his King, who lived in the hill near and was anxious lest his subjects should be molested by the humans. Toller gave the little hillman a cordial greeting and promised to do all he could to be a good neighbour. A most friendly relationship was established between the humans and the hillmen, and they did all they could for each other, with loans of pots or meal from Toller and his wife and help in every emergency from the little Trolls. And so they lived side by side for many prosperous years, until one day their first friend came to visit them very sadly, to invite them to a banquet. It was a magnificent feast, but a very mournful one, and at the end the King told them that the Troll people could no longer stay in Denmark because there were so many church bells everywhere. They were forced to migrate to the wilder, lonelier country of Norway, where they could hope for solitude. They said farewell, picked up their bundles and set out on their sad pilgrimage. But before they went they each gave Toller's daughter, over whose birth they had presided and who was by this time a full-grown maiden, a pair of stones, which by the next morning had turned into precious jewels. And these hillmen were the last Trolls in Denmark. So all the stories run about the departure of the Fairies, but for all that the last rumours of the Fairies linger on. We hear of them in Ireland and the Highlands of Scotland, and one is told anecdotes of their being seen in such sophisticated places as Kensington Gardens or rural Surrey. The fairies, older than the oldest gods of whom we have mythological records, still show here and there a flicker of their former life.

CHAPTER 4 – HOUSE SPIRITS

 N BRITISH FOLKLORE the Brownies are the most famous of the house spirits, though there were others scattered all over the British Isles, remarkably alike in some ways, but with considerable points of difference. They are not confined to these Islands, however, but range far in time and space. A manuscript in the British Museum (Harleiam 6482) gives a general but rather unfavourable picture of the house spirits, without mentioning their domestic labours, so that they seem rather more like Poltergeists than Brownies. They are also less solitary than the usual Brownie.

Of spirits called Hobgoblins, or Robin Goodfellows. 'These kinde of spirits are more familiar and domestical than the others, and for some causes to us unknown, abode in one place more than in another, so that some never almost depart from some particular houses, as though they were their proper mansions, making in them sundrie noises, rumours, mockeries, gawds and jests, without doing any harme at all; and some have heard them play at gitterns and Jews harps, and ring bells and make answer to those that call them, and speake with certain signes, laughters and merry gestures, so that those of the house come at last to be so familiar and well acquainted with them that they fear them not at all.'[1]

The author goes on to say that these spirits would be very dangerous both to body and soul if they were not restrained. As it is they are harmless though essentially malevolent. King James I in his *Daemonologie*[2] shows himself equally hostile to the fairy beliefs, but at least mentioned the Brownie as a devil who haunted the house, doing no evil, 'but doing as it were necessaire turnes up and down the house; and this spirit they called Brownie in our language, who appeared like a roughman: yea, some were so blinded as to believe that their house was all the sonsier, as they called it, that such spirits resided there.'

Here King James seems to accord a certain amount of belief to the Brownie, since he calls him a devil, and he certainly believed in devils, but a few pages further on (73–4) summing up the whole of the Scottish contemporary fairy belief, he seems more sceptical:

How there was a King and Queene of Phairie, of such a jolly court and train as they had, how they had a teynd, & dutie, as it were, of all goods: how they naturallie rode and went, eate and drank, and did all other actiones like naturall men and women: I thinke it liker Virgils *Campi Elysii* nor anie thing that ought to be beleeved by Christians.[3]

Here King James calls us back to classical beliefs and indeed we can find many similar traditions amongst the Ancient Romans, particularly those about House Spirits, which date back to very primitive times. Reginald Scot, whose *Discoverie of Witchcraft* James ordered to be destroyed by the Public Hangman when he came to the Throne of England, points out as James himself might do, the resemblance between the Roman and more modern beliefs.

Ritson cites Reginald Scot in the 'Dissertation on the Fairies' at the beginning of his book on *Fairy Tales*.[4]

The *penates* of the Romans, according to honest Reginald Scot (p. 16), were 'the domesticall gods, or rather divels', that were said to make men live quietlie within doores. But some think *Lares* are such as trouble private houses. *Larvae* are said to be spirits that walke onelie by night. *Vinculi terrei* are such as was Robin Goodfellowe, that would supplie the office of servants, speciallie of maides; as to make a fier in the morning, sweepe the house, grind mustard and malt, drawe water, etc., these also rumble in houses, drawe latches, go up and downe staiers, etc.

The Lares and Penates were indeed the primitive domestic gods of the early Romans. Their altars were set up on the hearth and given sacrifices of food, wine and animals. Libations of wine were poured out to them. The Penates were responsible for the supply of food in the house and the fertility of the fields. They were counted so important that they were called dii or divi, an honour not accorded to the *lar* or the *genius*. There were two to each household: their images were always brought to the table at each meal and set between the plates. The first helping was given to them. The Lar was solitary. He was the luck of the house, and his image was that of a young boy dancing, with a horn of plenty held above his head. His altar also stood on the hearth with the Penates, the genii of the household and Vesta. He was sacrificed to on all important occasions, by an incoming bride and after a funeral.[5]

It has sometimes been suggested that he may have been the spirit of a foundation sacrifice buried under the hearth, but there is no general agreement on this point. He is a very ancient spirit. His name is from an old Etruscan word, *Lar*, or *Lars*, meaning 'lord'. Everything that happened in the household, and the surrounding farm, was his concern. It will be seen how easily the more modern Brownies and other hobgoblins could have developed from this domestic spirit. The *larvae* of the Romans were the hungry, malevolent ghosts, who also have their counterparts in later folk tradition, the *Sluagh* of the Highlands, for instance, and the Devil's Dandy Dogs. There are, we notice, two types of hobgoblins, or helpful spirits—the Brownies, who actually live in the house, and the Good Neighbours, who live somewhere near, under a neighbouring knoll, who are responsible for the fertility of the land and might be equated to the Penates, though there are generally more than two of them. Like the Lar the Brownie is generally solitary and lives as a rule in the house or the outbuildings, though occasional Brownies haunt a pool or stream near, like Puddlefoot who haunted Altmor Burn near Cloichfoldich in Perthshire and paddled about in it until everyone in Cloichfoldich Farm had gone to bed, when he went up to the house and washed and cleared away all the dirty dishes, though he threw everything that had been cleaned on the floor. Milk was left out for him, which he took gladly, and left a gift of some kind in return. He was laid not by a gift of clothing but by a drunk man who called him by his name.[6] Like the Lar and the Penates, the Scottish Brownie expected a tribute of food, of good but simple quality, but the Scottish Brownies or those on the Border departed at once if other payment was offered them, and an almost standard way of laying them was to leave them a suit of clothes; although it was not quite an universal rule. In Lincolnshire, it seems, the annual wages of the Brownie was a white smock of fine linen, on New Year's Eve. In return for this he did all kinds of work for the farmer, not only working in the house but rounding up his sheep when they were scattered. He had one particularly arduous chase and he complained bitterly to the farmer that the little grey sheep had cost him more trouble than all the rest of the flock together. When the farmer went into the barn to count his sheep he found a terrified little hare amongst them. This anecdote is told about a variety of spirits who come to act as shepherd at a pinch. After a time, however, a new farmer succeeded to the farm, who grudged the Brownie his fine linen shirt and left one made of coarse sacking. The Brownie took it and sang out, so that all the house could hear him,

> 'Harden, harden, harden hamp,
> I will neither grind nor stamp:
> Had you given me linen gear,
> I had served you many a year.
> Thrift may go, bad luck may stay,
> I shall travel far away.'

And that was the last they heard or saw of him.[7]

Versions of this rhyme were known early, quoted by Reginald Scot and again in 1606 by William Warner in *Albion's England*. Warner thoroughly disapproved of Brownies and regarded them as plain devils, who tricked the housewives by getting them out of bed to clean the house in their sleep.

But he knew the stories.

> 'My Hampen Hampen Sentence, when some tender fool would lay
> Me shirt or slop, them greeved, for I then would go away.'[8]

In general through Scotland, England, Ireland and the Isle of Man, the
gift of clothing is enough to drive a house spirit away, though varying
reasons are given for this. In Ireland, in Patrick Kennedy's story of 'The
Phooka of Kildare', the Phooka, in the form of an ass, performs all the
drudgery of the house until it is rewarded with a gift of clothing. It
described itself as the ghost of an idle kitchen boy who was doomed to do
the drudgery of the house until he was considered worthy of a reward.[9]
OtherBrownie spirits were supposed to be ghosts, like the Cauld Lad of
Hilton, who was believed to be the ghost of a stable-boy, killed by one of
the past lords of Hilton in a fit of passion. He was always cold, and had a
disconcerting habit of getting into bed with people to warm himself, but
he performed household drudgery like a Brownie, and was finally laid by a
gift of clothing, and departed, singing:

> 'Here's a cloak, and here's a hood!
> The Cauld Lad of Hilton will do no more good.'[10]

Others there were who thought themselves too fine to work when they
had got new clothes. One example is the Pixy in Mrs Bray's story. An
interesting variant of this tale is given by E. M. Wright in *Rustic Speech and
Folk-Lore*. A poor young woman married a thresher who proved to be a
drunkard and never went to his work. In despair she dressed herself as a
man, and went to take his place. Every morning she found twice as much
corn threshed as she had left the night before. She was anxious to discover
who her benefactor was, so one night she hid herself and watched. Late at
night a tiny little pixy came into the barn and set to work on the corn. As
he threshed he sang:

> 'Little pixy fair and slim,
> Without a rag to cover him.'

And indeed he was quite naked. The woman was full of pity and gratitude.
She bought some stuff, made him a suit of tiny clothes, which she hung up
beside his flail. Then she hid to watch. The pixy came in, saw the clothes
and put them on, then he capered about joyfully and sang:

> 'Pixy fine and Pixy gay,
> Pixy now must fly away.'

Then he disappeared, and the poor woman never saw him again.

Fenoderee, the Manx Brownie, is another of the house spirits who is laid by a gift of clothing. He was a rough, hairy spirit, who was supposed to have been exiled from Fairyland because he had fallen in love with a human girl and was dancing with her in the merry glen of Rushen during the sacred festival of the Harvest Moon at which all the fairy court should attend. Keightley quoted the story from Train's *Isle of Man*. For this offence the poor Fenoderee was condemned to wear a hairy form and live in banishment until the Day of Judgement. He retained a great love of Mankind, however, and performed stupendous labours all over the Island. Once a gentleman was building a fine house near Snafield and he had quarried a number of fine stones, among them a particularly beautiful block of marble, too heavy for his men to transport. In one night the Fenoderee carried them all the way up to the proposed site, and the gentleman was so grateful that he had a handsome set of clothes made and laid out as a reward. The Fenoderee took them up one by one and said in Manx:

'Cap for the head, alas, poor head!
Coat for the back, alas poor back!
Breeches for the breech, alas poor breech!
If these be all thine, thine cannot be the merry Glen of Rushen!'

Then with a melancholy wail he disappeared and the Island has never been as merry a place since.[12]

According however to Dora Broome in her delightful *Fairy Tales of the Isle of Man*, he can be called back again by incantation to perform particular tasks. A man sent by his wife to invoke the Fenoderee to cure their little red cow says the correct incantation but forgets to cross himself for safety. The Fenoderee comes in a mischievous mood, cures the cow but begins to carry off the man, who remembers just in time to cross himself, but not before he had inadvertently devoted the cow to Fenoderee.[13]

Like the Fenoderee, the sixteenth-century German *Kobold*, Hinzelmann, was an exile from his native haunts in the Bohemian forests. A long account of him and his hauntings was written by a contemporary minister, Feldmann, of which a shortened account appears in Grimm's *Deutsche Sagen*. This is reproduced in Keightley's *Fairy Mythology*.[14] Hinzelmann began to haunt the old castle of Hudemühlen near Aller in 1584. From the first he talked freely with the inhabitants of the Castle and with visitors, but remained invisible. This terrified the servants at first, but they soon lost their fears and became friendly with him. In this way he behaved rather like Malekin, the little medieval house spirit described by Ralph of Coggeshall. Malekin, however, performed no Brownie labours.

Hinzelmann told his name to the household, and also his second name, Lüring, and his wife's name, Hille Bingels. It is most unusual for spirits to betray their names in genuine folk tradition, and the whole story seems to bear the marks of a ventriloquist's trickery.

The lord of the Castle did not become as easily reconciled to the invisible voice as the servants. He would gladly have rid himself of Hinzelmann, but the tradition of offering clothes to a Brownie did not seem to be active in Germany at that time, and he made no use of his knowledge of the spirit's name. The best expedient that occurred to him was to leave Hudemühlen. He set out with his convoy and travelled to Hanover, where he put up at an inn. They had all observed a white feather floating along beside the carriage, but could make nothing of it. On the next morning the Lord of Hudemühlen missed a very valuable gold chain that he usually wore and accused the inn servants of taking it. The innkeeper was indignant and defended his staff wholeheartedly. After an unpleasant interview the lord retreated to his room to think what he should do next. Suddenly he heard the voice of Hinzelmann quite near him. 'What is the matter?' it said. 'Are you anxious about your chain? Look under your pillow and you'll find it.' And there it lay. The lord knew Hinzelmann must have hidden it, for the bed had been searched already, so he said angrily: 'What right had you to get me into trouble with the landlord? It is because of you that I've had to leave my home.' 'There was no need to leave your home,' said Hinzelmann. 'Wherever you go I will go with you. Didn't you see me flying beside you like a white feather. Go back home, and so long as I am with you good luck will be yours.'

After weighing the matter the lord decided that the wisest course was to follow the spirit's advice, so back he went. Hinzelmann was delighted and set to work in a true Brownie fashion as soon as he got home. The cook had only to leave a pile of unwashed dishes when she went to bed and Hinzelmann would work all night, washing, polishing and putting them in their places. In return a bowl of sweet milk was left him for breakfast every morning. He took charge of the servants, scolding them for everything they did wrong and praising them if they were industrious. If anyone disobeyed him he picked up a stick and thrashed them, though all this time he was invisible. He groomed the horses and worked in the stable. In return for this he had a room allotted to him in the castle, furnished according to his own specifications with a table, an armchair and a bed. The chair he plaited himself of rushes and there was no sign that the bed was ever slept in except for a small dent such as a dog might have made curled up there. He expected a place to be laid for him at table, and food to be served. This disappeared but was generally found afterwards scattered about under benches. His glass of wine vanished for a time and was returned empty. He joined in the conversation at table, and welcomed guests, although he bitterly resented any attempts to lay him or imprison him. Like other house spirits he took an especial fancy to particular members of the family. These were generally young women, and Hinzelmann's favourites were the ladies Anne and Catherine, the sisters of the lord. It was perhaps an unfortunate preference, for he drove away all their suitors, and they never married.

He was fond of playing tricks and Robin Goodfellow jokes on the servants and on anyone who seemed to him conceited, but he took care to do no real harm. He called himself a good Christain, and was very angry with anyone who called him a devil or a Kobold. He was fond of the company of children and sometimes joined in their games in the form of a little, curly-haired boy. It was only to children that he showed himself willingly. After four years he came to the lord to say goodbye and gave him three presents, a little hollow cross made of curiously knotted silk, a straw hat woven by himself in the same kind of patterns as his chair and a glove embroidered with pearls. He said these three things must be kept together, and as long as they remained good fortune would stay with the castle. He advised the lord to give them into the care of the ladies Anne and Catherine, for they would know how to look after them. He left Hudemühlen in 1588, though the account of his activities makes his visitation seem longer than four years.

Another invisible Kobold described by Keightley was called King Goldemar of Vollmar.[15] He had much the same habits as Hinzelmann, expecting a place at table and conversing with the company. He was on very friendly terms with Neveling von Hardenberg and often shared a bed with him. He could be felt but never seen. His hands felt like a frog's paws, thin, soft and chilly. He sang beautifully and played on the harp. Like Hinzelmann he had a room in the castle and he also expected fodder and stabling for his invisible horse. He seems to have done no Brownie labours and he was much more ruthless than any of the British Brownies would be. Like all fairy creatures he could not endure to be spied upon. Once a servant strewed ashes and tares on the floor in the hope of finding his footprints; Vollmar came behind him as he was making a fire, hewed him in pieces and roasted him on a spit. His head and legs he put into a pot to boil. The cannibal meal was brought up to him and he ate it with cries of joy; but after that he left. Hutkin, who was attached to the household of the Bishop of Hildesheim is described as of a kind and obliging disposition, but he treated a kitchen boy who tormented him in the same savage way. All house spirits are rather touchy, but none are so dangerous to offend as the German Kobolds. The tiny, trooping house spirits of Germany, the *Heinzelmänchen*. were of a milder disposition.[16] They came into tradesmen's households, particularly tailors, and did wonderful work for them, finishing garments when they were pushed by work, and helping the housewives besides. Some tailors employed no journeymen because they were so well served by the Heinzelmänchen. At last a tailor's wife, devoured by curiosity, scattered dried peas on the stairs in the hope that they would fall and be lamed so that she could see them in the morning, the ruse failed, but after that the Heinzelmänchen left Cologne. The music of their departing was heard all night, but they never came to help the Burghers of Cologne anymore. Grimm (39) tells a similar story in his *Household Tales*, 'The Shoemaker and the Elves', but here the elves were laid like British house spirits by a gift of clothes, though they left good luck behind them.[17]

I have said that the British hobs and Brownies could be touchy and take offence easily, like most other fairy people, but they were never as ruthless as the German Kobolds. There were many thoroughly evil creatures in the spirit host, but the Brownies were generally well-intentioned. The Brownie of Cranshaws was a typical example of a touchy spirit. His story was told first by George Henderson in his *Popular Rhymes of Berwickshire*.[18] This Brownie was rather agricultural than domestic, and for several years he had reaped and threshed the corn at Cranshaws Farm until people began to take his services for granted. One evening one of the farm-hands remarked: 'The Brownie's getting lazy; the corn's no sae weel mowed nor stacked the year.' The Brownie who was dozing on one of the rafters of the barn, heard him and was furious. That night a great stamping and muttering was heard in the barn. The Brownie was going in and out of it carrying stooks of corn in his arms. As he went to and fro he muttered:

> 'It's no weel mowed! It's no weel mowed!
> Then its ne'er be mowed by me again;
> I'll scatter it owre the Raven Stane,
> And they'll hae some work ere it's mowed again.'

The Raven Crag was a great rock that stood above the burn some two miles from Cranshaw Farm, and all night long the furious Brownie stumped to and fro between the Crag and the barn until every blade of corn was whirled away by the stream. He never came back to work at Cranshaws again, but, angry though he was, he had hurt neither life nor limb.

The Manx Fenoderee, wounded by the farmer's criticism, took a rather more perilous course. The farmer complained that the corn was not cut close enough, so the angry Fenoderee followed him, stubbing up the roots so fiercely that the farmer's toes seemed in danger. However, here too the farmer was more frightened than hurt. The Welsh Bwca can be more energetic in his punishment according to the story told by John Rhys in *Celtic Folklore*.[19] It was however a punishment for a particularly nasty trick. Long years ago there was a strong, merry maidservant on a Monmouthshire farm, who was on particularly good terms with the Bwca who lived there. People had been afraid of the bogie before, but it was sometimes said that this girl had a touch of the blood of the Fair Family—the Tylweth Teg—in her and at any rate she knew how to get on the right side of a Bwca, and he did everything for her—washing, ironing, spinning, weaving, and only expected in return a bowl of sweet milk and some wheaten bread, set out for him every night. All went happily between them, but perhaps the girl really had a touch of fairy tricksiness about her, for one night, for sheer devilment, she filled the Bwca's bowl with stale urine, which is used as mordant for dyeing, instead of milk. She soon repented of the trick, for as she got out of bed in the morning he leapt on her, seized her by the throat and kicked and dragged her about the house, yelling all the time:

> 'The idea that the thick-buttocked lass
> Should give barley-bread and piss
> To the Bwca!'

The girl screamed for help as loud as she could. At length the men came running down from their lofts, and when he heard them coming the Bwca scampered away and was heard of no more at that farm. He went to another, where he and the servant girl made great friends. She fed him delicately, but unfortunately she was very curious to know his name, and at last by a ruse she learned it, Gwaryn-a-Throt, and taunted him with the knowledge. So she lost her helper and he lost his home. His third venture was luckier. He and the servant-man, Moses, became very fond of each other, and lived together happily for years, until Moses went to fight against Richard Crookback and was killed at the Battle of Bosworth Field. When poor Gwaryn-aThrot lost his friend he went down in the world and became a boggart instead of a Brownie. In the end a wise man was called in who raised a great wind and blew him away to the Red Sea, to keep company with all the other troublesome spirits.

The house spirits of Norway and Denmark are called *Nisse*. Those of Sweden are *Tomte*, small, slow and laborious but very lucky to have about the farm. The Nisse are also thought to be luck-bringers, but they are ready to give a pretty sharp punishment to anyone who offends them.

They are very small people, the size of a one-year-old child but with the face of an old man. They generally wear gray with a red pointed cap, except at Michaelmas when they wear a round peasant hat. The only reward they expect for their work is a nightly bowl of *groute*, a kind of porridge, enriched with a good pat of butter. They are punctilious in exacting this. One night a Nis began to eat up his groute and saw no butter in it. This so much enraged him that he went and broke the neck of the cow. Then he felt hungry and went back to finish his groute, meagre though it was. When he had nearly finished it he found that a large pat of butter had sunk to the bottom. He was filled with remorse; he had no power to bring the cow to life again so he lugged out a small, heavy treasure chest, filled with gold, and left it beside the carcase to make amends. There was enough gold in it to make the family prosperous for the rest of their lives. On the whole the Nisse were treated with great respect, but they seemed to suffer a good deal from troublesome and mischievous boys. There are several stories about this reproduced by Keightley from Grimm's *Teutonic Mythology*,[20] most of them from Jutland. The good luck of the farm patronized by a Nis was partly due to the Nis's habit of purloining grain and fodder from neighbouring farms and giving it to the farmer whom he favoured.

This trait may be found among English house spirits too. Once the Nis went out on one of these thieving expeditions accompanied by the farm boy. The Nis took as much as he thought he could well carry, but the boy was greedy for more. 'Come on,' said the boy, 'We can take a rest on the way.' 'What is this rest?' said the Nis, 'I've never heard of it.' 'I'll show you,' said the boy. So they took a great load, and half-way back the Nis began to be very tired. 'Come on, let's take our rest,' said the boy, so they sat down together, and after a time the Nis said, 'If I'd known rest was so good I'd have emptied the whole barn.' After a time, however, the boy began to tease and torment the Nis until he found it unendurable. He was sitting one day at the granary window with his feet hanging out into the yard when the boy ran at him and tipped him back into the granary. But that night the Nis took his revenge on the boy. He lifted him naked out of his bed and carried him down to the well, where he had arranged two planks across the top, and laid him on them, hoping that he would awake startled and fall down into the well. The boy was half awakened by the cold, however, and escaped without injury. It is doubtful whether the Nis meant to drown the boy or to give him a bad ducking and pull him out of the well.

There was another Nis in Vosborg who was very well treated by the people in the farm, and did all he could for them in consequence. One winter the weather was very cold and snowy some of the calves were completely cut off in their little shed, so that no one could get to them and the farm people lamented them as dead. When the thaw came, however, they found that the Nis had got through to them and the calves were well fed and groomed and in fine condition. The farm people could not make enough of the Nis after that. A roguish boy came to the place, however, who made a hobby of tormenting the Nis. One day the Nis was gambolling about in the loft when a rotten plank broke and his leg came right through into the cow-house below. The boy happened to be there and he picked up a fork and jabbed it into the Nis's leg. At dinner the boy kept chuckling to himself. 'What's the matter with you?' said the bailiff. 'Oh I gave the old Nis such a devil of a blow this morning,' said the boy. 'No', said the Nis outside the window, 'it was three blows, for there were three prongs to the fork. But I'll pay you out for it.' That night the Nis came up to the boy's bed, lifted him out, carried him down the yard and threw him right over the house. Then he ran round so fast that he caught him before he touched the ground, and tossed him back again. He did this eight times, and the ninth he let the boy fall into a deep pool just beside the house; then he laughed loud and long at the boy's ducking.

The little Tomte of Sweden took no revenge for ill treatment except to go away and take their luck with them. Keightley quotes an anecdote of one from *Sarge Häfdar* of Afzelius,[21] which seems to show them even smaller than the Nisse. He says they were given their wages on Christmas morning, a piece of gray cloth, tobacco and a shovel-full of clay.

In Sweden the Tomte is sometimes seen at noon, in Summer, slowly and stealthily dragging a straw of an ear of corn. A farmer, seeing him thus engaged, laughed and said, 'What difference does it make if you bring away that or nothing?' The Tomte in displeasure left his farm, and went to that of his neighbour; and with him went all the prosperity from him who had made light of him, and passed over to the other farmer. Any one who treated the industrious Tomte with respect, and set store by the smallest straw, because rich, and plenty regularly prevailed in his household.

The Tomte, like the Lincolnshire Brownie, does not seem to have been laid by a gift of clothes. On the contrary he accepted it as his right. The Lincoln Brownie already mentioned was banished not by a gift of clothing but by its poor quality, and the same offence seems to have been taken by the Hob of Hart Hall, whose story was uncovered by J. C. Atkinson in *Forty Years in a Moorland Parish*.[22] The parish which was the subject of his researches was Danby-in-Cleveland to which he was appointed in 1847 and where he continued to hold the living till his death in 1900. In

Cleveland the house spirits were generally called Hobs, and were believed to be entirely benevolent characters. Atkinson collected his information from an old parishioner who had once lived in the neighbourhood of Hart Hall, but after the time when the Hob had departed. He had gained from her account a very favourable impression of Hob.

In the barn, if there was a weight of work craving to be done, and time was scant or force insufficient, Hob would come unasked, unwarned, to the rescue, and the corn would be threshed, dressed and sacked, nobody knew how, except that it was done by the Hob. Unaccountable strength seemed to be the chief attribute ascribed to him. One did not hear of him as mowing or reaping, ploughing, sowing or harrowing; but what mortal strength was clearly incapable of, that was the work which Hob took upon himself. Another thing to be remarked about this Hob—at least in all the stories about him and his doings—was that there was no reminiscence of his mischievousness, harmless malice, or even tricksiness. He was not one of those who resent, with a sort of pettish, or even spiteful malice, the possibly unintended interference with elfish prerogative implied in stopping up an 'awfbore' or holes in deal-boarding occasioned by the dropping out of a shrunken knot, and which displayed itself in the way of forcibly ejecting the intended stopping, in the form of a sharply driven pellet, into the face, or directly onto the nose of the offender. Neither was he like the Farndale Hob told of by Professor Phillips, who was so 'familiar and troublesome a visitor of one of the farmers of the dale, and caused him so much vexation and petty loss, that he resolved to quit his house in Farndale and seek some other home'. No such tale was told of the Hart Hall Hob. The Hob's departure was due, like that of the Phooka of Kildare, to the curiosity of one of the farm lads. It was well known that creatures of his kind never liked to be spied upon, but one night this boy heard the thud of the flail upon the floor and he crept out in the moonlight to the barn and peeped through a hole in the wood. 'An he seen a lahtle brown man, a' covered wi' hair, spangin' about wiv fleeal lahk yan wud.' He had no clothes on to speak of but the boy saw a ragged old shirt lying near. He was spreading the corn and beating out the grain faster than two men could do it. The boy stole away without being noticed and told the other servants what he had seen, and they were full of pity for the little old man, making himself so hot with labour and then going out into the cold wind with nothing but an old ragged bit of a shirt to shield him from the blast. So they put their heads together and made a coarse smock, as like as they could to what the boy had described, and before nightfall they laid it in the barn, 'gay and handy for t'lahtle chap to notish.' They hid themselves to watch, and, when all the house should have been in bed, Hob came along and picked up the smock and turned it about to examine it. Then he burst out with:

> 'Gin Hob mun hae nowght but a hardin' hamp,
> He'll come nae mair, nowther to berry nor stamp.'

With that he took nimself off, and was never seen again.

Atkinson points out that this rhyme was very ancient. *Stamp* was in use as a dialect word for knocking off the heads of barley before threshing, but *berry*, meaning to thresh, had long been out of use, and *hamp* was an ancient name for the belted tunic that was often the sole garment worn by the medieval peasants. We have already seen that 'hempen, hampen' was part of the aggrieved Brownie's rhyme in the sixteenth-century tradition.

So we find the Brownie rhyme still alive in the nineteenth century, and probably well rooted in medieval times.

CHAPTER 5 – NATURE FAIRIES

T IS A MATTER of some conjecture whether the remaining nature fairies were once divinities, minor mythological deities, such as nymphs, dryads, naiads, fauns, satyres, tritons, or the helpful or malevolent spirits of the dead. It seems likely that they were of a mixed origin, as most fairies seem to be.

We might start with the most generalized and amorphous of the nature fairies, the fertility spirits. Here a mixed origin is very evident. The first that occur to us will probably be the Good Neighbours, mound dwellers who inhabit *shians* in an agricultural countryside. They are closely connected with the dead ancestors of the modern inhabitants, who, dwelling underground, control the growth of seed and the general fertility of the land. Kirk, in his *Secret Commonwealth of Elves, Fauns and Fairies*, says that the fairy mounds were set up near the churchyards to accommodate the souls of those who were waiting for the Day of Judgement to learn their final destination, and, in the meantime, were clad in bodies made of the good deeds they had performed while they were on earth.[1] This theory makes the fairy mound more recent than the church, but it witnesses to the strength of the belief that the fairies were the souls of the dead. They are propitiated by oblations of bread, of milk poured into the holes of cupstones and occasionally by sacrifices of the firstlings of the flock, though it seems that these last offerings may be made to dwindled gods. Sometimes they haunt farm houses as Brownies or other Hobgoblins, though it will be noticed that Brownies do not stay exclusively indoors, but commonly haunt a stream, or pool, or a tree. These are sometimes expressly described as ghosts, like the Cauld Lad of Hilton[2] or the Phooka of Kildare.[3] As would be natural to the dead, both the Good Neighbours and the Hobgoblins are notably conservative and are offended by innovation of any kind. These fairies belong, however, to a fairly recent stage of culture; they plough, mow, reap, spin, weave, even embroider.

There are also fairies and Hobgoblins who are more interested in stock. As we have seen in Chapter 4 there are some who specialise in rounding up the flocks and herds, and there are also fairies who are patrons of wild animals, and therefore belong to the earlier hunting culture. The Cailleach Bheur,[4] the Blue Hag of Winter, herds and protects the deer on the mountains, the Brown Man of the Muirs is the guardian of all the wild game on his territory of Elsdon Moors. Richard Surtees in volume IV of his *History of Durham*[5] reproduces a letter he wrote to Sir Walter Scott telling a story that he himself collected from an old lady, Elizabeth Cockburn, a tradition dating back to 1641. It tells how two young men were shooting on the high moors above Elsdon, and after good sport sat down together to eat by a mountain stream before they went on. The younger went down to drink at the stream and when he lifted his head from drinking, he saw, on the other side of the water, a small hideous dwarf, glowering at him with eyes as round and fierce as a bull's. He was squat, but very strongly made, with a ferocious face and red, frizzled hair. He was dressed in withered bracken, or some fabric like it, and he burst out into a torrent of abuse, asking the boy what right he had to slaughter the beasts that were under *his* protection. He himself, he said, though all the creatures were his, never tasted flesh or blood, but lived on nuts and berries and apples. 'I am strong enough on these,' he said; 'Come and see my diet.' The lad was just going to jump the stream when his companion called to him, begging him not to cross the water. It may be that he adjured him in God's name, for as he spoke the Brown Man vanished. They were both convinced that if the lad had crossed the running water that protected him he would have been torn limb from limb.

They were both shaken by this adventure and determined to shoot no more that day. They picked up their guns and their game and set out for home. But as they got further from the burn the spirits of the younger boy rose and he began to boast of what he would have done. A bird got up and he lifted his gun. His friend called: 'Don't shoot!' but he laughed and brought the bird down. As it fell a pang went through him, and by the time he got home, he was seriously ill. He lingered on for some time but he died before the end of the year, and all the neighbourhood believed that it was the Brown Man's vengeance.

Scott, in volume IV of *The Minstrelsy of the Scottish Border*,[6] described the Brown Man of the Muirs as a duergar and calls him a purely malevolent being; but the Brown Man, though an enemy of the human kind, was evidently devotedly attached to his creatures. His appearance seems to be much like that of a duergar; perhaps the duergar has the same prejudices in favour of the animal creation.

The little flower fairies of England, like those described in *A Midsummer Night's Dream,* seem to have been much like the Light Elves of Scandinavian mythology whose mission it was to tend the flowers. It will be noticed that Shakespeare's fairies have power over more than flowers. If they quarrel and jar together all the seasons go awry.[7] Mildew on crops and canker on the roses are fairy blights, and even the small Elizabethan fairies are particularly interested in fertility. They are patrons of true lovers and bring increase to human offspring as well as to flocks and herds.

When we come to Water Fairies we find creatures of very different kinds and origins. Many of them must have been originally mythological, ancient gods, spirits of streams, wells and lakes, some water-demons, some of them either ghosts or the euhemerized forms of hungry river spirits. Peg O'Nell is an example of this.[8] The story is that she was a servant girl at Waddow Hall near Clitheroe, and one frosty night they ran short of water, and the girl was very reluctant to go out. She said she would fall and break her neck. Her mistress said 'Get along with you! And may you break your neck indeed!' The ill wish was fulfilled. Peg fell on the icy stones, and has haunted Waddow Hall ever since. On every seventh year on Peg O'Nell's night the river claims a victim, and unless an animal has been sacrificed a human being is drowned. Peg Powler,[9] the spirit of the Tees, has been given no human form. She has long green locks and green teeth and pulls children down into the water. The cakes of foam on the upper reaches of the Tees are called 'Peg Powler's soap-suds'. She seems to be used as a cautionary bogy to keep children from playing too near the water. Particulars of both spirits are given by William Henderson in *Folklore of the Northern Counties*, who tells various bogy-beast stories at the same time, but these are shape-shifting tricks not closely associated with water. Though Peg Powler might well have been invented by cautious parents the Highland kelpie must have been taken more seriously. It is a bogy-beast which preys upon men, and belongs either to sea-lochs or rivers. It most usually appears like a pretty little horse which allures humans on to its back and then dashes away with them into the water, where it devours them, all except the liver which floats to shore. It can also appear in human shape.

There is one kelpie story, however, which is a version of type ML 4050, 'The Hour is come but not the Man'.[10] The setting is on the banks of the River Conan in Ross-shire, and it seems here, though it is not explicitly said that the kelpie took a female form, like a water nymph. Many years ago, when the little church by the ford was still standing, a party of reapers were cutting the corn on a sunny autumn day just near the false ford where the water ripples over seeming shallows before sweeping down into the deep lynn just below. All looked fair and still when they heard a voice crying out, 'The hour is come, but not the man!' and looking at the river they saw the figure of the kelpie standing in the false ford. Then she cried once again, and plunged like a drake diving into the great deep pool below. As she vanished they heard the sound of drumming hoofs and a rider came full-pelt down towards the false ford. Half a dozen of the men jumped out of the corn and ran to catch hold of him. They told him what the kelpie had said, they explained the dangers of the ford, but he seemed

neither to hear nor heed, and spurred on like a madman. They were determined to save him against his will, so they pulled him off his horse, and carried him, struggling and shouting to the little church where they locked him up, telling him that they would let him out when the hour of danger was past. He shouted and kicked at the door at first but he soon fell silent and they went on with their work and waited for the slow hour to pass. It was over at length, and they unlocked the door. 'You can go on now sir,' they called. 'The Ill Hour is past.' There was no answer, and they called again and yet again, and went into the church. There was an old stone trough near the door filled with water and the traveller was lying with his head in it. He had fallen in a fit and drowned there while they waited for the hour to go by. So the river had its victim in spite of them. Something of the same frantic haste is shown by the doomed riders who try to cross the Ribble on Peg O'Nell's night. This is an international Tale-Type, and many versions of it are found in Norway and Denmark as well as in other parts of Britain.

The Mermaids are perhaps the water spirits of which we hear most and of which people could make the most definite picture, and yet their general character admits of a good many different interpretations. The most common view in the straight line of English tradition is that expressed in that well-known folksong 'The Mermaid'.

> We there did espy a fair pretty maid
> With a comb and glass in her hand.[11]

At the very sight of her the whole crew abandons hope, the Captain bids farewell to the thought of his lady, the bo'sun to his wife, the little cabin-boy to his father and mother.

> Then three times round went our gallant ship,
>   And three times round went she;
> And three times round went our gallant ship
>   And she sank to the bottom on the sea.

The Mermaids of this type are so dangerous that the mere sight of them is enough to cause a shipwreck, and some, of the same type as the classical sirens, do their best to allure men to death. The fresh-water Mermaids are as dangerous as those from the sea. Chambers in his *Popular Rhymes*[12] tells the story of the Laird of Lorntie who had an encounter with one as he was returning to his castle with a single servant. As they passed the small lake that lies some three miles south of the Castle they heard a woman's voice screaming 'Lorntie! Lorntie! Help.' Lorntie rode quickly up to the water and saw a beautiful woman struggling in the lake. Without a moment's hesitation he leapt off his horse and plunged to the rescue. His servant, however, had quicker wits and almost as much readiness of action, for, just as the Laird was seizing the long golden locks that were floating on the water, he found himself seized and dragged out. 'Bide, Lorntie!, bide a blink,' said the man, 'Yon wauling madam was nae other, God sauf us! than the Mermaid!' Lorntie believed him, and the Mermaid confirmed it, for as they regained their horses she rose in the water and cried out in fury:

'Lorntie, Lorntie,
Were it na your man,
I had gart your heart's bluid
Skirl in my pan!'

Like the kelpie, this Mermaid was evidently a blood drinker. Other mermaids, even in Scotland, had more gentle reputations. Water spirits though they were they had great knowledge of land herbs, and some of them took an interest in the welfare of maidens. Cromek, who is always inclined to take a favourable view of the fairies, has an anecdote in his *Galloway and Nithsdale Song* of a young man who was lamenting the illness of his betrothed, who was wasting away in consumption, when a mermaid rose out from the water, and sang, clearly and sweetly:

'Wad ye let the bonnie may die i' your hand
And the mugwort flowering i' the land.'[13]

The young man at once rose up and gathered the flowers of southernwood, called in that country mugwort or muggins, dried them, infused them, and cured the girl by the infusion. Chambers gives a Renfrewshire tradition of a mermaid who rose out of a pool as the coffin of a young girl was carried over a stream and sang sadly:

'If they wad drink nettles in March,
And eat muggins in May,
Sae mony braw maidens
Wadna gang to the clay.'

The advice was cherished, though it came too late to save that patient.[14] Mermaids are generally supposed to have great medical skill and can confer the knowledge on chosen humans and their descendants. Hunt's story of 'The Old Man of Cury'[15] is an example of this. The stranded Mermaid restored to the sea by the old man is a gentle creature, though she gave her husband a more ferocious character, being anxious lest he should devour her children if he grew hungry in her absence. The gift of healing which she bestowed on the Old Man and his children was without strings and she left her comb with him, so that she could be summoned if he needed advice. 'Lutey and the Mermaid', a more sinister variant of the tale, is told by Bottrell.[16] The same bargain is made and carried out, but when they come to the sea the Mermaid tries to lure Lutey into the water, and would have succeeded if his dog had not begun to howl. As it was she had to leave him for nine years, and at the end of that time he was called into the sea. It was also said that one of Lutey's descendants was drowned every nine years.

In Ireland and the Highlands of Scotland Mermaids and Mermen are said to be anxious about their final salvation, like the Scandinavian water spirits. In Scotland salvation is always refused them, but in Ireland at least one Mermaid, Liban, became a saint, and though it must be admitted that she was not born a Mermaid, she had swum about Lough Neagh in that form for three hundred years.

In Scandinavia the attitude towards Mermen and other water spirits is specially tolerant. The *Neck* is a river spirit and a famous musician. Keightley cites a story which is known all through Sweden. The village pastor's children were playing by a stream when the Neck rose up out of the water and began to play most beautifully on his golden harp. One of the boys called to him, 'What is the use, Neck, of your sitting there playing? You will never be saved.' The Neck burst into tears, flung down his harp and sank to the bottom of the stream. The two boys ran in to tell their father, and he rebuked them for their unkindness. 'You were wrong.' he said, 'to speak to the poor Neck like that, who so earnestly desires salvation. Go back and tell him that there is hope for him still.' The boys went back to the stream where the Neck had risen to the surface again, and was crying and lamenting most bitterly. 'Neck, do not grieve so,' they said, 'Our father says that your Redeemer liveth also.'

At that the Neck snatched up his harp again and began to play with much rejoicing, so that the river echoed with the sweet sounds.[17]

In another version of the tale it is the priest himself who speaks harshly to the Neck, telling him that the dead staff in his hand will put forth green leaves again before the Neck's soul is saved. The Neck throws down his harp and bursts into lamentation, and the priest goes on his way, but he has not gone far before the green sap surges through his staff and twigs and leaves burst out. Deeply ashamed the priest turns back and shows the staff to the Neck, who picks up his harp again and breaks into a song of praise. Matthew Arnold's poem, 'The Neckan', ends with no such miracle but leaves the poor Neckan to his sorrow as in other stories of fairies seeking salvation. The Scandinavian Merman, the *Havmand*[18] is generally treated as a sympathetic character. *Havfrue* is sometimes thought of as kind and sometimes as dangerous and sinister, like the Mermaid of Scotland. In Denmark, which has no great rivers, the Neck story is told of the Havmand.

The Water-men in Germany are *Nixies*, and they often dwell on terms of some friendship with men. The Water-man is like a human man to look at, but has green teeth and wears a green hat. The female Nixies are very beautiful. They go to human markets to do their shopping, very neatly dressed, but can be recognised for what they are because one part of their dress, the corner of an apron or the hem of their skirt is sopping wet. Human midwives are often called to assist the labour of Nixie wives, though it is possible that these are generally human brides carried away by the Nixies. They do not seem as anxious as the Necks about their salvation. One story of a peasant and a Water-man quoted by Keightley is almost exactly the same as Crofton Croker's story 'Soul-Cages' about an Irish Merrow, in which the souls of drowned sailors are kept in cages rather like lobster pots.[19] There are many stories of sea spirits that raise storms and take the plunder of the sea, like Davy Jones, whose locker holds all that is lost at sea; there are other benevolent spirits, like Howlaa of the Isle of Man, who gives warning before the outbreak of storms.[20] The Breton Morgens are the same as our Mermaids, and Mermaids are also to be found in Italian folklore.

Among the river fairies of Europe are the medieval French *Dracs* recorded by Gervase of Tilbury. Like the Nixies their women come in human form to the market-place though the dracs were not identifiable by drenched hems to their garments. Gervase says of them:

> These, they say, have their abode in the caverns of rivers, and occasionally, floating along the stream in the form of gold rings or cups, entice women or boys who are bathing on the banks of the river; for while they endeavour to grasp what they see, they are suddenly seized and dragged down to the bottom: and this, they say, happens to none more than to suckling women, who are taken by the Dracs to rear their unlucky offspring; and sometimes, after they have spent seven years there, they return to our hemisphere.

Gervase goes on to tell the Fairy Ointment story and the one told of the Water Kelpy—'The Hour is come but not the Man'.[21]

A French story a little later than this, collected at the end of the fourteenth century, is that of Melusine, the serpent woman who was said to have married the Count of Lusignon.[22] She was a well-haunting spirit, one of the early Fairy Bridges, who turned into a serpent if she touched water. This transformation was said to be the result of a curse. At any rate it was the cause of a taboo imposed upon the husband, who was never to look at his wife while she bathed. The taboo was of course violated and the Count of Lusignon lost his bride. The Lake Maidens of Wales were other examples of fairy wives who imposed a taboo and were obliged to leave their husbands. They often bequeathed a knowledge of medicine to their children, for, like Mermaids, they were skilled in medicine. They brought with them a dowry of fairy cattle, who followed them back under water when the taboo was broken.

Water fairies are frequent everywhere, tree fairies are rarer. Some are attached to one species of tree. A well-known folk jingle runs 'Fairy folks are in old oaks' and in Britain the oak has a special potency, perhaps a survival from the early worship of the oak observed and recorded by Julius Caesar. The Oakmen, sinister characters with their red toadstool caps, occur in the longest and least-known of Beatrix Potter's books *The Fairy Caravan*.[23] Several folklore themes are treated in this, and though it makes no claim to be authoritative the legend is confirmed by the collections of Ruth Tongue in her *Somerset Folklore* where she gives a number of tree beliefs of Somerset. An old oaktree was often an object of veneration and it was considered wise to ask its permission to go into an oak-wood. The chorus of a Somerset folk-song gives some hints of the character of three trees.

> Ellum do grieve,
> Oak he do hate,
> Willow do walk
> If you travels late.[24]

The explanation of this is that the elm tree mourns for its companion if a neighbouring elm is cut down, and finally dies of grief, while an oak bitterly resents being cut. An oak is a lively tree and shoots spring up from the root when it is cut down. An oak copse which springs up when an oak-wood has been cut down is believed to be hostile to man and is dangerous to go through at night, particularly if it is a bluebell wood. Willows are supposed to have a sinister habit of following a traveller on a dark night muttering. Tolkien's Old Man Willow in *The Fellowship of the Ring*[25] probably had some foundation in folk belief. In most country places in England the elder tree was given a special personality as it was in Denmark. Hans Andersen's treatment of The Elder Flower Mother[26] will occur to many people. In some parts of England the elder tree was considered beneficent—a shelter to good fairies against witches; in other places it was thought of as witch or a form taken by a witch. In the legend of the Rollright Stones the witch who turned the invading king and his followers into stones herself took the form of an elder.[27] It used to be believed in the Cotswolds that an elder would bleed if it was cut. In *Lincolnshire Notes and Queries*, quoted in *County Folk-Lore: Lincolnshire*, we are given a formula to be used before cutting any branch from an elder tree. It presupposes an active spirit inhabiting the tree 'You just says,' said the informant,'*Owd Gal, give me of thy wood, an' Oi will give some of moine, when I grows inter a tree*.[28]

Almost exactly the same formula from Scandinavia is given by Keightley, quoting Thiele.

> A Danish peasant, if he wanted to take any part of an elder tree, used previously to say, three times—'O Hyldemooer, Hyldemooer! let me take some of thy elder, and I will let thee take something of mine in return.' If he took a piece of wood without asking leave he would be severely punished.

It was also thought unlucky to have any furniture made of elder wood, and the same belief was held in Lincolnshire. In Denmark the lime-tree was thought to be the favourite haunt of the Elves or Huldufolk, and it was unwise to go near it after sunset.[29]

William Craigie in *Scandinavian Folk-Lore* gives us some information about the Wood Elves or Wood Wives who were a special species of the Elle people. The females had pretty, smiling faces, but were hollow at the back, like the trunk of a hollow tree.

> 'In my young days,' said a wood-cutter, 'I saw the wood-fairy with my own eyes; she had a red knitted jacket, a green bodice, and blue gown. She ran past me with her long yellow hair flying loose about her; she was pretty in the face, but behind she was as hollow as a baking-trough. A thick vapour can sometimes be seen rising from the flat rocks, and one knows that she is boiling her clothes; and often during thunder loud noises can be heard coming from them, as if a whole load of stones were emptied down; this is her beating her clothes. She can sometimes be seen with a child on her arm; my own father saw this, and had heard that she had a husband, although she is given to enticing men to her.'[30]

Craigie gives a dialogue between a peasant and a wood-fairy which is a variant of the Scottish Ballad 'Meet-on-the-Road', where the interlocutors are the Devil and a little school-boy. It is in the same way a contest for the last word. A peasant had been working for a week in the woods, and was going home on Saturday evening when he met a wood-fairy who thought to get the better of him.

> 'I have been at your house' said she.
> 'Then you weren't at home that time,' said he.
> 'Your wife has had a child,' said she.
> 'It was her time then,' said he.

'She has got twins,' said she.
'Two birds in one egg,' said he.
'One of them is dead,' said she.
'Won't have to cry for bread,' said he.
'They are both dead,' said she.
'That's only one coffin then,' said he.
'Your wife is dead as well,' said she.
'Save her crying for the children,' said he.
'Your house is burned down,' said she.
'When the tail is seen the troll is known,' said he.
'If I had you out at sea,' said she.
'And a ship under me,' said he.
'With a hole in it,' said she.
'And a plug in that,' said he.[31]

The mention of the tail relates the wood-fairy to the Huldre who were very beautiful except for a long tail which they always tried to hide, as the Wood Elves hid their hollow back. The Huldre were mountain spirits who grazed their cattle on the mountain pastures and played beautifully on their pipes.

In Germany the Wood Wives or Moss People take the place of the Scandinavian Wood Elves. They are small, harmless people cruelly harassed by the Wild Huntsman, who makes them chiefly his quarry and can be heard hunting them high up in the air, like the English Devil and His Dandy-Dogs. Grimm gives a story in his *Teutonic Mythology* of a peasant who heard the baying and cheering above him and joined in the cry. Next morning he found his share of the quarry hanging on his stable door. It was the quarter of a Moss Woman.[32]

The animals domesticated by the fairies are of different species to those kept by mortals, and there are besides fairy creatures which appear to exist in their own right, black dogs, and such freakish things as the trash and the pad-foot and the ganconer, various kinds of bogy beast, as well as monstrous creatures like Nuckelavee[33] and the different kinds of worm or dragon. There are all kinds of water-horses, strongly inimical to man, as well as the gentler water cattle, some of them domesticated by the fairies, like those which I have already mentioned brought as a dowry by the Fairy Brides, and some which come up from the sea and mate with human cattle. Their offspring are recognised by their round ears, and are valuable members of a herd. The fairy dogs are usually white with red ears, a colouring which is also ascribed to fairy cattle in Irish legends. The fairy horses match their riders in size. Those ridden by the Welsh fairies visited by Elidor, were described as small. The horses of the Tuatha de

Dannan were unmatchable in power and swiftness but too fierce to be ridden by most mortals. Lady Wilde gives a most poetic description of the last of the fairy horses in her *Ancient Legends of Ireland*.[34]

Many of the fairies themselves went about in animal forms. The Selkies of the Highlands wore seal-skins to go through the sea but cast them off to dance on dry land and when they reached their underwater caves which had the same atmosphere as earth. These gentle seal people were perhaps the most frequent of the fairy brides, certainly in the Highlands.

A typical example is quoted from Gibbings by Douglas in *Scottish Fairy and Folk-Tales*. It is told of a fisherman of Unst in Shetland who happened on a party of sea-people dancing on a sandy voe. When they saw him the assembly broke up, and each dancer snatched a sealskin and plunged into sea. But the fisherman had seized a sealskin lying a little apart from the rest and carried it away. When he returned from hiding it the shore was clear except for one beautiful girl who was searching desperately for the skin that made it possible for her to return home. She guessed that he had taken it and begged him to give it back, but he only asked her to marry him and promised to be a loving husband to her. She consented at last, in despair, and she made him a good wife and was a tender mother to their children, but she was always searching for something, and on moonlight nights she would steal down to the shore and give a long cry which summoned a big dog seal to the edge of the water, and they would talk together earnestly in an unknown tongue. One day, when the fisherman was out in his boat, the children were playing hide-and-seek round the peat stacks, when one of them found an old seal-skin hidden away and ran with it to his Mother. Her eyes glistened with joy, she kissed her children tenderly and with a hurried goodbye, hastened down to the shore with the sealskin in her hand. The fisherman returned to find the children crying at the loss of their Mother. He ran down after her and was just in time to see her slip on the sealskin, and join the big dog seal who had come up to greet her. She swam away with him, but at the despairing cries of her mortal husband she turned and spoke gently to him. 'Farewell,' she said, 'and all good fortune go with you. I liked you well enough, but I always loved my first husband best.'[35]

This is not the only animal shape that the fairy people take. In *The Mabinogion* a fairy host takes the form of a great swarm of mice, among whom is the queen, slow and easily captured because she is pregnant.[36] The Little Bergpeople of Denmark take a less attractive shape, for they often appear in the form of toads, which indeed they resemble in their normal condition. The story is told in all the Scandinavian countries and is summarized in Reidar Christiansen's *Migratory Legends*.[37] A good version of it is given by William Craigie in *Scandinavian Folk-Lore*.

There lived an old woman in Andrup, of the name of Ann Ovster (Ove's daughter), who was employed as a midwife. One time during the summer she had been attending the wife of the farmer of Lille-kraens, and while returning home was passing the two mounds between which his fields lay. There she noticed an unusually large toad, of the kind they call 'padder,' with white stripes on its back. To this she said in jest, 'I shall come and help you too when you are in labour,' never thinking that her words had any significance. Some time after this she heard a waggon come driving up one night and stop before her house. She hurriedly rose, wondering who it could be that had come for her, as she did not know of any one likely to want her services so soon. She opened the door, and there entered a little man, with a beard so long that he almost trod on it, who explained his errand, and asked her to go home with him. 'You have made a mistake, my little man,' said she; 'you are none of my folk.' 'Yes,' said he, 'you must come with me, if you wish to be prosperous; you promised it to my wife fourteen days ago.' So she went along with him, not daring to refuse. He drove on for a long time, as she thought, and it was pitch dark too. Finally she entered a long passage, and found a little thick woman lying in bed, and so wretched was the place that she had nothing but straw to lie on. Ann aided her successfully, and she was delivered of a pretty boy. 'You are surely very poor here,' said Ann, while the man was outside. 'No, indeed, we are not so poor,' said the woman. 'There is a jar standing in the window there; dip your finger in it, and anoint your right eye with that.' As soon as she had done so, everything was changed; she was in a most beautiful hall, and had never been in any mansion that was so grand. The woman then, putting her hand into a pot, gave her a whole handful of gold coins, and said: 'When my husband comes to drive you home, you must spring off the waggon as soon as the horse seems to be going through soft ground, otherwise you will not escape him. You will be just at home then.' In a little the man came, and asked if they were ready. He drove off with her again, and a long time passed, so that she fell into a doze, but woke up with the horse dragging in mire up to its sides. Then she sprang out at once, and stood just at the end of her house.[38]

This tale continues with the usual Fairy Ointment story, the blinding of the seeing eye. In most of the Scandinavian stories the pregnant woman to whom the midwife is summoned is a human captive in Fairyland, and it seems likely that this is taken for granted in most of the stories. The husband in this variant is a particularly sinister character.

Another magical animal whose form is quite frequently taken by the fairies is the cat. In both the English and the Irish versions of 'The King of the Cats' it is uncertain whether the hero does not merely belong to the uncanny company of cats, but in the Zealand story of 'Knurre-Murre' it is quite clear that the hero was in his original form a young Troll. Between Pedersburg and Lyng there is a little hill called Bröndhöi which was said to be inhabited by some of the Troll people. At one time life was made very disagreeable inside Bröndhöi by a cross-grained old Troll nicknamed 'Knurre-Murre' (that is Rumble-Grumble) who quarrelled with everybody but finally picked a deadly quarrel with a brisk young Troll whom he suspected of being his wife's lover. He became so dangerous that the young fellow decided to move out for a time until the storm blew over, so he turned himself into a handsome tortoiseshell cat and moved into Lyng where he found an agreeable home in the house of an honest peasant called Plat.

One day Plat came home rather late and coming into the kitchen, where the cat was sitting comfortably in front of the fire licking clean a bowl of groute, he called to his wife: 'What do you make of this? Just as I was passing Bröndhöi a Troll called out to me:

> 'Harkee Plat,
> Say to your cat,
> Knurre-Murre is dead!'

At that the cat leapt down from the chair, upsetting his bowl, and ran to the door, on two legs like a man. As he went he cried shrilly:

> 'What, is Knurre-Murre dead?
> Then I can go home.'

With that he disappeared through the door, and was not seen at Lyng again. No doubt he was spending a happy time in Bröndhöi with Knurre-Murre's young widow.[39]

In Celtic folk-tales fairy ladies often turn themselves into white doves, as in the story of The White-Milk Deer reproduced from the Archives of the School of Scottish Studies in *A Dictionary of British Folk-Tales in the English Language*.[40] These transformations were sometimes not those of the fairies choice, but a malevolent enchantment, as in the Irish legend of Ossian's Mother.[41] The fairies have an almost unbounded power of self-transformation. We learn something of it in that very informative story 'The Fairy Dwelling on Selena Moor' which tells us so much about the Cornish fairy beliefs. There Grace, the captive in Fairyland, tells her lost lover that she has been rather happier since she discovered that she had the power to turn herself into a bird, so that she could fly round him. A price had to be paid for this power, for she returned to her own shape a little smaller every time, and was so gradually shrinking to the size of the small people.[42]

The standard fairy tales are full of these transformations either of oneself or of others. It was believed that mortal magicians could acquire the power by Art Magic, but fairies had it by nature.

CHAPTER 6 – FAIRY HABITATIONS ◞

HE FAIRY PEOPLE in the British Isles, not to say all over the world, vary so much in character, size, appearance and powers, that it is not surprising to find that they inhabit all kinds of places on land and in water, under the earth and above it. In Chapter 2, when we examined the theories of fairy origins, it will be remembered that in many of the British Celtic areas the fairies were given a theological origin: they were the less guilty of the fallen angels who were arrested on their fall through the universe towards Hell, and stayed where they fell, some in the air, some in rivers, the sea or lakes, some on earth, and some under the earth on their way to Hell. According to the other chief theory, in which the fairies and the dead are closely associated, their habitations are much the same. The place of the Good Neighbours is under the earth and in mounds, where they control fertility and from which they direct the activities of the living; the souls of unbaptised children, called Tarans in the North-East of Scotland and Spunkies in the Scottish Lowlands and in Somerset, haunt country roads and frequented woods, wailing, 'Nameless me! Nameless me!'.[1] There are some that live under inhabited houses, presumably their former homes when they were alive, and can bring good or bad luck to the present inhabitants. The evil dead, The Hosts or the *Sluagh*, as they are called in the Highlands, ride through the air and bring pestilence and ill-nortune wherever they are heard. Water spirits have various homes. Some of the sea-people, such as the *Merrows*[2] of Ireland, live in a sub-aqueous country beneath the waters, which form, as it were, a sky over their heads. To pass through it they have to use some magical property, the Merrows' red caps, the seal-skins of the *Roane*, the fish-tails of the Mermaids.

There are, however, some sea fairies, such as the *Asrai*[3] who are truly at home in the sea and who perish if they are exposed too long to the light of the sun. Such river spirits as Peg Powler or Peg O'Nell seem to be truly aquatic, some, like the Water Kelpie, the Dracs[4] and the Water Cattle,[5] are amphibious, more so indeed than natural amphibious animals.

There are also fairy realms across the sea like that Land of the Ever Young visited by Bran and Oisin, the mist-hidden Island of Man, made invisible at will by Mannanon the Son of Lir,[6] the three-legged wheel, and that invisible Island off the coast of Wales, the home of the Plant Rhys Dwfen,[7] the land where no treachery could grow. In Somerset too they speak of 'The Green Meadows of Enchantment' placed somewhere in the

Bristol Channel, which are visible only at the wish of the inhabitants.[8] Perhaps it is another version of the same belief.

The Middle Earth is shared between men and fairies, who inhabit woods, fields, hedgerows and glens. Others choose more inaccessible places, such as mountains and rocky clefts. They build fairy houses which are occasionally entered by men, and live in stone circles and fairy rings, where they are invisible unless a mortal accidentally puts a foot across the ring, when he is drawn into the circle, and sometimes disappears for a twelve-month and a day. Some of them frequent human markets where they purloin food, scraping pats of butter and stealing little cakes. They are invisible to human mortals, except to those whose eyes have been touched with the fairy ointment or who are carrying a four-leafed clover somewhere upon the head.

Some, though there are fewer of these, live in a sub-lunary world that is yet above the clouds, such as the land inhabited by the Giant in the story of 'Jack and the Bean-Stalk'. It will be seen that there is a wide choice of habitations for the fairy people, and it would be well to examine some of them in detail. Different as they are, they have a good many things in common.

Let us begin with the underground kingdoms. I have not yet mentioned the dwarfs and goblins who inhabit the mines, most of them metal mines—gold, silver, copper, iron ore, or precious stones; they do not seem to be so interested in coal. These were sometimes regarded as elementals, the earth was their element, and they breathed and moved in it as easily as mortals do in air. The German book on mining by Georgius Agricola[9] had a passage on these dwarfs or goblins which was much cited and quoted by the learned writers of the seventeenth century, Burton, Heywood and others. Hales' *Golden Remaines*[10] contains a short passage which was illustrated by a pleasant steel engraving on the title page. According to Agricola these mine spirits were heard and even seen performing all the operations of miners, blasting, mining, drilling, working with pickaxe or hammer and wheeling away the ore, yet in the end nothing came of all these prodigious labours, so that the phrase 'like goblins who labour in the mines' became proverbial.

On the other hand the smithy-works of these dwarfs, descended from the mythological World Picture of the Scandinavian peoples, were famous from very ancient times, and a weapon or breast-plate forged by the dwarfs—the Black Elves—was invincible against the work of any mortal smith. The dwarfs of the mines were generally supposed to be more sinister than the Kobolds, but they, on the whole, can be friendly to man, and there are tales of mutual borrowing and of rich gifts given by the

dwarfs to their protégés. To call them goblins is to load the name, for unless the friendly prefix of 'hob' was added goblins were thought to be almost as bad as Bogies. 'Gnomes' which is commonly used now is a later name derived rather from obsolete science than from folk tradition. When in the days of Paracelsus the universe was supposed to be composed in different proportions of the 'four elements'—Earth, Air, Fire and Water—the elementals attached to Earth were the Gnomes.[11] Like the Gnomes, the German Dwarfs and the Scandinavian Black Alfar, had their homes in caves in the mountains and in deep fissures under them. Those who visited them—and favourites were sometimes invited to do so—found themselves at length in great halls, the walls studded and glistening with jewels, and if they behaved modestly and with decorum they often carried gifts of gold or jewels or rich artefacts back with them. These riches appear to be actual and not the result of glamour, as many fairy palaces are.

The Cornish Mine fairies are the Knockers or Buccas.[12] They are supposed to work in the tin-mines and to make their homes in the caverns and adits of the mine or in neighbouring springs and wells. They are not thought of as elementals or goblins but as the dead, the ghosts of the Jewish miners who were placed in the mines as a punishment for their part in the Crucifixion. Like all fairies they dislike being spied upon, but they can make and keep friendly contracts with humans, and their knocking often leads the miners to the best lodes as well as giving warning of impending disasters. There is no record of any human having been invited to their houses, but it is probable that they are less splendid than those of the German Dwarfs, for the Knockers are not smiths or craftsmen, but homely, hard-working little miners. Mrs Wright, in her *Rustic Speech and Folklore* gives a list of the names given to the Cornish Mine spirits. They are 'Buccas, Gathornes, Knockers, Nickers, Nuggies and Spriggans'.[13] The Spriggans are rather different from the rest. They are not so exclusively dedicated to mining, but often inhabit stone circles, standing stones and even tumuli. They are not supposed to be the ghosts of the Jews but of the ancient giants of Cornwall, and though they are usually very small they are capable of swelling into a gigantic size. In Hunt's story of 'The Miser and the Fairy Gump'[14] the Spriggans were the bodyguard of the royal court. The tiny, exquisite fairies that they guarded were mound-dwellers and came out from under The Gump, the great earth-work that stands near to St Just.

Many stories are told of visits to the underground fairyland. The entrance to it is often by a cave, and occasionally the fairies live in the cave itself, as giants often do. These caves seem to be magnificent castles to the glamourized eyes of humans until their sight is cleared by a touch of the fairy ointment, when they are seen to be rough and primitive. We have a glimpse of this underground world connected to the upper air by a long cavern, in the anecdote of The Green Children set down by Ralph of Coggeshall in his twelfth-century chronicle.[15] Two pale green children were found dazed and wandering near Wolf Pits in Suffolk, and taken to the neighbouring castle. At first they would only eat green beans, and the boy pined and died, but the girl adapted herself to human food and manners, lost her green colour, married and lived long in the service of the knight. She told them something of the country from which she came. It was called, she said, St Martin's Land, and there was neither sun nor moon there but a perpetual dim light like that before dawn. The people there were Christians. One day the two children were watching the cattle when they came to the mouth of a cavern and went in to explore it. They heard a sweet sound of bells ringing and followed until they came to the mouth of the cave and out into the full light of day. The heat and glare of the sun overpowered them and they fell down in a daze. They were terrified by the sound of human voices and tried to escape, but could not see their way to the cave. This seems a cool, still, rural Fairyland, a quiet antechamber of the dead. We hear nothing in this brief summary of fairy revelry and feasting, though we are told that the girl was rather loose and wanton in her behaviour.

Often mortals were carried to Fairyland in a trance or swoon and knew nothing of their journey there. There are, however, two accounts of journeys to underworld Fairyland in British folk tradition, one to a quiet country house of Fairyland in the story of Cherry of Zennor[16] and one to the Fairy Court in the Ballad of Thomas of Ercildoune. Cherry of Zennor was led into Fairyland by a handsome, well-spoken gentleman who met her on the Lady Downs as she was setting out to hire herself for her first place at the Fair. Her courage had failed her at the thought of leaving her home, and she was sitting crying when the strange gentleman suddenly appeared to her and spoke to her so kindly that she was ready to go with him anywhere.

Away they went, he talking so kindly that Cherry had no notion how time was moving, and she quite forgot the distance she had walked.

At length they were in lanes, so shaded with trees that a checker of sunshine scarcely gleamed on the road. As far as she could see, all was trees and flowers. Sweetbriars and honeysuckles perfumed the air, and the reddest of ripe apples hung from the trees over the lane.

Then they came to a stream of water as clear as crystal, which ran across the lane. It was, however, very dark, and Cherry paused to see how she could cross the river. The gentleman put his arm around her waist and carried her over, so that she did not wet her feet.

The lane was getting darker and darker, and narrower and narrower, and they seemed to be going rapidly down-hill. Cherry took firm hold of the gentleman's arm, and thought, as he had been so kind to her, she could go with him to the world's end.

After walking a little farther, the gentleman opened a gate which led into a beautiful garden, and said, 'Cherry, my dear, this is the place we live in.'

Cherry could scarcely believe her eyes. She had never seen anything approaching this place for beauty. Flowers of every dye were around her; fruits of all kinds hung above her; and the birds, sweeter of song than any she had heard, burst into a chorus of rejoicing. She had heard granny tell of enchanted places. Could this be one of them? No. The gentleman was as big as the parson; and now a little boy came running down the garden-walk shouting, 'Papa, papa!'

Here they did not enter Fairyland by a cave but sloped gradually down through covered ways until they were underground before Cherry knew. They probably entered the fairy territory when Cherry was lifted across the clear, dark stream.

Streams play a part too in Thomas the Rhymer's entry into Fairyland, and like Cherry he is fetched by one of the fairies, though it was the Fairy Queen herself who fetched True Thomas. Thomas Rymour of Ercildoune was a real person who lived in the thirteenth century and whose prophecies were famous in Scotland for five hundred years. The earliest story of his meeting with the ₁queen of Elfame is found in a fifteenth-century Romance which forms a kind of introduction to a collection of his prophecies. The traditional ballads were recorded much later and are published in Child's *English and Scottish Popular Ballads*.[17] Child's introduction to the ballad is a mine of information, and he adds the first canto of the Romance as an Appendix. The first ballad, A, he believes to be the earliest, and thinks it is largely derived from the Romance, though there are some additions and variations. According to the Romance Thomas was lying pensive on Huntley Bank when he saw a lady richly attired and of unearthly beauty riding alone with her hounds and horn. She shone like the sun, so that he took her for the Queen of Heaven, and so yearned to speak to her that he ran down, hoping to meet her at the Eildon Tree, as indeed he did. She denied that she was Queen of Heaven, and said that she came from another country. Emboldened by her mildness and inflamed by her beauty he begged her to let him lie with her. She demurred, saying it would ruin her beauty, but in the end consented. When the intercourse was finished it became clear that she had spoken no more than the truth, for she was transformed into an hideous hag; but he had given her power over him, so that he was forced to go with her. She led him under Eildon Hill where it was as dark as midnight and for three days and nights he waded in water over the knee. At last he cried out that he was dying of hunger, and she led him out from the darkness into a fair arbour where all kinds of fruit were growing, but he might touch none of them, for the curse of Hell was on the fruit of that country. In the ballad the Queen had brought earthly food with her so that he could eat safely, and he ate and drank and was revived, but this is left out of the Romance.

Before they went further she told him to lay his head in her lap and she would show him five wonders. The first was the fair path that led up over the mountains to Heaven, the next was a valley road that led to Paradise, the third over a level plain led to the healing pains of Purgatory and the fourth plunged down to the fires of Hell. The fifth sight was a shining castle on a hill, where the King and Queen of the Fairies lived. Then he looked and saw that she was as fair as ever she had been, but before they went to the Castle she told him that she would rather be hanged and quartered than that the King should guess that she and Thomas had been lovers, and she begged him to speak no word to anyone there except to herself all the time he was in Fairyland. She would say that she had taken away his speech across the sea. Then she blew on her horn, the gates were opened and they went into Fairyland, full of music and revelry and dancing, thronged with lords and ladies. Thomas lived there in silent delight for what seemed to him three days, but it was three years of mortal time. Then the teind, or tribute, to Hell fell due,[18] and the Queen, fearing that the Devil would choose Thomas, took him back to Middle Earth and left him by the Eildon Tree with a parting gift of a tongue that could not lie. The Romance ends with a series of prophecies begged by Thomas from the Elf Queen before he parted from her, but the story does not end there, for it was long in oral tradition that Thomas was recalled to Fairyland in his old age, and indeed visitors to Fairyland were likely to see True Thomas, an old man and chief councillor of the fairies.

In the story of King Herla, given in Chapter 1, the entrance to Fairyland was by a cave and it was described as lit by a light 'seemingly not of the sun or the moon but of many lamps', and the Pigmy King's palace was 'a mansion in every way glorious, like the palace of the sun in Ovid's description.'

Occasionally the fairies are seen going in and out of their underground kingdom by a small hole, as in the last record of the Oxfordshire fairies they were said to do in the nineteenth century. The tradition was recorded by A. J. Evans in the *Folk-Lore Journal* of 1895. An old man, Will Hughes, recently dead when Evans wrote, said that he had seen them disappearing down a hole near the King Stone on the crest of the hill above the Rollright Circle. Betsy Hughes, his widow, knew the hole, and said that she and her playmates, when she was a child, used to put a stone over it when they wanted to play there, for fear the fairies should come out and frighten them.

The little captured fairy, who was called Skillywidden, disappeared underground with his parents when he escaped, and, according to Bowker's *Goblin Tales of Lancashire*[20] two poachers accidentally caught a fairy in their sack when they were ferreting for rabbits.

It is a common thing for underground fairies to live under human dwellings. It may be that they were the spirits of former inhabitants. Sir Walter Scott in *Minstrelsy of the Scottish Border* tells how Sir Godfrey Macculloch, a Galloway laird, was once accosted by a little old man in green riding a white palfrey who complained that Sir Godfrey's main drain ran into his 'chamber of dais', or dining hall. Sir Godfrey, guessing that he was one of the Good People, apologised courteously and had the course of the drain altered. Years later Sir Godfrey was involved in a fray and had the misfortune to kill a neighbouring gentleman, for which he was condemned to death. He was rescued from the scaffold by an old man on a white palfrey who carried him away in a flash, and he was never seen again.[21]

As for underwater fairylands, a detailed description of the land inhabited by the Merrows is given by Crofton Croker in 'Soul Cages'. Old Coomara, though an ugly creature to look at, was a friendly, sociable fellow with a good palate for drink, who did not realise the cruelty of catching the souls of drowned sailors and keeping them as curiosities. He inhabited a quiet underwater countryside not over-inhabited where he led a comfortable bachelor existence in a small, neat house of his own. Matthew Arnold, who was knowledgeable on Scandinavian tradition, describes a similarly sub-aqueous world inhabited by a King of the Merpeople in his 'Forsaken Merman'.

> We shall see, while above us
> The waves roar and whirl,
> A ceiling of amber,
> A pavement of pearl.[22]

Other Merpeople live in underwater caves with an atmosphere like that of earth as Grendel in the Anglo-Saxon tale of *Beowulf* seems to have done.

In the story of 'A Seal Catcher's Adventure', which is to be found in Grant Stewart's *Highland Superstitions and Amusements*,[23] the Seal Catcher is carried to an underwater cave, but it does not seem to have an earthly atmosphere, for the Seal Catcher has himself been temporarily transformed into a seal.

The Lake Ladies of the Welsh fairy wife stories rise up out of their lakes, but presumably they have an earthly atmosphere under the water, for the Lady of Llan Fan Fach did not swim ashore, but propelled herself across the Lake in a little skiff, and they and their cattle moved freely between land and water, as the Crodh Mara did, the sea cattle of the Highlands.

The Western Islands, Tir Nan Og, the Land of the Ever Young, and Emhaim, The Isle of Women, and others, were across the sea, not under it. It is to one of these that Oisin was called, but the fullest account of them is to be found in the story of 'The Voyage of Bran' which was referred to in Chapter 1 to illustrate the supernatural passage of time in Fairyland. Lady Gregory gives a description of Emhaim in the Song of the summoning messenger.

There are riches, there are tissues of every colour in the Gentle Land, the Bountiful Land. Sweet music to be listening to; the best of wine to drink.

Golden chariots in the Plain of the Sea, rising up to the Sun with the tide; silver chariots and bronze on the Plain of Sports.

Gold-yellow horses on the strand, and crimson horses, and others with wool on their backs, blue like the colour of the sky.

It is a day of lasting weather, silver is dropping on the land; a pure white cliff on the edge of the sea, getting its warmth from the sun.[24]

Fired by this description and by her urgent invitation Bran set out next morning in three boats, and when he at length reached the Island he found it no less beautiful than her song boasted.

On that they went into a grand house, where there was a bed for every couple, three times nine beds. And the food that was put on every dish never came to an end and they had every sort of food and of drink they wished for.[25]

Though subterranean dwellings, either in fairy mounds or in deep caverns, are most common in folk tradition there are fairy houses or castles above ground, generally invisible to mortal eyes. Robert Kirk, in *The Secret Commonwealth*, says of these houses: 'Their houses are called large and fair, and (unless at some odd occasions) unperceivable by vulgar eyes, like Rachland and other inchanted islands.'[26] Just before this, speaking of the fairies, borrowing of human food he says: 'for these subterraneans eat but little in their dwellings, their food being exactly clean and served up by pleasant children like inchanted puppets.'[27] As Kirk half suggests, these fine fairy houses or palaces were the result of glamour andwere called up by magic to deceive humans. A story of St Collen, a ninth-century Welsh saint, illustrates this well. The story is alternatively placed in Wales and in Somerset, for St Collen was a restless and stirring character and moved from one place to another. The resulting folk-tale is something of a hybrid. In the course of his journeys, St Collen was invited to become Abbot of Glastonbury, but he soon resigned his abbacy and sought for greater hardship as a hermit in a small cell at the foot of Glastonbury Tor. One day he heard two men outside his cell talking of the King of the Fairies, Gwyn ap Nudd, who reigned over the Kingdom of Annwn and had a magnificent palace on the summit of Glastonbury Tor. St Collen stuck his head out of the window and rebuked them for talking in that way of devils from Hell. The men were horrified and warned him to be careful how he talked of the fairy people, or the King would summon him to answer for it. St Collen stuck to his point, but a few days later a messenger arrived to invite him to come to dine with the King. St Collen refused, but the fairy repeated the invitation more and more urgently till he consented, but he picked up a flask of holy water and hid it under his habit. The great palace on the summit of the Tor was all as the men had described it. Light streamed out of it, gallant young knights on magnificent horses were riding round it, bevies of lovely young ladies came out to greet him, and he was led into the banquet hall, where the King received him and a splendid banquet was set out by pages in uniforms of red and blue.

'Come, sit and feast with me,' said the King, 'and if this does not please you, we have more.'

St Collen's eyes were not deceived by glamour.

'I do not eat the leaves of a tree,' he said with more truth than courtesy, and a shudder ran through the rich assembly seated round the long table; but the King spoke without anger. 'Tell me,' he said, 'what do you think of my pages? Have you ever seen any better dressed in their fine garments of red and blue?'

'They are suitably dressed,' said Collen, 'for what they are.'

'What do you mean?' said Gwyn ap Nudd.

'Red for the quenchless flames of Hell,' said Collen, 'and blue for the Eternal Ice!' And as he spoke he emptied his flask of holy water over them. There was a great shriek, the lights died out, the banquet, the castle and the company vanished in a flash, and Collen was standing alone on the crest of the Tor with the cool night air blowing round him.[28]

Many of the fairies lived in small, simple cottages, hidden away in woodlands or on mountains like that in which the Tacksman of Auchriachan took shelter from the mist when he was searching for his lost goats.[29] Some of these huts are glamourized caves, but many of them are solid enough, like that in which the Seven Dwarfs lived who received and watched over Snowdrop.

The superterrestrial fairylands are much less common than the subterranean, the watery or those of Middle Earth.

There are occasional stories of journeys to the Moon, inhabited by Mother Goose and the Man in the Moon.[30] A Giants' country is to be found above the clouds, the Fir Chlis, or Merry Dancers, dance in the Northern skies on winter nights, and Iris's rainbow is occasionally used by later fairies.

William Allingham makes the old Fairy King travel far above the roads usually taken by the Good People.

> With a bridge of white mist
> Columbkill he crosses,
> On his stately journeys
> From Slieveleague to Rosses;
> Or going up with music
> On cold starry nights
> To sup with the Queen
> Of the gay Northern Lights.[31]

The terrible hosts of the Sluagh sweep through the middle air and the Gabriel Hounds yelp through the sky on starry nights, but on the whole the skies are places of movement, and for places of settled habitation the fairies seem to prefer the quiet lands under the earth or even the men-haunted woods and hillsides.

CHAPTER 7 – FAIRY MIDWIVES AND FAIRY CHANGELINGS

NE OF THE EARLIEST of the traditions about fairies is that they coveted and stole human children and left substitutes in their place. These were of three kinds. Some of them were fairy babies who did not thrive, some of them were old worn-out fairies who were presumably tired of the perpetual bustle of fairy life, and were glad to lie passively in their 'mammy's' arms, wailing for food and being constantly caressed and cosseted. The third kind was 'the stock' a piece of wood roughly shaped into the form of the human baby and given by glamour a strong resemblance to it and an appearance of torpid life. After a while it would appear to die and would be buried. This stock was more commonly used when grown-up women were stolen to be wet nurses to the fairy children or to human babies taken into Fairyland, young men with special talents, musicians and singers or those beloved by fairy women, like Ossian, Bran or Lanval, but most commonly beautiful girls coveted particularly by the nobles and kings of Fairyland. The fairies seem to have been shy breeders, in spite of their interest in fertility, and they were always anxious to revive their powers with a human strain. It may be that human brides could not bear children without the help of human midwives, or it may be that human help was needed even for the birth of fairy children. At any rate the stories of midwives to the fairies are as common and widespread as those about changelings.

One of the earliest stories we have is told by the thirteenth-century Englishman, Gervase of Tilbury, who became Chancellor of The Holy Roman Empire and wrote a long book, *Otia Imperialis*, which contains among much interesting social history, some valuable folk tradition. This midwife story, complete with the fairy ointment is told about the Dracs of France, whom I have already mentioned among the water spirits in Chapter 4, who carried off women washing by the river to act as nurses to their children. He continues the story:

> We have ourselves seen one of these women, who was taken away while washing clothes on the banks of the Rhône. A wooden bowl floated along by her, and, in endeavouring to catch it, having got into the deep water, she was carried down by a Drac, and made nurse to his son below the water. She returned uninjured, and was hardly recognised by her husband and friends after seven years' absence.

> After her return she related very wonderful things, such as that the

Dracs lived on people they had carried off; and turned themselves into human forms; and she said that one day, when the Drac gave her an eel-pasty to eat, she happened to put her fingers, that were greasy with the fat, to one of her eyes and one side of her face, and she immediately became endowed with most clear and distinct vision under the water. When the third year of her time expired, and she had returned to her family, she very early one morning met the Drac in the market-place of Beaucaire. She knew him at once, and saluting him, inquired about the health of her mistress and the child. To this the Drac replied, 'harkye', said he, 'with which eye do you see me?' She pointed to the eye she had touched with the fat: the Drac immediately thrust his finger into it, and he was no longer visible to any one.[1]

This story crops up again and again in various places, generally joined to the blinding of the seeing eye, as in the Cornish story from Bottrell 'How Joan Lost the Sight of One Eye',[2] or in the gentler form recorded by Cromek in which the fairy vision alone is taken away and the mortal sight is spared. Among the many variants of the story there is one of particular interest told by Patrick Kennedy in his *Legendary Fictions of the Irish Celts*, 'The Fairy Nurse'.[3] This combines many elements of the story—the theft of a nursing mother to feed a fairy child, the services of a mortal midwife, the mother of the infant, who gives kind advice to the midwife because she herself was born a mortal woman; the encounter with the stolen wet-nurse, her rescue with the help of the fairy sight and the final blinding of the seeing eye. These motifs are all combined in a vivid and compassionate narrative.

Near Coolgarrow there was a farmer and his wife with three little children, the youngest of them newly born. They loved each other dearly and Molly was a good wife and mother and great about the house. There was only one fault about her, she was so taken up with her children and the house and her cooking that she was apt to scamp her prayers and go to sleep over them morning and evening. One saint's day it happened that all four of the family were going to church, and she let the three go on ahead of her and turned aside to consult a wise man, 'a fairy man' as they called it, about one of the cows that was ailing. This made her late for church, and she missed the best part of the service, and her husband was much grieved about it, and so was she too, for she was very sorry to have grieved him.

That very night the farmer was awakened by the children all crying out and the two elder ones calling, 'Mother! Mother!' He sat up and struck a light, and there was no wife beside him and the two children were at the door calling for their mother, and the baby was crying its head off. The two told him that they waked with a light in the room and it was full of little people in white and red and green, and their mother was walking away among them with her eyes tight shut, and she never seemed to hear them calling at all. The husband ran out of the house and searched all about in the darkness but there was no sign or sound of her. He searched all next day and asked about everywhere, and there was no news of her. You may think how sad his heart was, for he loved Molly as dearly as she loved him, and he was in a bad way besides, though the neighbours did all they could for him. The baby was put out to nurse, but the children were dirty and neglected and the house worse. The neighbours brought in what food they could spare; but for six long weeks things seemed to go from bad to worse. Then one morning as the farmer was going to work, a neighbour, one who used to help the women at their lying in, came up to him, and, falling into step beside him and speaking low so that the wind could not carry her voice, said to him: 'I have some word for you of your Molly.' He listened with all his heart and never missed a word though she spoke very low.

'Last night,' she said, 'as I was falling asleep, I heard a horse's tramp and a great knock, and when I went down there was a fine-looking dark gentleman on a great black horse, and he told me to go with him quickly, for a lady was in great need of me. As soon as I had on my things he took my hand and I was on the back of the horse behind him before I knew myself. "Where am I going, sir?" says I; "You'll soon know", says he, and he passed his hand over my eyes and all was blackness with not a glimmer of light. I took a tight grip of him and we seemed to be flying through the air, but whether we were going backwards or forwards not a one of me knew. Then he took a hold of me and I felt ground beneath my feet. "Here we are," he says, and he passed his hand over my eyes the other way across, and there we were in front of a fine castle. We went through the door and we were in a fine hall, the like of which you never saw, all painted with red and green and gold, with fine table and chairs and carpets, all about, and grand ladies and gentlemen in silks and satins walking here and there. And we went into a great room, finer than all the rest, and there was a beautiful lady lying in a rich bed with silk curtains. "Here you are," said he. "Now do all you can for her." And he went out of the room and it wasn't long before I helped a fine bouncing boy come into the world. The dark gentleman came in, and he kissed his wife and praised me and then he took out a green jar of ointment and he told me to rub the baby all over with it and not miss one piece. And I rubbed right enough, but as I was rubbing my right eye itched and I put up my hand to rub it, never thinking, and worra, worra, I nearly dropped the baby, for the whole place changed before my eyes. The great fine room was a big cave with the water oozing up between the stones and the silk-hung bed was nothing but a heap of dry bracken, and the lord and lady and the wee baby itself were poor, weazened, thin creatures looking as if they'd never had a good meal in their lives, and all their fine clothes were just rags and bits of weeds. But thanks be to Mary I kept my courage and went on rubbing the wee babe as if nothing had happened. Then the black gentleman came up and told me to wait in the next room and he'd see me home. As I went in I saw your Molly standing pale and frightened, looking through the door, and she whispered to me, "Don't let on we're speaking. I'm a prisoner here to give suck to the Queen's baby, but there's one hope for me yet. All the court will pass the cross near Templeshambo on Friday night, for we're all going to visit the fairies of Old Rosses, and if John will grip me tight and hold me I'll be safe. Here's the King! Don't let on anything to him. I saw what happened with the ointment." With that she slipped away, and the King never seemed to suspicion that she'd spoken me. He took me out and there I saw that his grand castle was only the old Rath of Cromague, and the black horse was waiting, only with my right eye I saw it was no more than a stalk of ragwort, and I was in dread every minute of the way I'd fall off, but we landed at my door, and he thanked me civilly and slapped five gold guineas into my hand, and I tumbled into bed without looking at them, but in the morning when I looked at them they were no more than five withered oak leaves—bad scran to him!'

John was half crazy with joy and the fear of failure, so he drew the midwife into his botheen so that no breath of the outside air could come to them, and together they made their plans for the rescue. The next Friday they met at Templeshambo Cross before midnight and stood looking towards the Rath of Cromague with their hearts fluttering within them. After a while the woman said, 'By this and by that here they come! With bridles jingling and feathers tossing!' But he could see nothing. She stood watching and trembling, at last she said: 'They're close on us now, and Molly is riding to this side, all ready for you to catch her. We must make no sign that we are watching, but we'll turn our backs and walk slowly, slowly as to reach the Cross when they come to it, so as to look as if we had no notion at all that they're there; but when Molly comes just against us I'll give you a great push, and if you don't catch on to her and hold tight whatever happens you'll have no more luck in this world, and you'll not deserve it.'

So they moved on slowly, slowly with their poor hearts fluttering inside them, and at length she gave him the nudge, and he put his arms out and clasped his wife's waist as if his arms were a band of iron.

Then you'd have said all hell broke out, with the thundering and the quaking and the flashes of flame and the ugly shapes all round them, but he never slackened his grip and he made the sign of the cross with his fingers and defied them in the name of God. And a great silence came and the whole show vanished and Molly lay fainting in her husband's arms, and he and the good neighbour carried her back to her home and children, and you may be sure that she paid better heed to her prayers from that day on, and never again went to ask advice from a fairy man.

But the midwife, who had been so wise and brave, had a price to pay, for one day, when she was off her guard, she saw the dark man stealing butter at the market at Enniscorthy and let him know that she saw him, and he tricked her cunningly into saying which was the seeing eye, and struck the sight out of it with a switch.

This story is slightly shortened in the retelling, but there are so many points of interest in it that it cannot be much curtailed. We have here the story of the abduction of a nursing mother and her rescue from Fairyland, combined with the full Fairy Midwife story, complete with the blinding of the Seeing Eye, as a kind of appendix. It seems likely in this story that the fairy lady was a native fairy, not a captured bride, for she made no effort to warn or assist the midwife nor to secure a real reward for her as the captive mortals in Fairyland often do, and the fairy ointment revealed her as haggard and wan like the other fairies.

Kennedy gives a fairy midwife story in the same book in which we are warned of the danger of eating and drinking in Fairyland and of taking any fairy gifts except cures of illnesses caused by enchantment.[4] The midwife is warned of this by a captive in Fairyland, and she refuses money, jewels and food; her patient seems genuinely sorry to be unable to give her anything, and asks if there is anything she can do to reward her for her kindness. It happened that the midwife had a daughter who had been suffering for more than a year from a mysterious sore place on her leg for which they could find no cure, and she asked if the Queen could heal it. The Queen grew angry and said it was the daughter's own fault for straying to the kitchen one night after twelve when all decent mortals were asleep, and putting her great flat feet bang on top of the Queen's tea-set when she was enjoying a quiet invisible tea party. So the Queen had thrown the spout of her broken tea-pot into the girl's leg, and it had been there ever since. After a little pleading, however, the Queen relented, and gave the midwife an ointment with which she healed the aching leg at once. Since the fairy ointment motif does not occur in this story we have one example when a midwife's visit to the fairies does her nothing but good.

Another very full Fairy Midwife story is given by John Rhys in the first volume of *Celtic Folklore*.[5] It is unususal because we know the antecedents of the bride chosen by the fairy father.

An old woman and her husband lived at Garth Dorwen a long time ago. They went to Carnarvon Market to hire a servant-girl as the custom was in those days, and picked a girl called Eilian, who stood a little apart from the others and had a great wealth of shining golden hair. She was a good worker, but she had some strange ways. In the long winter nights when most people were spinning by the fire she used to carry her wheel out to the meadow where the Tylwyth Teg danced, and she would bring back a great quantity of spun-up thread of a very fine quality. For long after her time the meadow was called 'The Maid's Meadow', or 'Eilian's Field'. As time went on she stayed longer with the Tylwyth Teg and when the spring came she went away and came back no more.

The old woman of Garth Dorwen used to act as midwife to the neighbourhood, and it happened some time after this that she was summoned to help a lady and was taken by the old man who fetched her to a ruined fortification called Rhos-y-Cwrt and led through a great cave into a most beautiful room where a lovely lady lay in bed. The story followed the ususal course. She was given ointment to anoint the baby and when she inadvertently rubbed one eye she saw not only that the rich room was a large, damp cave but that the lady on the bed was her former servant Eilian.

In the end, as usual, the Seeing Eye betrayed her and it was put out by Eilian's husband. Here we see clearly that the half-human baby needs the ointment to give its eyes the fairy vision.

Keightley gives a Scandinavian story 'The Troll Labour' written down and attested in 1671 which gives the outline of the fairy midwife story, but without the episode of the ointment:

In the year 1660, when I and my wife had gone to my farm (Fäboderne), which is three quarters of a mile from Ragunda parsonage, and we were sitting there and talking a while, late in the evening, there came a little man in at the door, who begged of my wife to go and aid his wife, who was just then in the pains of labour. The fellow was of small size, of a dark complexion, and dressed in old grey clothes. My wife and I sat a while, and wondered at the man; for we were aware that he was a Troll, and we had heard tell that such like, called by the peasantry Vettar (spirits), always used to keep in the farmhouses, when people left them in harvest-time. But when he had urged his request four or five times, and we thought on what evil the country folk say that they have at times suffered from the Vettar, when they have chanced to swear at them, or with uncivil words bid them go to hell, I took the resolution to read some prayers over my wife, and to bless her, and bid her in God's name go with him. She took in haste some old linen with her, and went along with him, and I remained sitting there. When she returned, she told me, that when she went with the man out at the gate, it seemed to her as if she was carried for a long time along in the wind, and so she came to a room, on one side of which was a little dark chamber, in which his wife lay in great agony. My wife went up to her, and, after a little while, aided her till she brought forth the child after the same manner as other human beings. The man then offered her food, and when she refused it he thanked her, and accompanied her out, and then she was carried along, in the same way in the wind, and after a while came again to the gate, just at ten o'clock. Meanwhile, a quantity of old pieces and clippings of silver were laid on a shelf, in the sitting-room, and my wife found them next day, when she was putting the room in order. It is to be supposed that they were laid there by the Vettar. That it in truth so happened, I witness by inscribing my name. Ragunda, the 12th of April, 1671.[7]

PET. RAHM.

This is interesting because of its matter-of-fact narration and is a signed, dated attestation. There is no fairy ointment nor any traditional variation.

There is one tale which is a variant of that quoted in Chapter 5, in which a woman goes to act as midwife to a toad. It is to be found in a modern version given by Sean O Súilleabhain in *Folktales of Ireland*,[7] published in The Folktales of the World, edited by Richard Dorson. It is a curiously savage tale and it is difficult to make reason out of it. It begins like the Scandinavian story of The Toad Fairy. A girl coming home one night saw an enormous frog and said jokingly to it 'I hope you won't give birth to your young until I'm present.' That night a stranger came to fetch her, saying she was needed. The girl of course was no midwife and was unwilling to go, but the stranger persuaded her, promising to bring her back safely. She rode behind him to a fairy palace where she was taken to a small room where a woman was in labour with two women attending her. The girl was much frightened, but not long after she arrived the baby was born. The two women raked up the fire, put the baby at the back of it, and left it there till it was burnt to ashes. Then they took the ashes out, and put them in a dish which stood in the room. The man who had brought her came to tell her to come home with him. 'And you'd better give her a present,' he said to the woman.

'I'll give her a present right enough,' she said, and she gave the girl a purse full of money and a shawl. The girl noticed that all who were leaving the room dipped a hand into the dish of ashes and rubbed their eyes with it. She thought she would do the same and rubbed the ash onto one eye. They got on horseback, but on the way home the man drew up near a big tree and told the girl to tie her shawl round it. She did so and the tree split in two. 'If you'd tied that shawl round yourself it would have been the same with you,' said the man. He set the girl down at her own door, but before he went he told her to change every bit of money in the purse in a different house, and not to keep a coin for herself. She did so, and the morning after she had changed the money she heard that every house in which she had left a coin had been burned down. The story ends with the blinding of the seeing eye. Presumably the frog fairy was so bitter against the girl because she blamed her for a long and painful labour.

There are many variants of the Fairy Midwife story, most of them containing two or three of the common motifs, but these that I have given are among the fullest.

The changeling stories are almost as common, with on the whole less variation, though there are unususal features in some of them. The earliest is the most unususal of all. It comes from the twelfth-century chronicle of Ralph of Coggeshall[8] and it is the account of a little fairy girl called Malekin who haunted the Castle of Dagworthy in Suffolk. She said that she was a human child, stolen from the cornfield while her mother was at work. She had been with the fairies for seven years, and in another seven she hoped to return to the human world. She was generally heard but not seen; she talked to the servants in broad Suffolk, but spoke to the Chaplain in Latin and conversed with him about the scriptures. One chambermaid was her particular friend, who always put out food for her in an open armoire. This girl was the only person who claimed to have seen her; she had often begged her to appear, and at last Malekin consented after a solemn promise that the girl would neither touch her nor try to detain her. The girl said that she was like a tiny child in a white linen tunic. Presumably the human food would be very important to her because it was believed that captives who tasted fairy foods could never again regain their humanity. The anecdote shows the other side of the coin. It would probably be supposed that a fairy changeling would be left in Malekin's place so that she would not be missed. It was not usual for the fairies to steal little female babies, though they often stole beautiful girls or nursing mothers.

A story which might well be a pendant to the Malekin tale is given in Grimm's *Teutonic Mythology*.[9] A woman was reaping corn at the Dosenberg in Hesse with her baby beside her when a Dwarf-woman came and changed it for her own hideous child. When the mother saw the creature that had been left she cried out and made such a roaring and disturbance that the Dwarf-woman brought the child back, and only prayed the human mother that she would put the little changeling to her breast and give it suck. She did so and the Dwarf took her own baby back, quite satisfied. In Germany it was recommended that the suspected changeling should be abandoned in some fairy spot or thrown into a stream. The method of detecting a changeling was the wide-spread 'Brewery of Eggshells' and several examples of it are cited by Grimm from Germany as well as from Breton and Danish sources. The eggshell story is combined in one of the German legends with the belief that if the changeling can be made to laugh it will leave, and the real child will come back. Keightley quotes a story from Grimms' *Kinder und Haus-Märchen* in which the Mother breaks an egg in two, fills each half of it and puts it down to boil. 'Well!' the thing in the cradle exclaims, 'I am as old as the Westerwald but I've never seen anyone cooking in an eggshell!' With that he bursts out laughing and the true child is laid in his cradle as he shoots up the chimney.[10]

In other tales the changelings betray themselves through their love of music and revelry, which is natural enough, for many of them are old fairies, with hundreds of years of fairy merriment behind them, and, however comfortable they may be, well fed and assiduously tended by a loving mother, it naturally palls for a time, and they yearn for their old amusements. A number of changeling stories, both Scottish and Irish, centre round this incident, usually with a travelling tailor as the hero. A good example of a modern version is among those to be found in the archives of the School of Scottish Studies. It was recorded by Hamish Henderson and told by Andrew Stewart. The name of the Tale is 'Johnny in the Cradle'.

A man and his wife were not long married, and they had a wee kiddie called Johnnie, but he was always crying and never satisfied. There was a neighbour near, a tailor, and it came to market day, and Johnnie was aye greeting, and never growing, and never growing. And the wife was wanting to get a day at the market so the tailor said he'd stay and watch wee Johnnie. So he was sitting sewing by the fire, and a voice said, 'Is ma mother and ma faither awa'?' He couldn't think it was the baby speaking, so he went and looked out of the window, but there was nothing, and he heard it again. 'Is ma mother and ma faither awa'?' And there it was, sitting up, with its wee hands gripping the sides of the cradle. 'There's a bottle of whiskey in the press,' it says, 'Gie's a drink.' Sure enough, there was one, and they had a wee drink together. Then wee Johnnie wanted a blow on the pipes, but there was not a set in the house, so he told the tailor to go and fetch a round strae from the byre, and he played the loveliest tunes on the pipe through the strae. They had a good talk together, and the wee thing said, 'Is ma mother and ma faither coming home?' And when they came, there he was, 'Nya, nya, nya,' in the cradle. By this time the tailor knew it was a fairy they had there, so he followed the farmer into the byre, and told him all that had happened. The farmer just couldn't bring himself to believe it; so between them they hit on a contrivance. They let on that a lot of things had not been sold at the market, and there was to be a second day of it, and the tailor promised to come over again to sit by the bairn. They made a great stir about packing up and then they went through to the barn, and they listened through the keek hole in the wall. 'Is ma mother and ma faither gone?' said the wee thing, and the mother could just hardly believe her ears. But when they heard the piping through the corn-strae, they kent it was a fairy right enough, and the farmer went in to the room, and he set the girdle on the fire and heated it red hot, and he fetched in a half bagful of horse manure, and set it on the girdle, and the wee thing looked at him with wild eyes. When he went to it to grip it and put it on the girdle, it flew straight up the lum, and as it went it cried out, 'I wish I had been longer with my mother, I'd a kent her better.'[11]

In this story we heard of the banishing of the changeling, but nothing at all of the return of the real child. Perhaps they should have set out to rescue it from the fairies as the Father did in J. F. Campbell's story, 'The Smith and the Fairies'. There was a Smith on Islay who was a widower but had an only son, a boy of about fourteen, lively and merry and likely to be a good help to his father. One day, however, he took to his bed, and lay on it listless and silent, with a prodigious appetite but otherwise with little sign of life, and however much he ate he still got thinner, yellower, more withered until he looked like an old man, and the smith and all his neighbours thought that the boy would soon die. One day he was visited by an old friend, a man of great wisdom, and when he had taken him into the forge and told him all his trouble the old man went benn to look at the boy on his bed, and coming back he said: 'That boy is none of yours. Your boy has been carried away by the Deena Shee and it is a sibreach in his place.' Then he told the smith what he must do. First he must test the boy to make sure that he was indeed a changeling. This was done by the brewery of eggshells, and the changeling fell into the trap, for he sat up and exclaimed with a shout of laughter, 'I have lived 800 years and I have never seen the like of that before!' Then the smith built up a great fire and threw the changeling on it, and it flew up through the smoke-hole and

away; but the smith's son did not return, so the wise man sent him into the
fairy hill to rescue the boy.

On a certain night of the full moon the hill rose up on columns, lights
streamed out of it, there was the sound of music and festivity. The smith
armed himself with a Bible tied securely across his chest, a living cock
hidden in the folds of his plaid and a dirk in his right hand. So protected he
boldly approached the hill. At the arch by which he entered he paused for
a moment to stick his dirk into the turf, then he went in. The place was full
of merriment, feasting and music, except for one far corner where a group
of slaves worked at a forge, and among them was the smith's son. The
fairies came angrily around him but they could not touch him because of
the Bible. They cried out the word which would shut the hill, but there
was one door which would not shut because of the dirk in it. They asked
him what he wanted and he demanded his son. They surged around him,
screaming and shouting, and the noise awakened the drowsy cock, which
climbed to the smith's shoulder and crowed. At that they scattered, some
shoved the boy towards the smith, he drew him out through the door, the
dirk was shot out after them, and they were outside and safe. The fairy
spell hung over the boy for a year and a day, but then he was himself again
and became the finest smith in the country.

In a Hereford story collected by E. M. Leather the changeling held on
to his position for twenty-five years, and would have done so until he tired
of the game, but the boy's elder brother, a soldier, returned from the Wars
after years of service and banished the changeling, and he was replaced by
a fine young man. He was one who had been happy in Fairyland and was
only called back by his mother's yearning.

Perhaps the happiest of the changeling stories is one told by Lady Wilde in
her *Ancient Legends of Ireland*.[12] It is a strange, confusing story, full of dual
experiences which seem to contradict each other, but the conclusion of it is
that the fairy queen, whose son had been left with the woman as a changeling wanted her own child back again, so that each mother had her own.

'Take him,' said the Queen, 'he is your own child, that we carried away,
for he was so beautiful; and the boy you have at home is mine, a little
elfish imp. Still, I want him back, and I have sent a man to bring him
here; and you may take your own lovely child home in safety, for the
fairy blessings are on him for good.'

And so it proved, for the truce was so complete between mortals and
fairies that the mother could safely partake of a fairy banquet set out for
her, and sprinkled with salt to make it fit for human use. And, as the
Queen said, the child blessed in Fairyland was fortunate and happy all the
days of his life.

CHAPTER 8 – CAPTIVES IN FAIRYLAND

I N SOME OF the earlier chapters we have come across instances of captives in Fairyland and of their rescue from its sad revelry, but the subject is large enough to deserve a whole chapter to itself. The story of 'The Fairy Nurse' with its successful rescue from a fairy rade will be found in Chapter 7 and so will J. F. Campbell's story, 'The Smith and the Fairies'. As will be seen, these attempts at rescue were not always successful, but, on the other hand, the fairies' attempts at the capture were often thwarted before their victims reached the fairy strongholds. A Highland legend mentioned by Grant Stewart,[1] and included in Keightley's *Fairy Mythology*[2] gives an example of one of the laws that are supposed to bind the fairies in their dealings with human beings, and also shows the magnanimous hospitality of the Highlander at its best.

It is one of the laws which govern the fairies that if a human being offers to exchange anything he has for anything of theirs they cannot refuse, however bad the bargain may be. John Roy of Glenbroun in Badanoch knew this, and when the time came he used his knowledge to very good effect.

One night, when he was up on the hills looking for his cattle, a flight of fairies passed him with something in their midst. They went so swiftly by him that he had no time to look at what they carried, but he feared that it might be some unhappy human creature borne away to captivity beneath the knowes. So like a flash he threw his bonnet into the thickest of the swarm, and cried out in Gaelic: 'Mine be yours and yours be mine!'

The fairies gave a cry of rage and scattered, taking with them John Roy's bonnet, and leaving at his feet a human lady in fine white linen. She was between sleep and waking, sick and fevered; but when he had restored her and carried her back to his clachan he could get no word of Gaelic out of her. It was clear she was no Highlander.

His wife was as noble in hospitality as John Roy himself and they kept the poor lady with them for many years. In that time the lady learned the Gaelic and John Roy had learned a little English, so that they could talk together. She told him that she came from England and that she had been carried off on her sick bed. John Roy had no hope that her husband would ever search for her, for he knew that the fairies would have left a stock in her bed, which would soon seem to die and be buried.

So the poor lady lived on without hope of ever seeing her own people again, until at last King George sent his redcoats to build new roads all over the Highlands, and to civilize the Highlanders whether they would or no. These redcoats were little liked, as you may imagine, and it was difficult for them to find any lodging; but John Roy had taken a kind of liking for the English because of his stolen lady, and he was a hospitable man besides; so he took the Captain and his son into the house. The English lady was stirred to the very heart to hear the English spoken again, and she looked at the two Englishmen as if she could never look away. They too were glad to hear the English spoken again in so outlandish a part; and the son, after looking at her closely, said to his father: 'Sir, if I did not know that my dear Mother was dead these many years I should say that I saw her here now.'

'Do you say so?' said the lady. 'And if miracles could happen I should say that I saw my little child grown into a man and standing before me.' Then the father broke in and said:

'You are like what my dear wife would have been if these years had passed over her. Do you know where we lived then and what the house was like?'

Then, weeping with joy, she told him, and they fell on each other's necks and wept together, and went over every particular of their parting and her rescue by good John Roy. So the poor stolen lady was restored to her husband, and they all remembered their gratitude to John Roy for as long as they lived.

It is unusual for the Highland fairies to wander so far from their own district, though Kirk says that they change their habitations continually, commonly moving at Quarter Days.[3] It almost looks as though these might have been the *Sluagh*, the wicked, ravening Fairy Hosts.

Another story of a rescue from fairy abduction, 'Jamie Freel and the Young Lady', was collected in Donegal by Letitia Mackintosh and is to be found in Yeats, *Fairy and Folk Tales of the Irish Peasantry*.[4] Jamie Freel was a dutiful and hard-working son to his widowed mother and seemed to have no other thought except that he was always fascinated by the sound of fairy music which came out of a ruined Castle close at hand, said to be the home of a tribe of fairies, who were never seen except on May Eve and Halloween. He had often looked and listened at those times, when light streamed out of the windows and little figures were seen moving exquisitely in the dance. At last one Halloween he said to his mother, 'I'm awa' to the Castle Hill to get my fortune.' And out he went, in spite of all his mother could say. He went boldly in through the open door, and got a grand welcome, with all crying throughout the furthest corners of the Castle, 'You're welcome, Jamie Freel! Come and join the dance with us!'

Jamie danced with them as happy as a king, but after what seemed a short time they said 'We're away to Dublin to fetch a young lady. Will you come with us, Jamie Freel?' 'Aye will I,' said Jamie, and they all went outside to where a fine troop of horses was waiting. They all mounted, and Jamie with the rest. Then they cried out something and all rose up in the air over hills and mountains and above Lough Swilley, and then over Derry, and each place they came to they cried out its name, and it seemed a great journey they took. However at last he heard the little, twittering voices crying out 'Dublin! Dublin!' and they came steeply down and flew into one of the finest houses on Stephen's Green. They went into a rich bedroom, where Jamie saw a beautiful pale girl lying on a bed. The fairies lifted her out and laid a piece of wood in the bed, which immediately changed to an exact likeness of the lady, so that she seemed to be still in the bed, and the fairies whisked her out of the window seated behind one of them. They took turns in carrying the lady until they came near to Jamie's home, when Jamie asked that he might carry her for a little. The fairies were agreeable and the change was made, but when they got directly above his cottage Jamie steered his horse to the ground and landed, holding the lady tightly in his arms. The fairies came screaming down round him, and he had need to hold tightly, for they turned her in his arms to all sorts of shapes, but he still held on, till it came near to daylight and they were forced to go; but the smallest of them all said, 'You'll get no good of your trickery, Jamie Freel, for it's deaf and dumb she'll be from this day on.' And she threw a handful of powder over the lady who had no power to speak, but stood trembling and tongue-tied.

Jamie took the lady into his cabin, where his mother was puzzled to think how they could feed and wait upon so grand a lady, but she greeted her kindly and Jamie said he would work for both. So she lived with them for a year, very sad and unable to speak a word, but so gentle and sweet and eager to help that she won both their hearts.

At the end of the year it was Halloween once more and Jamie Freel determined to visit the Castle again. His mother was terrified at the thought, and did all she could to dissuade him, but he went and hid close to the Castle walls to hear what the wee folk were saying. They were talking of what had happened the last Halloween and of the shabby trick that Jamie Freel had played them; and the smallest one of all said: 'Ay but I punished him weel, for there she sits a dumb thing by his hearth, but he does na know that three drops out o' this glass in my hand wad gie her hearing an' her speech back again.' Jamie waited a short while and then he went up into the hall. His heart beat fast; but the fairies cried out: 'Here's Jamie Freel again. You're welcome, Jamie Freel! You're

welcome!' And when the clamour had died down the wee fairy said: 'You must drink to our health, Jamie Freel, out of this glass I hold in my hand.' Jamie took the glass, but instead of drinking it he made one leap out of the Castle Hill, and away, with the fairies after him. He never knew how he got home; but he burst open the door and slammed it behind him, with the glass in his hand and three precious drops still in it, though the greater part was spilled on the way. The young lady drank them, and speech and hearing came back to her, and the first words she said were of thanks to Jamie Freel for all he had done for her. The three of them talked till sun up, and then the young lady said that she must write to her father and mother, who would be breaking their hearts over her. She wrote, and they waited, and no answer came; and she wrote again, and at length they decided to go on foot to Dublin. It was a hard journey for the gently-bred girl and when they got to Stephen's Green they got a hard reception, for her parents were sure that they had seen their daughter die and had buried her more than a year ago, but at length a ring on her finger and a mole on her neck convinced both mother and father that this was indeed their daughter and then they could not thank Jamie Freel enough. But when he prepared to take his leave the daughter said he could not go without her, and the parents were so filled with gratitude that they consented more easily than might have been expected, and a fine coach was sent to carry Mrs Freel down to Dublin; and after the wedding the two families continued to live together in great harmony.

Crofton Croker's story 'Master and Man' is on the same general plot, more farcically treated.[5]

One example among many of prevention of fairy theft is sufficient to show the stratagems they were supposed to use. Cromek's story of Sandy Harg's Wife is a good and short version of a tale told at more length in Gibbings' *Folk-Lore and Legends, Scotland*.

Alexander Harg, a cottar, in the parish of New Abbey, had courted and married a pretty girl, whom the fairies had long attempted to seduce from this world of love and wedlock. A few nights after his marriage, he was standing with a *halve* net, awaiting the approach of the tide. Two old vessels, stranded on the rocks, were visible at mid-water mark, and were reckoned occasional haunts of the fairies, when crossing the mouth of the Nith. In one of these wrecks a loud noise was heard, as of carpenters at work; a hollow voice called from the other; 'Ho, what're ye doing?' 'I'm making a wyfe to Sandy Harg!' replied a voice in no mortal accent. The husband, astonished and terrified, throws down his net, hastens home, shuts up every avenue of entrance, and folds his young spouse in his arms. At midnight a gentle rap comes on the door, with a most courteous three-times touch. The young dame starts to get up; the husband holds her in a forbidding silence and kindly clasp. A foot is heard to depart, and instantly the cattle low and bellow, ramping as if pulling up their stakes. He clasps his wife more close to his bosom, regardless of her entreaties. The horses, with most frightful neighs, prance, snort, and bound, as if in the midst of flame. She speaks, cries, entreats, and struggles; he will not move, speak, nor quit her. The noise and tumult increases. but with the morning's coming it dies away. The husband leaps up with the dawn, and hurries out to view his premises. A piece of moss-oak, fashioned to the shape and size of his wife, meets his eye, reared against his garden-dyke, and he burns this devilish effigy.[6]

Before we tell some happy stories of rescues from Fairyland, some attention must be paid to the failures. It was commonly believed that, if humans carried into Fairyland could somehow obtain human food and refrain from tasting any fairy food or drink, they could be rescued before seven years had passed. It will be remembered that little Malekin, in Ralph of Coggeshall's story, seemed to think that every seven years gave her a chance of escape, and this is a variant of the belief. It used to be said that every part of the human body is completely changed at the end of seven years, and this may be a version of the same tradition.

Jeremaiah Curtin in *Tales of the Fairies*[7] gives a long and circumstantial story of a woman, Elizabeth Shea, who was carried off by the fairies and was not rescued because of her husband's indifference. The old man who told the story said that he was the step-brother of Elizabeth Shea's husband, James Kivane.

When Elizabeth was brought to bed for the birth of her second child she was nursed by her mother-in-law and her mother, but it happened that they both fell asleep and were waked by Elizabeth calling out that her bed was on fire. The mother sprang up, and looking towards the fire saw a cat with a man's face on it and was frightened, but was too busy putting out the fire to look a second time. Afterwards, when she looked, the cat was gone and she never saw it again. Two days later the child died and after a few days more Elizabeth Shea began to complain of a terrible pain in her foot and her leg swelled up, and then her whole body, and no cure could be found for it. After a month of intense suffering she died, and her body was so swollen that a great box had to be made for it instead of a coffin. They thought it was fairy stroke for they lived near the Fairy Castle of Rahonain. A year passed without incident, and James Kivane married a second wife. At the end of the year a neighbour of Kivane's called Pat Mahoney came to see him with a strange story. Mahoney had been at

Listowel Market when a stranger came up to him and asked him if he lived near Rahonain and if he knew James Kivane, 'For I have a message for him from his wife,' he said. 'His wife died a year back,' said Mahoney. 'She did not,' said the stranger, 'for she lives in the fairy fort close to Lismore, and has been coming to my house to get food every night.' And he told the whole story about how food set out for the servants at night had been eaten, and how after that they saw her every night when she came to eat food, and she told them who she was and every particular of what had happened. She had been stolen by fairies on the night when the man-cat was seen, and had been carried away to Rahonain to nurse a fairy child, and then the whole tribe had moved to Lismore. 'But I have not tasted food in the fort,' she said, 'but at the end of seven years I'll be forced to taste it, unless someone comes to rescue me, for I cannot escape myself;' and she told the man what must be done to save her, and sent messages to all her family begging them to come.

Mahoney went at once to Kivane's house and told him the whole story, but Kivane would do nothing, because of his new wife. The narrator, however, and Elizabeth's father and brother and another neighbour—for the rescue had to be by four men with a horse and car—got ready to go, but before they started they went to consult the priest, but he advised so strongly against it that three of them decided not to go and the whole project fell through. Elizabeth Shea was told of the second marriage, and sent messages that she would never trouble her husband, but would live quietly with her father and mother and the child, but nothing was done and she was forgotten for two years. Then urgent messages came again, saying that there was still time to save her, but these were smothered up by the second wife's kin, and seven years passed while nothing was done. Then Elizabeth Shea appeared again, but this time she was like an avenging ghost. She walked silently beside her father for nearly a mile, and at parting gave him a blow that blinded him for two days. But before he went blind he saw Elizabeth come and give a blow to her child, who died strangely shortly after. Then Kivane's wife fell sick and lay without pain but without movement, and her daughter died too; but the three sons were spared.

Too hasty a re-marriage is often the cause of failure to rescue a captive in Fairyland. A fairly recent version of such a tragedy was reproduced by T. G. F. Paterson in *Ulster Folk-Life* (1938). A woman of Creggan died leaving a sorrowing husband and a little baby boy behind her. Her husband grieved for her sorely, but his sorrow was transient, for another woman soon took his fancy and he married her, but the marriage was not a happy one, for she was bitterly jealous. She knew that he still loved his first wife the best, and the household and his poor little boy suffered for it. One October night his first wife appeared to him and told him that she was not dead at all, but had been carried away to fairy hill. She was sad and anxious because her poor little baby was ill-used, and she begged her husband to rescue her, which he could easily do in a few days time. When Halloween came the fairies would be riding past the farm and she would be on the third grey horse. As she passed he was to throw over her a pail of milk, taken from one cow whom she named, with no other milk, and above all without a drop of water in it, for if there was one drop the spell would be broken, and the fairies would murder her in their rage. The farmer was sorely put about and flustered at the thought of having two wives about the place, but she promised earnestly that she would not interfere between the man and his wife if she might have the little boy as her own.

The farmer consented and promised that he would not tell anyone about what they had arranged; but the foolish man let it all out to his new wife, and she secretly put a cupful of water in the pail. The farmer waited up in the byre, and about midnight he heard the tinkling of fairy bells and the trampling of hoofs. He picked up the pail and went out to the farm-end. The first grey passed him and the next, and he threw the pailful over his wife as she came level with him. There was a terrible cry and screaming, his wife fell from her horse, all was darkness and turmoil, and when daylight came they found the trampled ground all soaked with blood. The fairies had murdered her as she feared, and when the new wife boasted that she had watered the milk you may judge if they lived happy ever after.

This is the only story I know in which the fairies murdered a captive, though the vengeance was often cruel. Frequently it is human cowardice not human malice which is the cause of failure. Sir Walter Scott, in *Minstrelsy of the Scottish Border*,[8] tells the story of a Lothian farmer's wife who had been carried away by the fairies. During her year of probation she used to appear in her old home on Sundays, combing the children's hair and looking after them. One day her husband spoke to her, and asked her if there was any way in which she should be freed. She said that the Fairy Rade would pass near the house on Halloween, and begged him, for her temporal and eternal salvation, to use all his courage to rescue her. He had only to seize her and hold her fast through whatever strange transformations were laid on her and she could return to the human world again. The farmer loved his wife tenderly, and late on Halloween he set out to a little clump of furze, and waited impatiently for the Fairy Rade to pass him. Presently he heard an unearthly jangling of bells and a wild chant, and the Fairy Rade passed. It was such an uncouth, uncanny procession that, though he saw his wife among them, he stood frozen with terror until the ghastly show had passed. Then, as they vanished, loud shouts of laughter and exultation came back to him, and among them he heard the voice of his wife lamenting that she was lost to him and to the human world for ever.

Sometimes the attempt at rescue came too late. James Craig, in *Scandinavian Folk-Lore*,[9] tells of a girl who was carried off by huldre-folk. Her father and mother searched and asked everywhere, but no one could tell them anything until her father went to a neighbouring priest who was said to have much occult knowledge. The priest received him kindly, and the man begged him to find out if his daughter was alive or dead. The priest told him that she had been taken by the fairies, and though he could take her father to see her he would get no joy from the sight. But the father begged so vehemently for help in rescuing her that at length the priest fixed on an evening to make the attempt.

The man came at the appointed time, and the priest made him mount behind him on a horse that was waiting, ready bridled and saddled. They rode together till they reached the sea and then into it and on until they came to a little island of high cliffs in which a bright light shone out, and inside all was as clear as day. They saw a number of people moving about, and among them was a woman with a bluish face and a white cross upon her forehead. 'How do you like the woman with the cross?' said the priest. 'Not at all,' said the man. 'That is strange,' said the priest, 'for she is your own daughter and we can free her and take her home with us if you wish it, but you will have no joy in her, for she has taken on the troll nature by living among them.' 'I don't wish it,' said the man, 'Take me from this dreadful place. I cannot bear to look any longer.' So they went back the way they had come, and no one had missed them. The man went very sadly back to his home and no more is told of him after that. It was love that had failed here rather than courage, but presumably the girl had eaten fairy food and would return to them without her soul. The cross on her forehead, however, would seem to show that her baptism had still some power to protect her.

Another perpetual prisoner in Fairyland, who might have been rescued but for a failure of nerve, is said to be Robert Kirk, the author of *The Secret Commonwealth of Elves, Fauns and Fairies*. He often used to wander round the fairy hills at night, pursuing his researches, and his neighbours must have thought it a perilous occupation for when he was found unconscious one morning by the Fairy Hill at Aberfoyle the rumour went round that it was not he that was carried home but a stock, and that he had been carried away into the Fairy Knowe. The story, told by Walter Scott in *Demonology and Witchcraft*, is that shortly after his funeral and immediately after the birth of his posthumous child his apparition appeared to a cousin and told him to go to Grahame of Duchray, another cousin, 'Tell him,' said the vision, 'that I am not dead but a prisoner in Fairyland, and that there is yet a chance to rescue me. When my newly-born child is christened in the Manse I will appear to Duchray, and if he throws his dirk over my head I shall be freed from my enchantment.' The message was given to Duchray, who held his dirk ready in his hand, but when the apparition appeared he was so much afraid that he had no power to throw it, so Robert Kirk was lost to the world of men. In 1943 a memory of the legend still survived, for it was said that, if a child was born and christened at the Manse, and if, during the christening someone stuck a dirk into Robert Kirk's great chair, which still stood in the room, Robert Kirk would be freed from Fairyland. No doubt he would crumble into dust, but his immortal soul would be saved. So the legend went, but it was likely that the husband who was stationed near Aberfoyle would be posted before the child was born, and so the belief would never be put to proof.[10]

However, not all the attempted rescues ended in failure. Burd Janet set out to rescue Young Tamlane on Halloween by the same method as the Lothian Farmer was told to use, and held him undauntedly through the most terrifying changes. She successfully used milk in the disenchantment as the Ulster Farmer tried to do.[11] A redemption story of a later date is reproduced by Sir Walter Scott, in *Minstrelsy of the Scottish Border*,[12] from a chap-book of his period. An interesting variation is that it is the woman's brother, not the husband, who has to perform the rescue.

A girl called Mary Campbell had lately married a goldsmith, John Nelson, and the young couple moved into Aberdeen where he set up a business. They lived together in great happiness until she was brought to bed of a child. John Nelson hired women to attend on her, and on the night when her labour started they were all sitting round her when a great tumult arose in the room and all the candles went out. The nurses were much flustered and took a long time to find tinder and relight the candles. When they could see again they found to their horror that Mary Nelson was lying dead. It was a terrible grief to her husband, but all he could do was to make preparations for a costly funeral. People came from all round to it, and among them was the Minister, the Rev. Mr Dodd, who said, as soon as he saw the corpse: 'That is not Mistress Nelson; it is no Christian that is lying there, but some senseless substance that has been shaped to look like her.' And he refused to celebrate the funeral, which was delayed for a day and a night until they found another minister.

One evening a little time later John Nelson was riding round his fields outside the city when he heard a pleasant sound of music and saw a woman coming towards him closely veiled, and he rode up to her and asked her kindly what she was doing walking alone there so late in the evening. She lifted her veil and burst into tears, saying 'I am not permitted to tell you who I am'. He at once recognised his wife and asked her in God's name what was troubling her and what caused her to appear at that hour. She said that hours made no difference to her, for she was not dead but was taken away by the fairies on the night of her delivery. Her husband asked what means he should take to win her. 'I can be recovered,' she said, 'but not by you. The greatest dependence I have is on my brother Robert. His ship will be in port in ten days. Look in your desk on Sunday morning and you will find a letter written to him. Give it him unopened and he will know what he must do. I can be freed, but I doubt if we can get my child back; he has three nurses to attend him and is treated like a prince. As for me, I have the attendance of a queen; look over my right shoulder and you will see some of my companions.'

He did so and saw a king and queen sitting on a throne at the foot of the motte—that is a prehistoric, man-made mound—which was on John Nelson's land. Guarded as she was he would have tried to rescue her, but she told him not to attempt it, for it would only mean that she was lost to him for ever. As it was she was threatened with heavy punishment for speaking to him, but he could free her from that if he rode boldly up to the motte and threatened to burn all the thorns and brambles around it unless they promised that no harm should come to her. He did so, though he saw no one, but a voice came out of the motte asking him to throw away the book he had in his pocket, and then they could speak to him. He refused to do so, for it was the Bible, but told them he would not leave a thorn-tree standing or a furze or bramble round the place. Then they answered that they would promise if he would promise to leave the thorns alone. He promised, and a pleasant sound of music was heard, and he rode home and sent to ask Mr Dodd to visit him. Mr Dodd heard the whole story, and stayed with him till the next Sunday, when he looked into his desk and found the promised letter. Robert Campbell, who was the captain of a small merchant ship, came to port a few days later, and John Nelson at once took him the letter. As soon as he read it he called his crew together and told them what had happened to his sister and of his determination to save her. They all at once volunteered to go with him, but he thanked them but said that it was he alone that had to go.

In the course of her letter Mary Nelson had said: 'I request you will (the first night after you see this) come to the motte where I parted from my husband: let nothing daunt you, but stand in the centre of the motte at the hour of twelve at night, and call me, when I, with several others, will surround you; I shall have on the whitest dress of any in the company; then take hold of me, and do not forsake me; all the frightful methods they shall use let it not surprise you, but keep your hold, suppose they continue till cock crow, when they shall vanish all of a sudden, and I shall be safe, when I will return home and live with my husband.'

Acting on these instructions, Robert Campbell left his boat at ten o'clock that night and set out for the motte. As he got to shore a great lion came roaring towards him; he drew his sword and made a cut at it and it vanished into air. This was a great encouragement to him, for it showed not only that he was formidable to the fairies but that all their threats were no more than appearances, so he walked briskly on and climbed to the centre of the motte. He found a white handkerchief spread out, took his stand upon it and called out for his sister. He was at once surrounded by a crowd of girls wearing white dresses and looking much alike. There was one, however, whose dress was whiter than the rest, so he caught her firmly by the hand and called her by her name. At once a great clamour broke out, he stood in the middle of a circle of flame and all round him were hideous shapes, making towards him. He kept firm hold of his sister's hand, whatever it felt like. For an hour and a half they stood there, with thunder and lightning all round them and invaded by a rush of hideous shapes and a narrowing circle of flames. At length the sky began to lighten and distant cocks called out from the neighbouring farms. Robert Campbell knelt on the ground, with his arm still round his sister to return thanks to God for their deliverance. He felt her shiver in the cold air of dawn and put his coat round her. 'I am safe now,' she said, throwing her arms round him. 'Now you have put some of your own clothes round me they can do nothing. Let us go home!'

So they went home full of rejoicing and were received with still greater joy, but Robert Campbell was not content that the baby should be left as a lost soul, and as he and his brother-in-law were sitting discussing what should be done, he said: 'We will burn and dig up the whole motte if we cannot get him back!' Suddenly a voice spoke from the air. 'You shall have back your child safe and well if you promise solemnly that you will not till the ground for three perches round the motte, nor harm any thorn or plant upon it.' 'We promise solemnly' said the two together, and at once the baby, bonnie, well and merry was set on his mother's knee. They had no further trouble with the fairies after that, and indeed Mary Nelson said that she would never have been stolen if the women hired to nurse her had not been drinking too much as they sat up watching her.

The beautiful medieval poem, *The Romance of King Orfeo*,[13] translates the Kingdom of Pluto into Fairyland, following the tradition which makes Finvara, the Irish King of the Fairies, a ruler over the dead. It is a grim Fairyland into which King Orfeo penetrates to bring back his queen, Dame Meroudys. The dead, especially those who died violent deaths, are standing in massed ranks round the palace walls, but the company have their courtly pleasures like the Trooping Fairies of all sizes. Bevies of fairy ladies ride out hawking, knights go out on hunts; there is dancing and feasting and minstrelry as in human courts. And there is honour—what the fairies promise they will perform. Here as elsewhere, courage, courtesy and firmness win their way. This tale of rescue ends happily. There is no glance backwards, no final deprivation and despair, no terrible death, torn apart by maenads. Orfeo and Meroudys go home to his palace; after his sad years of wandering he is recognised and reinstated by his faithful steward, and the two live together for the rest of their lives in prosperity and mutual love.

Humans were not always carried into captivity in Fairyland, but occasionally taken out nightly in their sleep to work for fairies, and to wake in the morning wearied and unrefreshed, as people turned into horses and ridden by witches were said to do. In Craigie's *Scandinavian Folk-Lore* there is a story 'Working for the Bergfolk'[14] which illustrates this belief.

There was once a girl at service with the midwife in Vallö, who always complained of having such pains in her arms, as if she was quite killed with work, and yet her place was an easy enough one. One time the midwife had been sent for, but as she was driving past a mound, there came out one who took her out of the waggon, away from the man who had been sent for her, and carried her down through the mound to a large cave below it, where she had to assist a woman. When this was done, she noticed a girl standing and grinding malt with a quern, looking exactly like her own maid, and even wearing a pelisse the very same as one she had given her. She talked a little to the girl, who said that she was so tired, and had a great deal to grind yet before she would be finished. Meanwhile the woman slyly cut a piece out of her pelisse. In the morning her own maid was lying asleep in her bed, but by and by she came, and complained that some one had cut a piece out of her pelisse. Her mistress now brought the piece she had cut, and it fitted exactly, so she told the girl that it was no wonder her arms ached, seeing that she had to stand and grind away at the troll's quern by night. With that she told her the whole story, and advised her to repeat the Lord's prayer, and cross herself every evening on going to bed, before she laid herself down to sleep. This proved effectual.

Sometimes the fairies were not so greedy and arbitrary about their captives, but allowed people to come and go according to their whim. There is a pleasant story told in Simpkin's *County Folk-Lore VII*[14] which shows them in a very benevolent mood. There was a poor woman in Tullibody who was cursed with a drunken good-for-naught of a husband. Perhaps his trade made him thirsty, for he was a salt-man, but at any rate he was notorious and was generally known as 'the drunken Sautman o' Tullibody'. His wife tried all ways to reform him, but neither coaxing nor scolding was of any use, so at last in despair she called out to the fairies to come and fetch her away. They heard her right enough, and in a moment they whisked her up the chimney, singing:

> Deedle dinkum dodie,
> We're aff wi' drunken Davie's wife,
> The Sautman o' Tullibody.

They carried her to Cauldhame—the palace of the fairies in that district—and there she lived like a queen. But after a while she began to yearn after her old drunken husband, and the fairies were so kind as to carry her back, singing:

> Deedle Dinkum dodie,
> We're back wi' drunken Davie's wife,
> The Sautman o' Tullibody.

And what is more before they left her a little wee man gave her a small stick saying: 'As long as ye have this by you yir gudeman'll never be the waur o' drink.'

It was true enough, and the gudewife kept it by her all her days and never failed to bless the kindness of the fairies.

It seems from this that the Good Neighbours are not always as black as they are painted.

CHAPTER 9 – POWERS EXERCISED BY THE FAIRIES

THE DIFFERENT TYPES and tribes of fairies vary in the powers they have over humans and over their own fortunes.

The least powerful are the small fairies, living in isolated families, such as Skillywidden or Coleman Gray. They can move quickly, but they seem to have no power of levitation, nor of variation in size, nor of shape-shifting, and no available means of offence. They are helpless victims of their captors. If the little fairies who are sometimes obliged by mortals, who mend their broken baking peels or milking stools, are of the same species as these little captured fairies, they seem to have one power, that of giving continued good fortune to those who accept the food they offer in reward, and they may even be able to give a never-emptied bag of seed or pound of flour in return for a friendly loan; and these are not mean powers. A relevant story is told by Grant Stewart in his *Popular Superstitions of the Highlands of Scotland*.[1] A farmer of Strathspey was sowing his fields one fine morning and singing merrily as he sowed when he was approached by a beautiful fairy lady, carrying a small 'poke' in her hand. She greeted him courteously and asked him if he would be so kind as to sing her an old Gaelic song *'Nighan Donne na Bual'*. He was delighted to do so, and she listened with equal delight. Then she asked if he would fill her poke with some of his seed. He did not refuse, but asked what benefit he would get for it. She told him that he would not miss the grain he gave her, so he crammed her little bag full, and she thanked him and went. He sowed the whole field, and then found with surprise and delight that the bag was still full. He went on to the next field and the next, and still his poke was as fat as ever. Full of excitement he sowed one field after another and his supply was still undiminished when he carried it back to the granary. Unfortunately he met his wife at the door, and she was a foolish, chattering creature.

'What, gudeman,' she said, 'have ye done nothing the day, or have ye borrowed frae a neighbour. Yir bag's as full as when ye set out the morn.' By the time she had finished speaking the bag was as empty as her own brain. 'Ye menseless, chattering creature!' cried the farmer. 'Ye've emptied what would have been half a king's ransom to us with one idle, senseless word!'

It may have been that the fairy who gave this valuable gift—which would have been priceless if one of the best-known of the fairy taboos had not been violated—belonged to the fertility fairies who were concerned with agriculture. It is more probable, however, since the story was collected by Grant Stewart, that she was one of those whose gain was human loss, burnt grain and milk spilt on the ground belonged by right to them. As Robert Kirk put it, 'When we have plentie, they have scarcity at their homes.'[2] Grant Stewart has a story of a fairy who came to borrow some oatmeal from the wife of one of the tenants at Del-na-bo, promising to return it very soon as she was expecting a good supply very shortly. The wife knew better than to disoblige one of the Good People; she measured out the firlot that was borrowed, gave her guest a dram and a piece and began to convey her home. When they got near to Craig-el-nan, the mound in which the fairies lived, the Ben-shi paused and said: 'Ye may take yir meal home, mine's arrived sooner than I thought for.' The goodwife took back her loan with thanks, but as she turned to go home she saw that a neighbour's cornstack was blazing merrily, and in a few minutes it was all destroyed. After that she knew where the good neighbours got their supplies.[3] The smaller, powerless fairies steal the corn ear by ear as a mouse might do, as in Keightley's story, 'The Hampshire Farmer and the Fairies'.[4] The operation is more laborious but the underlying principle is the same.

The first of the general powers which is common to all fairies is that of glamour, by which people see what the fairies wish them to see and see nothing when the fairies wish to be invisible. We have seen good examples of this power in some of the Fairy Midwife legends and other tales of visits to the Fairy Hills. The spell is neutralised by the application of fairy ointment, or by such personal holiness as that of St Collen, whose eyes were proof against glamour.

In the modern story told in Chapter 7 from Seán Ó Suilleabháin's *Folktales of Ireland*, the disenchanting salve is a gruesome powder made from the ashes of an incinerated baby, but as a rule fairy ointment is supposed to be made of four-leaf clovers,[5] and a four-leaf clover itself gives the power of penetrating both witches' spells and fairy glamour. Robert Hunt's story of 'The Fairies and the Cow' is well known, but a short illustration of the same belief in the other end of the country, South Northumberland, is given in Volume II of *The Denham Tracts*.[6]

Many years ago, a girl who lived near Netherwitton, returning home from milking with a pail upon her head, saw many fairies gambolling in the fields, which were invisible to her companions, though pointed out to them by her. On returning home and telling what she had seen, the circumstances of her power of vision being greater than that of her companions was canvassed in the family, and the cause at length discovered in her weise, which was found to be of four-leafed clover—persons having about them a bunch, or even a single blade, of four-leafed clover being supposed to possess the power of seeing fairies, even though the elves should wish them to be invisible.

A weise is a round pad or a twist of grass which a milkmaid puts on her head to cushion it against the hardness of the pail.

Even the very small trooping fairies had power of the weather and seasons, and brought blight on corn and mildew on plants. Murrain on cattle was also attributed to them.

The Pixies, Piskies and Pisgies of the West Country were credited with more powers. One of their chief activities was to mislead travellers and these powers they shared with the Pouks of Central England. In Devon and Somerset people are often 'pixy-led', in the Midlands it is 'pouk-ledden', and the Will o' the Wisp is variously called 'Hunky-Punk,' 'Hobbedy', 'Kit-with-the-Canstick', 'Joan-with-the-Wad', 'Jenny Burnt-Tail', and so on. Pinkets and Spunkies are more often thought of as ghosts than as tricksy fairies. In Wales it is the Pwca who misleads travellers and leaves them in the dark and on the edge of a chasm.[7] In the Scottish Border it is Shellycoat who plays the same trick.[8]

To turn one's coat inside-out was a spell often used against pixy-leading. Thoms gives a report of a Devon girl on an occasion when this practice proved effectual. 'She once knew a man who, one night, could not find his way out of his own fields, all he could do, until he recollected to *turn his coat*; and the moment he did so, he heard the Pixies all fly away, up into the trees, and there they sat and laughed. Oh, how they did laugh! But the man then soon found his way out of the field.'[9]

As a rule Pixies and Hobgoblins seem to play their misleading games as a practical joke, out of sheer mischief; but Ruth Tongue in *Somerset Folklore* has a tale of a blackguardly old farmer, unpopular with the neighbourhood and presumably with the fairies as well, who was pixy-led to his death.

They'll tell 'ee three things 'bout an Exmoor Pony 'can climb a cleeve, carry a drunky, and zee a pixy'. And that's what old Varmer Mole's pony do.

Old Varmer Mole were a drunken old toad as he lived out over to Hangley Cleave way and he gived his poor dear wife and liddle children a shocking life of it. He never come back from market till his pockets were empty and he was zo full of zider he'd zit on pony 'hind-zide afore' a zingin' and zwearin' till he rolled into ditch and slept the night there—but if his poor missus didn't zit up all night vor'n he'd baste her and the children wicked.

Now the pixies they did mind'n and they went to mend his ways.

'Twad'n no manner of use to try to frighten the pony—he were that foot-sure and way-wise he'd brought Varmer safe whoame drunk or sleep vor years, wheresoever the vule tried to ride'n tew.

This foggy night the old veller were wicked drunk and a-waving his gad and reckoning how he'd drub his Missus when he gets to whoame when her zee a light in the mist. 'Whoa, tha vule!' says he, 'Us be to whoame. Dang'n vor lighting a girt candle like thic. I'll warm her zides for it!'

But pony he wouldn't stop. He could a-zee the pixy holdin' thic light and 'twere over the blackest, deepest bog this zide of the Chains—zuck a pony down in a minute 'twould, rider and all.

But the old man keeps on shouting, 'Whoa, fule, us be tew whoame!' And rode straight for the bog—but pony digged in his vour liddle veet 'n her stood!

Varmer gets off'n and catches'n a crack on the head and walks on to light. He had'n goed two steps when the bog took and swallowed 'n!

Zo old pony trots whoame. And when they zee'd 'n come alone with peat-muck on his legs they knowed what did come to Varmer—and they did light every candle in house and dancey!

After that Missus left a pail of clean water out at night vor pixy babies to wash in, pretty dears, and swept hearth vor pixies to dancey on and varm prospered wondervul, and old pony grew zo fat as a pig.[10]

Presumably these Pixies were able to make themselves invisible, but shape-shifting does not seem to have been among their accomplishments. Shakespeare's Puck, how ver, who played a Will o' the Wisp's part, was able to turn himself into a toasted crab-apple or a three-legged stool; or he could take the shape of a filly foal or as many changes of form as a Hedley Kow or a Picktree Brag, or any other counterfeiting bogy-beast. The Spriggans, who are the goblins of Cornwall, are as a rule small and hideous, but they can swell themselves into an enormous size, as we learn in Hunt's story of 'The Miser on the Fairy Gump'.[11] They were sometimes said to be the ghosts of the old giants which were destroyed by Brut and his companions.[12]

The Scandinavian dwarfs have the power of invisibility, but this is dependent on their mist caps, as are the magic caps of the Brown Dwarfs of the Isle of Rügen. Keightley gives a full account of the three tribes of Rügen dwarfs, founded on Arndt's *Märchen und Jugenderinnerungen* (Berlin 1818).[13] The White Dwarfs are the most innocent and gentle of all, something like in character to the small English fairies of *A Midsummer Night's Dream*. Like all the Dwarfs they are expert artificers and spend the cold winter days and nights underground, making such exquisitely delicate artefacts that they are invisible to mortals. In the nights of spring they come above ground and make their homes in trees and bushes and at night they spend their time in dancing and revelry. Their music is heard by travellers, but they are themselves invisible. They do not go out in companies in the light of the sun but individuals come out in the shape of birds and butterflies, and in these forms they seek out good men and reward good deeds with happiness and fortune.

The Brown Dwarfs are less than eighteen inches high. They wear brown jackets and brown caps, each with a little bell on it. It is these brown caps which make them invisible and give them magical powers. Any mortal who gains possession of a Brown Dwarf's cap is his master, and as long as he wears it he has great power in the Brown Dwarf's mounds. The Brown Dwarfs are, as a whole, good-natured and cheerful, but they have a habit of stealing human children whom they can hold as bond slaves for fifty mortal years.

The Black Dwarfs are supreme artificers, and any weapons or arms they make are worth a king's ransom, but they are morose, grudging and solitary, live together in only ones or twos and have no dancing or revelry. It is said that they have no music or song, but only wail and howl like screech owls or wolves. They have in general a dislike of mankind, and their marvellous weapons and corselets have to be dearly paid for.

All these dwarfs are shape-shifters and have powers of invisibility. The Hedley Kow, however, was the champion among shape-shifters. Jacobs has a delightful story of an old woman whose invincible and innocent optimism triumphed over every trick he could play. He appeared first as a pot full of gold coins, then as a bar of silver, after that as a lump of iron. When she got it home it was a large stone, and when she stooped to roll it in as a door-stop, it put down four lank legs and galloped away whickering. But to her every change was a change for the better.[14]

Pixies and Hobgoblins and Bogies do not invariably mislead by an *ignis fatuus* but confuse the senses of those that they wish to torment by hiding familiar gates and stiles and making a farmer wander in bewilderment through his own well-known fields until they choose to release him. Ruth Tongue gave me two comparatively modern versions of this, recorded in *The Fairies in Tradition and Literature*.[15] They were collected during a talk on Folk Tradition to a Women's Institute. A much more elaborate practical joke was played on a small Irish farmer in Curtin's story 'John Connors and the Fairies'.

John Connors had never had a son born to him, though he had seven small daughters, one after the other. He grew more furious at the birth of each daughter, and at the end he wouldn't do so much as to fetch a sponsor for the child, nor go into the house to say a kind word to his wife. At long last, however, they came into the field to tell him that a fine boy had been born to him, and then he nearly went mad with joy. He invited a great christening party, and sent out for enough food and drink to feed the whole parish, and in the end he said that no one in that poor place was good enough to be a godfather to his son, so he set off to ask some friends in Beaufort, near Killarney, to be the sponsors. The Inn was on his way, so he looked in there to tell the good news and stand a drink to the company. He had ridden on for quite a time when he met a fine-looking gentleman on a grand white horse, who asked him about his errand. 'I'm riding to Beaufort,' said John Connors, 'to find god-parents for my new-born son.' 'You're a foolish man,' said the stranger, 'you passed the cross-roads half a mile back; ride back and take the first turn to the left.' John Connors turned round, and rode on for more than an hour, but could find no trace of a cross road. At length he met the gentleman again. 'Aren't you the man I met an hour or more ago,' he said, 'looking for the road to Beaufort? You're a foolish fellow indeed! Turn back and take the first turn to your right.' John Connors turned back, more and more bewildered, and after a long ride met the gentleman again, who rated him for a fool, but said it was no use to knock up people at that hour, so he had better c me to spend the night at his house and he could look for sponsors in the morning. The poor man was so worn out and bewildered that he was glad to obey, and in a short time they came to a great castle. The stranger told John to leave his horse to the servants, gave him a grand meal and took him to a bedroom. John Connors undressed and went to bed and slept for three weeks. While he was asleep strange things were happening. The stranger took his clothes away and put them on something that looked like the dead body of John Connors, tied it onto the horse and sent it home where it caused great grief and consternation. The whole village came to the wake and John Connors was buried with all honours. Nearly three weeks later the strange gentleman roused John Connors, accusing him sternly of spending three days and nights in drunken slumber. His horse, he said, had broken out and run home, his child was already christened and they were all awaiting his return. John Connors looked for his clothes, but the stranger said he knew nothing of them, all he wanted was to have the drunken sot out of the house. He could put the sheet round him if he wanted covering, and go. John was quite cowed by the anger of his host, so he put the sheet round him and went out of the great door. When he'd gone some paces he looked back and there was no castle to be seen; nothing but fields and ditches, so he went home as best he could, hiding in the hedges for shame of being seen naked. But when he did get home there was no getting into the house or any other, for the word ran round like wildfire that the ghost of John Connors was raging round the place, banging at doors and yelling outside windows, and every door was banged and bolted against him, until he managed to get into the priest's house, and the priest listened to him and was convinced in the end, that it was Daniel O'Donohue, the Fairy King of Lochlein, that had played tricks on him, and serve him right. He gave him a bit of a talking to and then went back with him to his own house, and persuaded his wife in the end that it was John Connors himself that was there. And though John had a long family after that he never went out of the place to look for a sponsor again.[16]

Here we have a neat example of the fairy powers of misleading and of glamour. It was a painful experience for all concerned, but a salutary lesson was taught and digested. The same cannot be said of the next fairy power, the power of stealing the goodness imperceptibly from human food and leaving only an appearance behind. Kirk puts it with his usual felicity. 'Others feed more gross on the foyson or substance of cornes and liquors, or on corne itselfe, that grows on the surface of the Earth; which these fairies steall away, partly invisible, partly preying on the grain as do Crows and Mice.'

A very good example of this stealing of the foyson of both cattle and flour is the tale of The Tacksman of Auchriachan[17] told at some length by Grant Stewart and condensed by Keightley. What follows is an even shorter version.

It is well known that the fairies can steal the substance from our food and cattle and yet leave them apparently unimpaired, unless spells are used to prevent it. The Tacksman of Auchriachan near Glenlivet knew this, and was always most careful to use the spells taught him by his grandmother so as to preserve his food for his own use. One evening, however, his goats had strayed, and as he followed them up the sides of Glenlivet a thick mist came down, and he began to fear that he would never see the morning. He sat down to wait until the mist had cleared; but presently in the distance he saw a light, and when he came up to it he saw that it came from a curious dwelling, almost as if a part of the hill had been raised upon pillars. He knocked at the open doorway, and a woman came to the door whose face he knew well. He had been at her funeral a few months before.

'What in the name of wonder are you doing here, Auchriachan?' she said. 'Get you home at once, for my companions are unchancey people for you to meet if they come back before you are gone.'

'I cannot go, Janet woman,' he said. 'The mist is thick around me, and I cannot stir a foot without falling down a cliff. You must make some hiding place for me and take me in.'

Janet was an old friend, so she hid him in a corner of the room and piled peats round him. In a little time the fairies came in, led by an old man, with a long white beard and a silver chain whom the rest called True Thomas, so that Auchriachan knew him to be no other than Thomas the Rhymer, who had disappeared into fairyland two hundred years before.

The fairies came in very hungry, and began to ask each other how they should dine.

'The Tacksman of Auchriachan has a fine fat ox,' said True Thomas. 'The old miser guards it carefully enough with his spells as a rule; but our friends the goats have led him away tonight, and his son has forgotten the spell; let us fetch it and roast it.'

The others shouted with joy, and in a minute some of them came back with the body of Auchriachan's poor ox, which was roasted under his eye.

'But what shall we do for bread?' said one fairy, as the ox was cooking.

'I noticed that Auchriachan's wife had forgotten to make a cross on her bannocks,' said one who had brought the ox. 'We can take those.'

Poor Auchriachan could hardly contain himself at this second theft; but for the love of life he had to lie quiet; and as the fairies were about it Janet hurried him out, for the mist had blown aside. Auchriachan hurried home to see how much damage had been done. There he found his ox and his wife's bannocks looking as well as ever; but the bannocks had no cross on them, and his son confessed that he had forgotten to say any words over the ox that night.

So Auchriachan felled the ox, and threw it and the bread out on the brae side, where neither cat nor dog came near them, for indeed all the good had been taken out of them to the fairy knowe.

Another example of cattle killed or devoured by the fairies and afterwards apparently resuscitated is to be found in the stories attached to the first edition of Henderson's *Folk-Lore of the Northern Counties*, 'The Three Cows'.[18] It is reproduced in Jacob's *More English Fairy Tales*, but there is nothing in it of the fairies' extraction of goodness from human bread.

An interesting point in 'The Tacksman of Auchriachan' is the mention of True Thomas, now fully integrated into Fairyland. It is strange to find him in the Highlands, for Ercildoune is in the Border Country, but his prophecies were as widely spread as those of Mother Shipton or Merlin.

The power of bestowing good or ill luck has already been mentioned, and even the smallest and least powerful of the Fairies can exert some influence in this direction. Transgression of a fairy taboo can result in continued illness and dwining among stock and humans, a run of unexpected ill-luck or a series of disastrous accidents. In Ireland, for instance, it was thought very important that a new house should not be inadvertently built across the track of a fairy road, for the fairies were great travellers, and moved constantly from place to place, always following known routes through the air, invisible to mortal eyes, as birds do when they migrate.

D.A.MacManus in *The Middle Kingdom*[19] gives several instances of ill-luck which were said to follow the breach of this taboo and of such prohibitions as extending a building to the westward or into open country instead of into a piece of land that was already enclosed. Sometimes these violations were only punished by poltergeist manifestations, loud noises or localised raging winds, but sometimes the punishment was out of all proportion to the crime. MacManus gives one instance which came to his notice in 1935. A farmer with a family of six children had lately extended his house to the west into a neighbouring field when one of his children fell ill of a mysterious malady, and died after a few days in spite of all the doctor could do. Then another sickened and died, and another and another. Then the fifth child sickened, and became rapidly worse till the doctor despaired of his life. Next morning, however, the parents called at the house to say that the child was well again and would not need the doctor. It seems the father had despaired of any help from the doctor and called in a wise woman, who immediately told him that the new extension was the cause of the trouble and unless he pulled it down before sunrise his fifth child would die. The poor father worked desperately all night demolishing his building and when he went in at sunrise, found the child in a healthy sleep.

The uprooting of hawthorns or other fairy trees is also supposed to bring down ill fortune. In Scotland, where fairies often live underneath human houses, they naturally objected to slops or drains trickling down to foul their living quarters, but they generally gave a civil warning about this before proceeding to extremities.

Many illnesses were supposed to be caused by fairy agency. The most notable was the 'fairy stroke', a name which still survives in common use. This was thought to be caused by elf-shot, flint arrowheads which pierced the skin without leaving a mark and caused paralysis or lameness. These were shaped by the elves but generally directed by humans who were carried about by the evil fairies on their flights for that purpose. Isobel

Gowdie, in her strange, mad confessions of her visits to the elf-hills, said that the Devil himself shaped the elf-arrows and delivered them to little 'boss-backed' elves to be sharpened and polished.[19] Some illnesses were ascribed indiscriminately to witches and fairies. Tuberculosis is an example. People who suffered from wasting and perpetual tiredness, who waked every morning unrefreshed from a night's sleep, might either be 'hag-ridden', that is, turned into horses and ridden by witches to their nightly meetings, or they might be called every night into the fairy hill, either to dance there or to work like the women used by the Bergman in the Scandinavian story quoted in Chapter 8. A somewhat similar cause of perpetual tiredness was suggested by William Warner in *Albion's England*,[20] who said that the Brownie did no household work himself, but got the housewife out of bed in her sleep to do the household chores for which he got the credit. Rheumatism, cramps and bruising were also blamed on the fairies.

A merrier power was that of levitation. Not until comparatively modern times were fairies credited with wings, but they had other means of travel. Often they moved by a magic spell alone. Aubrey and Walter Scott both tell us that in Scotland 'Horse and Hattock' is the operative word, though the *Shetland Folk Book* (Vol. III)[21] gives a rather more elaborate one:

> Up hors, up hedik
> Up with ridin bolwind,
> An I kin Ise reyd among yu.

In Ireland, the word is 'Boram, Boram, Boram'.[22]

In the adventure of the Laird of Duffus 'Horse and Hattock' was sufficient. One day as the Laird of Duffus was walking in the fields, a whirl of wind and dust passed him and he heard voices crying 'Horse and Hattock!' which he knew for the word used by the fairies when they were riding. Being a bold man, he cried 'Horse and Hattock!', and in a moment, was sweeping through the air surrounded by a crowd of riders. They went on and on to the coast, and by the time the sun had set they were over the sea and in France. It was dark night when they got to the King's Palace, in through the keyhole, Duffus and all, and down to the French King's cellar, where they revelled, drank and sang. How long it went on the Laird of Duffus never knew, for when the cry of "Horse and Hattock!" was raised again, he was fast asleep, and was found by the butler drowsily wandering through the cellar with a rich cup of curious workmanship in his hand. Things looked black for him, but his courage and good breeding stood him in good stead; the King remembered the ancient friendship between France and Scotland, and not only sent him home, but allowed him to carry the fairy cup back with him, which was kept in the House of Duffus for many generations.[23]

It was more usual, however, for the fairies to use some apparatus for their flight. Ragwort stalks were most commonly used both in Scotland and Ireland, but any 'kecksies', or dried stalks of weeds, could be transformed into flying horses. Fergusson's *Ochil Fairy Tales* gives an example in the adventure of The Black Laird of Dunblane, reproduced in a shortened form in Simpkin's *Folklore of Fife, Clackmannan, and Kinross* (F.L.S.).[24]

The Black Laird of Dunblane, returning late one night from Alloa, met in Menstrie Glen with the Fairies, who invited him to go with them. They mounted bundles of windlestrae, and he a plough-beam left in a furrow. Crying 'Brechin to the Bridal' they flew hither through the air on white horses, entered a mansion where a banquet was prepared, and ate and drank, invisible to the guests. Then crying 'Cruinan to the dance!' they passed out again through the keyholes 'like a sough of wind' and went in the same way to Cruinan. At length the Laird could not help exclaiming, 'Weel dune, Watson's auld plough-beam!' and at once found himself alone, astride of the plough in the furrow whence he started.

In the Irish story of Guleesh,[25] collected by Douglas Hyde, the fairies and the hero, taken with them by the fairies to help in the capture of the King of France's daughter, appeared to be mounted on splendid white horses, and only when Guleesh has used the name of God to rescue the Princess do they appear in their real form, bundles of grass ridden by the fairies, and a plough-beam, fitter to bear the weight of human beings, for Guleesh and the Princess.

Magic caps were used by both fairies and witches for transport as well as for invisibility as we have seen in the Hereford story told in Chapter 2.

It is not only living creatures that can be levitated, but objects. Scott[26] tells a story of a group of boys who were whipping their tops near the church of Duffus when they saw a small cloud of dust approaching from a short distance. It passed near them and most of the boys blessed themselves, for these little whirlwinds were supposed to be made by a troop of fairies, but one, bolder than the rest, called out 'Horse and hattock with my top', and at once the top rose up and disappeared in a cloud of dust. It was found at last in the churchyard at the other side of the church. More ponderous things than tops can be lifted. There are many foundation stories in which the eccentric position of a house or church is accounted for by the removal of building materials and diggings from the place where they were originally planned, by the Devil or a monstrous pig or cat; but occasionally the fairies are believed to be the operators. Once, according to George Henderson in his *Popular Rhymes, Sayings and Proverbs of the County of Berwickshire*,[27] they tried to levitate the finished and inhabited Langton House.

The rhyme they were chanting was:

> 'Lift one, lift a',
> Baith at bak and for wa'
> Up and awa' wi' Langton House
> And set it down in Dogden Moss.'

Fortunately a wakeful guest heard the invocation, and just as the house began to heave up he thrust his head out of the window and nailed it to the ground with a hastily uttered prayer.

I have spoken much of the fairies' power of bestowing good luck and ill-luck and have several times referred to their interest in agriculture and fertility. It would be as well to illustrate this by a specific example, a longish story quoted by J. E. Simpkins from an article 'Folk-Lore of Clackmannanshire' which appeared in *The Scottish Journal of Topography* in 1848.[28]

Nearly seventy years ago, David Wright rented the farm of Craiginnin. His servants, on cutting the grass of the meadow, were in the custom of leaving it to the management of the fairies. These aerial beings came from Blackford, Gleneagles, Buckieburn, etc., and assembling on the summit of the 'Saddlehill' descended to their work among the hay. From morning till evening they toiled assiduously. After spreading it out before the sun, they put it into coils, then into ricks, when it was conveyed into the adjacent farm-yard, where they built it into stacks. This kindness of the fairies David Wright never forgot to repay, for, when the sheep-shearing came round, he always gave them a few of the best fleeces of his flock. He flourished wonderfully, but finding his health daily declining, and seeing death would soon overtake him, he imparted to his eldest son the secret of his success, and told him ever to be in friendship with the 'gude neebors.'

The old man died, and was succeeded by his son, who was at once hard, grasping and inhospitable. The kind advices and injunctions given him by his father were either forgotten or unattended to. Hay-making came round, but young Wright, instead of allowing the 'green-goons' to perform what they had so long done (thinking thereby to save a few fleeces), ordered his servants to the work. Things went on very pleasantly the first day, but on going next morning to resume their labour, what was their surprise to find the hay scattered in every direction. Morning after morning this was continued, until the hay was unfit for use. In revenge for this, he destroyed the whole of their rings, ploughed up their green knolls, and committed a thousand other offences. He had soon reason, however, to repent these ongoings.

One day the dairymaid having completed the operation of churning, carried the butter, as was her wont, to the 'butter well,' on the east side of the house, to undergo the process of washing, preparatory to its being sent away to the market. No sooner had she thrown it into the well, than a small hand was laid upon it, and in a second the bright golden treasure disappeared beneath the crystal waters! The servant tried to snatch it; but alas! it was lost—irrecoverably lost for ever! and as she left the place a voice said:

> Your butter's awa'
> To feast our band
> In the fairy ha!

The horses, cows, and sheep, sickened and died; and to complete all, Wright, on returning from a Glendevon market, night overtook him in the wild pass of Glenqueich. He wandered here and there, and at last sank into a 'well-e'e,' in which he perished. After his death the farm-house went gradually to demolition, and only its bare walls are now to be seen.

CHAPTER 10 – FAIRY DEALINGS WITH MORTALS

I N THE TRADITIONS of fairy lore there is evidence of constant interdependence between fairies and mortals. In some of the earlier chapters I have laid a good deal of emphasis on gifts of fertility and good fortune to farms and to people who provided hospitality to the fairies without intruding on their privacy, and who showed a general respect for them.

In Ireland, almost more than any other country in Europe, the fairies have, or had till recently, an almost god-like status. In Evan Wentz's exploration into Celtic Fairy Beliefs, *The Fairy Faith in Celtic Countries*, published in 1911, we have a report collected near Ben Bulbin in County Sligo, which gives this staus to The Gentry. The speaker was an old man whose ancestors had lived for four hundred years under the shadow of Ben Bulbin and who was thoroughly imbued with the traditions of the county.

> The *gentry* take a great interest in the affairs of men, and they always stand for justice and right. Any side they favour in our wars, that side wins. They favoured the Boers, and the Boers did get their rights. They told me they favoured the Japanese and not the Russians, because the Russians were tyrants. Sometimes they fight among themselves. One of them once said, 'I'd fight for a friend, or I'd fight for Ireland.'

It was considered very important to retain the goodwill of the fairies, and careless talk about them was to be avoided, particularly out of doors, for the wind would carry anything that was said to fairy ears.[2] Seemingly impossible tasks could be performed with fairy help, but this was often dearly paid for, as in the Rumpelstiltskin stories, Tom Tit Tot,[3] Hard Weather[4] and Whuppity Stoorie.[5] However some of the boons bestowed were purely benevolent like the spinning of Habetrot, the tutelary fairy of spinning.[6] Another skill frequently bestowed by the fairies is that of piping or fiddling.

A tale called 'Finger Lock' is in the archives of the School of Scottish Studies, recorded by Hamish Henderson from Walter Johnson. It is a variant of the Cinderlad story and is woven round the McCrimmon Brothers, the famous Scottish pipers. 'Finger Lock' is the name of a well-known pipe tune.

> There were three McCrimmon brothers and two of them were great pipers, and used to go piping about everywhere, but they just kept the youngest one for a slave. Once at the time of the Games the youngest

one asked if he might go too to hear the piping. The eldest hit him across the face, and told him to bide at home, and mind the cows. So the two went off and locked the door so that the laddie shouldn't steal any food, and left him at the burnside, watching the cows. He was lying there very sadly when a wee green man came up and asked what was the matter.

'I wanted to the games with my brothers, to hear the piping,' said the laddie.

'I'll give you a piping,' said the fairy, and he played the loveliest tune on a strae. 'Now you play,' he says.

'I canna play,' says the laddie, 'not even the chanter, and my brothers has the pipes with them, and the door of the house is locked forbye.'

'That's easy enough,' said the fairy, 'just blow in the lock, and put your wee finger in and turn it.' The laddie did that and the door opened. 'Look in the old kist,' said the fairy, 'and you will find your pipes.'

There was an old kist there he had never seen before. He opened it, and there was a set of pipes mounted in gold and the finest kilt you ever saw. The laddie put it on and he looked grand.

'Play a tune on your pipes,' said the wee green man. The laddie played, and a tune seemed to come out of his head, the like of which he'd never heard before. 'The name of that tune is "The Finger Lock" ' said the wee green man.

He went off to the Games, and everyone sat in a dream, listening to him playing 'The Finger Lock'. He got the prize before everyone, but the fairy had told him to be home early, so he slipped away and when his brothers came back, everything was back in the kist, and there he was in his old clothes, watching the cows by the burn. He asked his brothers how the playing had gone and they said the grandest player had come and played the finest tune that ever was heard.

'What was the name of it?' said the laddie.

'It was called "The Finger Lock" '.

'Ach!' says he, 'I can play that tune mysell.'

'You!' says they. 'You canna so much as play on the chanter.'

'Wait here a wee minute,' he says and he went off to the kist, and put on his kilt and took up the pipes, and played 'The Finger Lock' over to them. After that the two elder McCrimmons never went to the Games and Gatherings, but the youngest went to them, and was the best piper of the three. And that was how 'The Finger Lock' was first played.[7] Another fairy power was that of healing, and the fairies sometimes benevolently bestowed that on poor men, though the well-intended gift occasionally turned into a source of danger. Such a double-edged gift entered into history and was twice mentioned in informal accounts of witch trials. It is the story of The White Powder.

Durant Hotham mentions the incident in the Preface to his *Life of Jacob Behmen*, published in 1654,[8] which contains several passages of some interest, and Webster in his *Displays of Supposed Witchcraft*,[9] more than twenty years later expands the account, for he himself had been present at the trial.

He tells us that the man was a very ignorant, poor person, who had found means to keep himself and his family by the use of white powder, which brought him under the suspicion of witchcraft. He goes on:

The judge asking him how he came by the powder, he told a story to this effect. 'That one night before the day was gone, as he was going home from his labour, being very sad and full of heavy thoughts, not knowing how to get meat and drink for his wife and children, he met a fair Woman in fine cloaths, who asked him why he was so sad, and he told her it was by reason of his poverty, to which she said, that if he would follow her counsel she would help him to that which would serve him to get a good living; to which he said he would consent with all his heart, so it were not by unlawful ways; she told him that it should not be by any such ways, but by doing of good and curing sick people; and so warning him strictly to meet her there the next night at the same time, she departed from him, and he went home. And the next night at the time appointed he duly waited, and she (according to promise) came and told him that it was well he came so duly, otherwise he had missed of the benefit, that she intended to do unto him, and so bade him follow her and not be afraid. Thereupon she led him to a little Hill, and she knocked three times, and the Hill opened, and they went in, and came to a fair hall, wherein was a Queen, sitting in great state, and many people about her, and the Gentlewoman that brought him, presented him to the Queen, and she said he was welcome, and bid the Gentlewoman give him some of the white powder, and teach him how to use it; which she did, and gave him a little wood box full of white powder, and bid him give 2 or 3 grains of it to any that were sick, and it would heal them, and so she brought him forth of the Hill, and so they parted.' And being asked by the Judge whether the place within the Hill, which he called a Hall, were light or dark, he said indifferent, as it is with us in twilight; and being asked how he got more powder, he said when he wanted he went to that hill, and knocked three times, and said every time 'I am coming, I am coming,' whereupon it opened, and he going in was conducted by the aforesaid Woman to the Queen, and so had more powder given him.

The jury either believed his story or judged it to be a harmless delusion, for they acquitted him. The judge was harsher or more critical, for he said that if he had had his way he would have had the man whipped to the Fairy Hill, but fortunately he did not have his way, and no one took up the man's challenge to go with him to the Hill.

Here we have a legend of purely benevolent fairies, who did good to a poor man out of pity and without payment. If the story of a fairy association was an attempt to put a more favourable gloss upon help given by a herbalist who might have been suspected as a witch the man selected a story which gained a certain amount of credence. It seemed the fairies were accepted as more creditable associates than even white witches would have been.

Skill in crafts was sometimes bestowed as well as in music or dancing. Evan Wentz collected a legend from an old piper in the Isle of Barra about skill in boat-making bestowed on a young prentice. A boy apprenticed to carpentry was working with his master on building a boat on the shore. He found he had forgotten a tool and ran back to the workshop to fetch it, but disturbed a crowd of fairies hard at work on carpentry. They scattered as he ran in, and one little fairy woman was so flustered that she dropped her silk girdle as she ran, and the boy picked it up and put it in his pocket. In a minute the little woman came back to look for it and asked the boy to give it to her. He refused, and she promised to give him full skill in his trade without further apprenticeship, so he restored it to her, and she ran away with it happily. Next morning the boy got up very early, and fitted two planks into the boat so perfectly that the master asked him if he knew who had been there, for they were set in by a master who could teach *him* his trade. So the boy told the master his story, and his skill stayed with him all his life, in spite of his mention of a fairy gift.[10]

There are various other boons given by the fairies, though good luck and health are generally the best tokens of their favour.

However valuable fairy help might be to mortals, yet it will be seen that the fairies were in many ways even more dependent upon human help and nourishment. The food served at their banquets may appear delicious, but it is spiced and dressed by glamour. It can serve no human need and is insufficient even for the fairies, unless it is reinforced by thefts from human food, the 'foyson' or goodness stolen out of mortals' milk or cheese or grain, or the food itself stolen away as if by birds or mice. According to St Collen, the fairies, if left to themselves, fed upon the glamourized leaves of a tree;[11] J. G. Campbell gives them rather more choice of diet, for grain they grew barley in their subterranean world, roots of silverweed, stalks of heather and milk of red-deer and goats made up the rest of their diet. The medieval Green Children had a more austere world with an exclusive diet of green beans, traditionally the food of the dead. The foyson of human food had presumably been transformed into food proper to the fairies, which was unsuitable for human consumption, for those who ate it became fairies themselves and unable to return to the human world. It may be that some of the fairy individuals who depended on human food were, like Malekin, captives in Fairyland who were still hoping to return to humanity, but the instances of fairy thefts were too frequent to lead us to suppose that this would always be so. In the tale of The Tacksman of Auchriachan two of the inhabitants of the fairy house had once been human, but all of them made their meal from the foyson of the Tacksman's ox and cakes, and there are so many evidences of fairy thefts as to make it seem their most usual custom. D. A. McKenzie in his *Scottish Folk-Lore and Folk Life* quotes a story from a book published in Inverness in 1891 which records a large-scale theft of milk.[12] This was given as part of the evidence at Lord Lovat's trial in 1746.

John Fraser prospered for a time and supplied milk of excellent quality to his Inverness customers. Then suddenly 'a famine of milk set in'; the cows gave little or no milk. At last no more could be supplied for sale to Inverness. The very bairns in the town cried out for milk which could not be had. 'Through summer, autumn, winter and spring the scarcity of milk continued.'

One evening 'early in the summer of the year following that when the dearth began ', Fraser was standing near a rowan tree near his mill. He saw approaching a strange dwarfish man clad in curious attire. The careworn and elderly aspect of his face contrasted with his 'youthful locks of brown hair'. This stranger carried over a shoulder 'a long tapering sapling of hawthorn that seemed as if it would break beneath the load of some invisible burden that was attached to its slenderest end'. He did not speak to Fraser when he reached the rowan tree, nor did Fraser speak to him.

Fraser suddenly suspected that the stranger had some evil intent and, seizing the end of the hawthorn sapling severed a portion of it with his gulley knife. The old man walked on as if unaware of Fraser's action and 'disappeared over the rising ground towards the Leachkin'.

The narrative continues:

'As he vanished from the sight of Fraser, a rushing sound came from the cut twig that had fallen . . . Rich, creamy milk flowed as in a stream—it overspread in all directions the field where the miller stood . . .' A rivulet of milk flowed towards the River Ness, giving it for a time 'a milky appearance'. Thus did John Fraser 'cut the fairy spell and let loose the milk that had been stolen from the cows of the valley for so many months. No longer did the cows refuse their milk, but gave it even more plentifully than before, and it was noticed that the field where the switch had been cut from the old man's wand yielded a richer crop of grass for years after.'[12]

This is the tale of theft on a large scale, often the fairies proceeded in a gentler way of borrowing, and a willing loan brought a blessing with it.

Lady Wilde gives two stories of fairy dealings with cows in her *Ancient Legends of Ireland*.[13] One is the straightforward anecdote of the milking of a cow by a fairy woman. Like the cow *Daisy* in the Cornish story a cow refuses to let her milk down and goes night and morning to stand under a hawthorn tree. One day the farmer watches and sees an old woman in red come out of the trunk of the hawthorn and milk the cow. He consults a 'fairy doctor', who brings the trouble to an end by singing, incantations, a herbal draught and a red-hot ring drawn round the hawthorn tree. No ill fortune follows this treatment. In the second tale, however, there is cooperation and good feeling between mortals and fairies. A cow was being lured into a fairy rath and the little herd boy, the son of the farmer, was trying to drive it back when an old fairy woman appeared and coaxed him to lend the cow for a year, for their queen needed the taste of fresh milk. At the end of the year, she said, the cow would come back to him with a beautiful calf. She spoke so pleasantly that the boy was willing to do anything for her, so he took a hazel stick as she asked him and tapped the cow three times with it, and the old woman and the cow vanished together into the rath. The boy had to go back and tell his father as best he could. The father kept the date in mind, and on that very day next year he sent the boy to the rath, and there was the cow waiting quietly for him, with a beautiful little white calf beside her. So all was well between that farmer and the fairies.

Fairies are always grateful for human help in mending or making utensils for them. There are several variants of 'The Fairy Ped' and 'The Fairy Peel', always ending in a gift of food from the grateful fairies, and good luck following on its acceptance. A short version of this legend is to be found in Leather's *Folklore of Herefordshire*.[14]

One day a man was working in the fields when he heard the fairies talking over their baking; they said they had no peel. He said 'I'll find a peel.' He made one and left it out in the field where they could easily get it. Next day it was gone, and in its place the fairies had given him a batch of delicious cakes. But they were invisible all the time: he never saw them, only heard them talking. A peel is a flat iron shovel, with a long wooden handle, used for putting bread or loaves into an oven and taking them out.

One of the most widespread of the traditions about intercourse between fairies and humans is that of their visits to human houses by night. In a way it cannot be described as intercourse because the fairies wanted the living quarters left to them, neat and clean, ready for their use, with water set out and a clear fire burning. The owners of the house were supposed to be upstairs, with their eyes tight shut and preferably asleep. This is well illustrated in *Fairy Faith in Celtic Countries*, in the evidence taken by Evan Wentz in the Isle of Man.

The Fairy Dog—This used to happen about one hundred years ago, as my mother has told me:—Where my grandfather John Watterson was reared, just over near Kerroo Kiel (Narrow Quarter), all the family were sometimes sitting in the house of a cold winter night, and my great grand-mother and her daughters at their wheels spinning, when a little white dog would suddenly appear in the room. Then every one there would have to drop their work and prepare for the company to come in: they would put down a fire and leave fresh water for them, and hurry off upstairs to bed. They could hear them come, but they could never see them, only the dog. The dog was a fairy dog, and a sure sign of their coming.[15]

All was well when things were performed in order in this way, but the fairies can take a grim revenge if their desires were not met. Wentz collected an example of this from Glen Rushen in the Isle of Man.

A Fairy-Baking—At night the fairies came into a house in Glen Rushen to bake. The family had put no water out for them; and a beggar-man who had been left lodging on the sofa downstairs heard the fairies say, 'We have no water, so we'll take blood out of the toe of the servant who forgot our water.' And from the girl's blood they mixed their dough. Then they baked their cakes, ate most of them, and poked pieces up under the thatched roof. The next day the servant-girl fell ill, and was ill until the old beggar-man returned to the house and cured her with a bit of the cake which he took from under the thatch.[16]

Here the fairies behaved like vampires; and though they do not often suck human blood they are supposed to have a constant need to reinforce the dwindling stock of fairy life and energy. This is the explanation generally given of the fairy theft of human children and of beautiful girls to be wives to fairy men and bear their half-human children. It is constantly said in Ireland that humans are borrowed to take part in fairy games of hurling and in faction fights. This belief is tersely illustrated in evidence given to Evan Wentz in North Galway.

Fairy Warfare.—When the fairy tribes under the various kings and queens have a battle, one side manages to have a living man among them, and he by knocking the fairies about turns the battle in case the side he is on is losing. It is always usual for the Munster fairy king to challenge Finvara, the Connaught fairy king.[17]

In this short extract the phrase 'living man' seems significant, and the introduction of Finvara, King over the Dead, as one of the combatants. The sense of the dwindling powers of the fairies is strongest where the connection between the fairies and the dead is strong. In Cornwall the fairies are generally described as the pagan dead, who were not bad enough for Hell and not good enough for Heaven. In Ireland Finvara of Connaught is always described as leading a host of the Dead. He and his wife, Oonagh, are a kind of Pluto and Persephone. This dependence of the fairies upon human strength and the illusory nature of the fairy delights may be a part of that strand of fairy belief which identifies or connects them with the dead.

CHAPTER 11 – FAIRY PATRONS AND FAIRY WIVES ᔕᔕᔕᔕᔕᔕᔕᔕᔕᔕᔕᔕ

HE FAIRY GODMOTHERS who play so large a part in the courtly French Fairy Stories, the first of them adapted by Perrault from genuine folk-tales and later burgeoning out into all the extravagances of the *Cabinet des Fées*,[1] were already at a remove from the fairies of tradition, though they were not entirely unrooted. As pointed out in Chapter 2, the medieval fairies were originally the Fates—the *Fata* of Italy, the *Hadas* of Spain, the *Fées* of France. These, generally as three persons like the Classical Fates, visited a child at birth, and gave it good or ill fortune. The Greek legend of Meleager might be considered as the forerunner of the christening tales.[2] Meleager, who came of the line of Endymion, was six days old when the Three Fates visited his mother, the two first, as was their custom gave him good gifts, generosity from Clotho, great strength from Lachesis, but Atropos said that he should live only till the log then burning on the fire was consumed. His mother, Althaea, leapt up and drew the log from the fire, quenched it, and put it for safe keeping into a chest where she kept it till Meleager grew to manhood, generous and of great strength according to the gifts of the two Fates, and one of the most famous heroes from Greece. He went with other champions to conquer the wild boar that was ravaging Caledon. Between them he and Atalanta, the warrior maiden, killed the boar, and Meleager gave its carcase to Atalanta. His two uncles claimed it, and tried to take it from her by force. Meleager attacked them, and had the misfortune to kill them both. Althaea, when she heard of their death, took the log from its hiding place and put it on the fire. As it fell into ashes Meleager died. Myths are commonly more tragic than fairy tales.

The Fays were the descendants of these Fates. They make their appearance in the twelfth-century humorous play *Le Jeu d'Adam* written by the Troubadour Adam de la Halle.[3] The three Fays came not to a name giving but to a summer hall set up for them in the churchyard with the proper accompaniment of drink and food and white-handled knives. Two of these Fays are in an amiable mood but the third is determinedly ill-tempered because she has not been properly summoned. Since the play is a farce not a tragedy, there is no fatal issue to it; Adam is simply cursed with baldness.

The real forerunner of the Fairies at the Christening is to be found in the fifteenth-century romance, Huon of Bordeaux, translated into English by

Lord Berners in 1558. One of the chief characters in this romance was Oberon, the King of the Fairies, beautiful and virtuous but no bigger than a three-year-old child. This is a common size for fairies, but the Fays were at that time most usually of at least human size and his dwarfishness is accounted for by a fairy curse.

When Huon is persuaded by Oberon's beauty and his readiness to speak the Name of God to hold conversation with him, Oberon tells him of his birth and lineage. He was the son of Julius Caesar by the Fairy Lady of the Hidden Isle, called Chapalone by Lord Berners, though its most usual name is Cepholonia. Centuries before she had married a King of Egypt, Nactabanus, and had been the mother of Alexander the Great. Oberon goes on to tell of the fairy visits at the time of his birth.

> Thus I have shewed you who was my father. At my birth there was many princes and barons of the fairy, and many a noble ladie that came to see my mother whiles she travailed of me, and amonge them there was one not content, bicause shee was not sent for as well as the other; and when I was borne, shee gave mee a gift, the which was, that when I should passe three yeares of age, I should grow no more, but thus as you see mee nowe: and when she had thus done, and sawe that she had thus served me by her words, she repented herselfe, and would recompence mee another way. Then shee gave me another gift, and that was that I should be the fairest creature that ever nature fourmed, as thou mayest see me now . . .[4]

He goes on to tell of other fairy gifts bestowed on him, the power of knowing whatever men were thinking or doing, the power of travelling great distances in a moment, of rearing golden palaces at a thought and of producing any meat or drink in a moment at his need. Huon accepts his offer of nourishment, for he and his men are starving in the wilderness, and they are sumptuously feasted in a golden palace. No harm comes of this tasting of fairy food, there is no long enchantment into Fairyland, and this although Huon has been warned by a wise and good man not to speak to Oberon nor to suffer himself to be delayed. No gifts of Oberon turn to harm, he is a steady and faithful patron, and when his time comes to die and he is summoned to Paradise he bestows his crown on Huon and gives the Realm of Fairyland into his keeping. Oberon is as virtuous as Liban, the saintly mermaid. Before the witchcraft fever struck Europe one comes occasionally upon this more tolerant attitude towards the fairies, which returned in the 18th century with the wearisome and unconvincing morality of the Fairy Godmothers.

It can be seen that in the Romance of Huon of Bordeaux the distinction between the supernatural and humanity is tenuous and shifting. Oberon, the King of the Fairies, owes his dwarfish size to a spell and his magical powers to a fairy gift. Like the classical heroes he is the child of a supernatural being and a mortal. Huon of Bordeaux is a mortal born and a fairy by adoption. One may surmise that the nearer the medieval fairies were to the classical Fates the more supernatural they were; as we move towards the fifteenth century the process of euhemerisation gains in strength. Morgans were once water spirits, by the time we come to Malory Morgan le Fay, the half-sister of Arthur, has learned her grammarye in a convent.[5]

We have a clear example of this tendency in two versions of the Romance of Sir Lancelot du Lac.[6] The earliest of the Lancelot Romances which has survived is *Lanzelet* by Ulrich V. Zatzikhoven, a translation of an early French Romance with an interesting literary history. It was left in Austria by Sir Guy de Morville who came as hostage in 1194 to replace Richard Coeur de Lion in the prison of Leopold of Austria. It was in French, though possibly English in origin. This is an early version of the legend, before Lancelot became the chief knight of Arthur's court and before he had any connection with Guinevere. Jessie Weston in her analysis of the Lancelot Legend points out that its main theme is the capture of a king's son in infancy by a water fairy, in fact an early version of a changeling story without the substitution motif. The object of the theft is to find a champion to protect the Lady's cowardly son, Mabuz, from the assault of an enemy. Here we find an example of the fairy dependence upon mortals. Lancelot is brought up in an Isle of Maidens like that in the Irish legends. The inhabitants are ten thousand maidens who have never known a man. The land is one of perpetual May-tide, and none living in it could know sorrow. Here the child was brought up, without training in arms or warfare or even the manage of a horse, until he reached the age of fifteen when he grew anxious to try his strength in the world of men. The Lady of the Lake gave him magnificent armour and equipment, but let him depart completely untrained, telling him that when he had conquered Iweret, the most powerful knight in the world, she would tell him his name and parentage. He owed his training to the kindness of a mortal knight, Joherit de Liez, who took him into his castle and gave him knightly skills. From here he is launched on his first adventures and becomes famous. In the course of his adventures he reaches the Castle of Mabuz, the magician, the cowardly son of the Lady of the Lake, is captured by magic and is sent out to conquer Iweret, which he does. The Lady of the Lake accordingly appears, tells him who he is and lets him know that he is Arthur's nephew and Gawain's cousin. After this the poem degenerates into a series of episodes, in the course of which Lancelot rescues and marries a number of ladies who are promptly forgotten by the chronicler and Lancelot alike. It is clear that the main plot of the story is in the carrying of a mortal child into fairyland for the sake of the human strength he can import into a battle. This early Lanzelet is obviously a fairy story in the old Celtic manner. By the time we get even to the thirteenth century the fairies had been euhemerised. The author of the later prose Lancelot explicitly tells us:

> The damsel who carried Lancelot to the lake was a fay, and in those times all those women were called fays who had to do with enchantments and charms—and there were many of them then, principally in Great Britain—and knew the power and virtues of words, of stones, and of herbs, by which they were kept in youth and in beauty, and in great riches, as they devised.[7]

In this later Lancelot Romance the Lady of the Lake was Nimue the treacherous damsel who learned Merlin's secret from him and imprisoned him beneath a great rock. This causes much confusion in the later Arthurian legends, for the Lady of the Lake was a patroness of Arthur as well as of Lancelot. The Lake, in this later Lancelot, was a 'faerie':

> The lady who reared him conversed only in the forest, and dwelt on the summit of a hill, which was much lower than that on which King Ban had died. In this place, where it seemed that the wood was large and deep, the lady had many fair houses, and very rich; and in the plain beneath there was a gentle little river well-stored with fish; and this place was so secret and so concealed, that right difficult was it for any one to find, for the semblance of the said lake covered it so that it could not be perceived.[8]

In spite of this the Lady had abundance of company, knights and dames and maidens, and Lancelot was well trained in the technique of chivalry, and when he was old enough he was introduced to the court of King Arthur by the Lady herself. It is arguable, if we accept this Fairy as the wicked Nimue, that the whole adoption and training of Lancelot was part of an evil design to bring sorrow and tragedy on the Round Table by his love with Guinevere. Like Morgan Nimue seems generally bent on shaming and discrediting King Arthur's knights, although in Malory's *Morte d'Arthur* the confusion between her and the Lady of the Lake makes her one of the Guardian Queens who bore Arthur to the Isle of Avalon to be healed of his wounds, as well as the donor of the magic sword Excalibur. This dual character may however be called typical of the fairies. A very similar fifteenth-century Romance in which an abandoned baby is adopted and reared by a good fairy is *Le Roman de Maugis d'Aygremont et de Vivian son Frère*, which is cited by Keightley in his *Fairy*

Mythology.[9] The stolen baby is lying under a hawthorn tree when the slave who has stolen him is devoured by a lion and a leopard, who then destroy each other in fighting for the baby. Oriande la Fée, who is in the habit of visiting the tree, hears the child's distressful crying and adopts him in God's name. She nicknames him Maugis and, recognising from a rich earring he is wearing that he is of noble birth, sets her nephew Espiet, to discover his parentage. This Espiet, like Oberon, is a dwarf, only three feet in height, with golden hair and the appearance of a child of seven, though he is a hundred years old. Unlike Oberon he was one of the falsest knaves in the world. However he discovers that the child is the son of Duke Bevis of Aygremont, and the fairy takes him to her castle of Rosefleur where he is christened Maugis and is tenderly reared by her. He is educated by her brother Baudris who knows all the arts of necromancy. When he became a man the fairy fell in love with him and took him for her paramour. He performed many feats of arms, won the magic horse Bayard, slew the Saracen who attacked Oriande's Castle of Rosefleur and gained from him the sword Flamberge. It is doubtful whether Oriande was a true fairy or one of the later Fays, a mortal skilled in magic arts and glamour. She and all her kin seem to have the fairy longevity, but she at least confesses herself a Christian and can attend a mortal christening. We might describe her as a half-fairy, like Melusine. She was at any rate an indeterminate figure, half-way between a Fairy Patron and a Fairy Mistress.

There are a great number of fairy wives of varying nationalities and of dates ranging from early classical times through the Dark Ages, medieval times and down to the comparatively modern Seal Wives and the Welsh Lake Maidens. Some of these were attached to actual historical personages, whose wives were called fairies in their own day. One of them, Wild Edric, was known in Shropshire at the time of the Norman Conquest.[10] He long held out against William the Norman, but at last he made his peace and brought his wife, the Lady Godda, whose beauty was famous, with him to court. The story was that while hunting with his little page in the Forest of Clun he came on a fairy house, and looking in through the window saw women of more than mortal beauty dancing there. One was more beautiful than any of the rest, and enflamed with desire, he broke in and carried her out with the help of his page. After days of courtship she at last broke silence, and consented to be his wife on one condition, that he should never reproach her with her sisters. This imposition of a taboo is a constant feature in all fairy wife stories and is almost always infringed. The most famous knight with a fairy wife is perhaps Bertrand du Guesclin, the pattern of knighthood in medieval

France, born near the beginning of the fourteenth century.[11] He married
Tiphaine Raguenel of Dinant, rich, beautiful and learned, generally
called la Fée. They were devotedly attached to each other, and no rumour
of a broken taboo separated them. They were separated only by du
Guesclin's fame and the constant call to arms. Shortly after his marriage
he wished indeed to retire to his estates to enjoy the company of his
beautiful wife, but she re-inspired him with martial ardour and sent him
to fight for the cause of France against the English.

Another fairy woman, Melusine,[12] was claimed by the Counts of
Lusignan as an ancestress. The traditions about her were collected
towards the end of the fourteenth century and later polished and
amplified by a Dominican friar, Stephen. It is a complicated story, for as I
have said, Melusine was only half a fairy; the true fairy wife was a fountain
fairy, Pressina. She is first mentioned by Gervase of Tilbury in the
fifteenth century. Only her husband's name is given, and the story is
comparatively brief. Elinas, the King of Albania, was mourning for the
death of his wife and to console himself spent his time in hunting. One day
he was thirsty, and went to a fountain to quench his thirst. As he
approached it he heard a most beautiful voice singing. It was Pressina,
and the king fell at once deeply in love. He haunted the fountain, and at
last she consented to marry him, but on one condition, that he would not
visit her when she was in child-bed. They married and were entirely
happy. After a year she gave birth to three beautiful little girls, Melusine,
Melior, and Palatina. The King's eldest son by his first marriage ran to
tell his father the news. Elinas, forgetting all about the promise in his
excitement, burst into the room and saw Pressina bathing the children.
She cried out: "You have broken your word! I must go!" And snatching
up her three children she disappeared. Pressina took refuge in
Cephalonia, the Hidden Island, which had been the home of so many
Fairies and Enchantresses. There she reared her children and took them
every morning up a high mountain from which they could see Albania,
telling them that they might be living there in great happiness if it had not
been for their father's treachery. Presumably she was still yearning for her
husband, though she had not forgiven him, but it was not the best way of
endearing him to his children. When she was fifteen Melusine asked her
mother what her husband had done, and when she learned the truth she
determined to punish him. She took her two sisters to help her, they
crossed to Albania, and by their magic arts they imprisoned their father
with all his wealth, under the great mountain of Brandelois. When they
returned proudly to report their action to their mother she was furious,
and punished all her daughters severely, but the worst punishment she

laid upon Melusine, the ring-leader. The curse laid on her was that every Saturday she would become a great serpent from the waist downwards, and this curse could not be loosed until she found a man who would marry her on a Saturday, and would keep the vow. Another version of the tale has it that when she bathed she would become a serpent, and presumably, since she was a child of a water spirit, bathing was necessary to her.

Poor Melusine wandered over the world seeking for a husband who would be willing to make such a vow, and at length in the Forest of Colombiers she and her sisters stayed for a time, and there Raymond de Lusignan saw the three dancing and playing in the moonlight, and fell in love with the great and strange beauty of Melusine. He courted her and was ready to vow anything to have her for a wife.

They were married with great festivity in spite of the warnings of Raymond's friends. They loved each other tenderly, but there was one thing which greatly troubled them—Melusine's serpent nature showed in the deformities of her children. One of them, Geoffroi du Dent, was deformed in character as well as appearance. He had a monstrous tusk like a boar's sticking out of his mouth but his depravity caused his parents much more grief than any physical handicap. Perhaps it was this unhappiness which made Raymond vulnerable to the suggestions of a cousin, who kept insinuating to him that these children could be the offspring of a demon lover who visited Melusine every Saturday. At length he was persuaded to hide himself, and watch his wife on one of the forbidden days. He was horrified to see that below the waist she became a monstrous serpent, but his horror was less than his grief and shame at having broken his solemn vow and risked the loss of his beautiful wife, whom he still loved passionately. He resolved to keep his knowledge secret. So they went on together for some time, until the evil temper of Geoffroi burst out uncontrollably. He quarrelled with his brother Freimund, who took refuge in a monastery and refused to come out. Geoffroi burned the monastery to the ground. Freimund, the Abbott and a hundred monks died in the fire. Count Raymond was weeping in his closet when Melusine, followed by some of the Court, came hastily in to comfort him.

In his agony he cried out to her: 'Out of my sight, pernicious snake, contaminator of my children!'

So the curse came on Melusine, and she was forced to leave Count Raymond for ever, and he died a hermit at Montserrat, but Melusine became the banshee of Lusignan and returned to the castle which had been built by her magic to wail before the death of each of its Lords. When Raymond's race died out and the castle of Lusignan passed to the Crown

she appeared in the same way, both in her serpent and her human form
before the death of each King of France, until the Castle of Lusignan was
destroyed in 1574.

Melusine was the most famous of the fairy wives of France, but she was
not the only one. Keightley in the chapter devoted to the French fairies
mentions other fairy wives. One of the lords of Argouges in Normandy
married a fairy who only stipulated that the word Death should not be
mentioned in her presence. All unpleasant subjects were banished and the
pair lived together in great merriment and pleasure until one day, after a
long time of happiness, they were preparing to attend a tournament. The
lady was so tardy in dressing herself that when she at length appeared her
husband said in the words of a proverb: 'Madam, you would be a good
person to send in search of Death, you would take so long over the errand.'
At his words she gave a long shriek and disappeared, leaving the mark of
her hand on the gate. Every night afterwards her spectre appeared in the
Castle reiterating, 'Death! Death!' with piteous groans. But she herself
never returned to her home.[13]

A somewhat similar story is told in Spain, though the prohibition here
is the utterance of any holy name.[14]

In another of the French stories the castle of Pirou in Normandy was
built by a bevy of fairies, who when put to flight by Norsemen, turned
themselves into wild geese and flew away. But it was their habit to return
in great flights to the Castle before the birth of any child to the lords, and
men could tell by their behaviour whether the child would be male or
female. We seem here to have a trace of the Swan Maiden story, which is
even more widespread than the version of the Fairy Wife legend which we
have been examining.[15]

In the Fairy Wife tales and legends the fairy is wooed and consents to
the marriage with a stipulation, which is generally not arbitrary, but
arises out of the conditions of her being. This is almost always
contravened and the wife departs. Hartland gives a comprehensive review
of both the Fairy Wife and the Swan Maidens in two chapters of his *Science
of Fairy Tales*.[16] Here he gives a few instances, chiefly from the tales of
primitive tribes, in which the husband regains his wife by long travelling
and the performance of arduous tasks, as in the Cupid and Pysche Tales in
which the wife has to seek for her lost husband; but it is most common for
her to be lost to him for ever. The second type of tale, and the most
wide-spread is the Swan Maiden, in which the bride is detained against
her will by the theft of her feather coat if she appears as a bird, her skin if
she is a seal, or a magic cap or other method of flight. As soon as she
regains her skin or clothing she escapes back to her natural element,

though she sometimes returns at night to nurse or help her children, and even in some stories lays out her husband's clean clothing when he is asleep.

In the beautiful Middle English Romance of Sir Launval,[17] translated and expanded by Thomas Chestre from the French poem written by Marie de France, the fairy Lady Tryamour lays a taboo of silence upon her paramour, Sir Launval, which he breaks in defending himself against the advances of Guinevere, so that he loses Tryamour and all the magical riches that she bestowed on him, but when he is in danger of death from the Queen's false accusation she appears in all her splendour to vindicate him. She then takes him with her to Fairyland, from which on one night of the year his horse is heard to neigh, and he appears challenging any knight who dares to combat with him; but none has dared the supernatural adventure, so Launval has never since the day when he followed Tryamour into Fairyland been known to speak to mortal man.

This happy ending may well have been a literary innovation and not have belonged to the original legend.

CHAPTER 12 – FAIRY MORALITY 〜〜

T HE FAIRIES are commonly divided into the Good and Evil Fairies. Even the Good Fairies can be formidable and have as a rule rather different ethical standards from God-fearing human beings, but they are on the whole well disposed towards those who obey their laws and they are not without kindly impulses. The Evil Fairies are wholly hostile to mankind. Let us first deal briefly with the the Evil Creatures of the Supernatural World. These can be divided into two main classes, the Hosts and the individual bogies and monsters. The Highland *Sluagh*, the Unforgiven Dead who have already been mentioned in the chapter on Trooping Fairies, are typical of the Evil Hosts of the British Islands. As well as their nightly flights over the earth, spreading sickness and injury beneath them, the *Sluagh* engage in war among themselves, and they can be seen on frosty nights advancing and retiring against each other, and their blood rains down on the earth. The bright red lichen called *crotal* is supposed to to be the blood of the *Sluagh*.[1] But they are not content with fighting among themselves. They swoop down from the sky and snatch up mortal men and employ them to shoot darts at their fellow men, and at cattle and horses, dogs and cats. These human puppets, Carmichael says, were shockingly ill-treated by the *Sluagh*. 'They would be rolling and dragging and trouncing them in mud and mire and pools.' He heard a story of the beautiful daughter of a King of France who was lifted up by them, carried over land and sea, and at length left mortally injured on the Isle of Hestamel, where she died, after telling the people what she had suffered.[2]

In England the Wild Hunt, the Ganconers and the Devil and his Dandy Dogs, took the place of the *Sluagh*; in Germany there was Hecea's Hell-Wain and the Wild Hunt, in France Herlequin's Rout;[3] and Scandinavia was well supplied with various flights of the Evil Dead.[4] There were the Sea Draugs, the souls of those unsanctified men who had perished in the sea. Reidar Christiansen, in his *Folktales of Norway*,[5] has a legend of a farm-boy attacked by a host of Sea-Draugs who escaped through a churchyard calling on the sanctified Christian souls buried there to arise and protect him. He escaped safely to the farm, and in the morning the disturbed and littered churchyard was a witness that he was no liar.

The spirits of the Air were the Oskorei,[6] the 'terrible host'. They were not unlike the Wild Hunt of the West Country in England, but like the

'People of Peace' in Scotland they could feed upon any human food which was for any reason unhallowed. They had a special fear of the sign of the cross. Christiansen gives a legend recorded in the nineteenth century of a man who heard the Oskorei in the air above him asking each other where they could find food, and being told by their leader, Guro Rysserova, that at Natadal they would find Friday-baked bread and Sunday-raked hay. He was horrified because Natadal was his own farm. He could not hope to get there before them, so he ran ahead, flung himself on the grass and stretched out his arms on either side of him. The Oskorei came above him and swooped down: then their leader cried out 'The cross! The cross!' and they all started aside and made a wide detour. This gave the farmer time to get to the farm before them, and protect every entrance with the sign of the cross.[7] In Ireland the malevolent fairies are the subjects of Finvara, the King of the Dead, whom we meet in such stories as Lady Wilde's 'November Eve' in *The Ancient Legends of Ireland*,[8] though here there is often one well-disposed neighbour, recently dead, who will warn and advise the unfortunate guest who has been decoyed into their macabre festivities. In the same way an old friend, Janet, hid the Tacksman of Auchriachan when he took shelter in a fairy house.

There are hundreds of malignant creatures among the solitary fairies of the British Isles and of the continent of Europe—supernatural hags like those in the Irish legends of the Fianna Finn,[9] Black Annis of Leicestershire,[10] Baba Yaga of Russia,[11] monsters like Nuckelavee of the Scottish Highlands,[12] Seven-headed Ogres, Dragons and Worms, the Border Red-Caps[13] or the murderous Duergar;[14] but our chief business is with those who are optimistically called 'The Good Fairies'. These vary considerably in their ethical standards and their general benevolence, but all of them are capable of gratitude and ready to reward kindness done to them and to show approval of conduct which seems to them admirable.

Most of these fairies, like many human beings, have a double morality; they think themselves entitled to take whatever they need of human provender, to abstract by invisible magic the foyson from grain and milk, or to steal it away, preying on it like mice or birds. Sometimes they send their fairy bulls to entice earthly cows into their mounds, or they openly borrow them, as in the instance given from Lady Wilde in Chapter 10. The theft of human beings, either mortal babies, replaced by changelings, beautiful girls, strong young men, or people with special qualifications—musicians, poets, wizards or skilled craftsmen—has already been dealt with in earlier chapters. There are also legends of humans whose faults have made them vulnerable being employed as slaves in the subterranean Fairyland, as if it were a kind of Purgatory.[15]

We are even told in one of Lady Wilde's more gruesome tales that the fairies served up the body of an old hag—a notorious miser—as the chief course in one of their banquets.[16] As we have seen in Chapter 10, they were occasionally accused of mixing their cakes with human blood if clean water had not been set out for them, but this was perhaps by way of punishment rather than a matter of diet.

Some of these visiting fairies were called 'Good People', 'Good Neighbours', 'The Men of Peace', rather from the anxious courtesy of fear than from any real affection, as the *Eumenides* in Ancient Greece were called 'the Kindly Ones'. The best that we can say of them is that compliance with their wishes and the code of conduct laid down by them led them to tolerate the mortals that shared the land with them, to promote the fertility of the soil and even to reward special acts of kindness by gifts of money and by service. If however the tribute they expected was unpaid they exacted a heavy penalty for this neglect.

An example of this type of good fairy is given in one of Mrs Balfour's *Legends of the Cars* contributed to the early numbers of *Folk-Lore*. It is about 'The Strangers' and is presented in a rich dialect which I have here modified. The Fen-Men of the Lincolnshire Cars were accustomed to very hard conditions, and made no great demands upon the comforts of life. *The Strangers* were the nearest to good fairies that they could envisage. This tale was told to Mrs Balfour by a unnamed Lindsey man.

But 'bout the Strangers, Thou knows what they be—ay—thou's gettin' ready with the word, but it 'bain't chancey to call 'em such! No; and if thou'd seed as much on 'em as I done, thou'd twist thy tongue into another shape, thou would. Folk in these parts they called them mostly 'the Strangers', or the tiddy people, because they were none so big as a new-born babby; or the 'Greencoaties', fro ther green jackets; or mebbe the 'Yarthkins' since tha dwelt in the mools. But mostly the 'Strangers', as a said afore; for strange they be—in looks an' ways, an' quare in their likein's, an strangers in the mid of the folk. Hev I seed un?— ay that I hev; often an' often, an' no later than last spring. They be main tiddy critters, no more nor a span high, wi' arms and legs as thin as a thread, but great big feet an hands, an heads rowlin' bout on ther shouthers. They wears grass-green jackets an breeches, an yaller bonnets, fur all the world like toadie-stools on ther heads, an queer bit faces, wi' long nosen, an wide mouths, an great tongus hangin' out an' flap-flappin about. I never heard un speakin as I can mind on; but when they be fratched with owt, they girns an yelps like an angry hound, an' when they feels gay and croodlesome, they twitters an chirps as soft an' fond as the tiddy birds.

O' summer nights they danced i' the moonshine on the great flat
stones tha sees about; I don't know where they comes from, but my
granther said how his granther's granther told em at long agone the folk
set fire on they stones, an smeared em wi' blood, an thought a deal more
on em than of the passon bodies an' the church.

An o' winter evens the Strangers ud dance o' nights on the fire-place,
when the folk were to bed; an' the crickets played far em with right
goodwill. An they were allus there, whatever were going on. In the
harvest field they pulled about the years of corn and tumbled mid the
stubble an' wrastled with the poppy heads; an' in the spring of the year
they went to shaking and pinching of the tree buds to make 'em come
open; an' tweaking the flower-buds, an', chasing the butterflies, an
tugging the worms out of the yarth; allus playing like tom-fools, but
happy mischeevious critters, so long as tha worn't crossed. Thou'd ony
to hold quiet and keep as still as death an thou'd see the busy tiddy
things running an', playing all round tha.

Folk thought as the Strangers helped the corn to ripen an all the
green things to grow, an as they painted the purty colours o' the flowers,
an the reds and browns o' the fruits in autumn, an' the yallering leaves.
An they thought as how, if they wor fratched, the things ud dwine and
wither an', the harvest ud fail an the folk go hungered. So they did all
they could think on to please the tiddy folk, an keep friends wi' em. In
the gardens the first flowers an the first fruit an the first cabbage, or
what not ud be took to the nighest flat stone, an' laid there fur the
Strangers; in the fields the first years of corn, or the first taters wor put
to the tiddy people; an' to hoam, afore they gan to yeat their vittles, a bit
of bread an a drop of milk or beer wor spilled on the fireplace, to keep
the greencoaties from hunger an thirst.

So the old Lindsey man reckoned that as long as this was kept up all
went well with the Fen Men, but bit by bit men went more to church and
attended less to the flat stones, until a generation grew up that knew
nothing about them at all, and then the Strangers grew angry, and crops
began to fail and stock to sicken, and then children died, and money grew
scarce, and what there was of it was spent by men at the ale house and by
the women on opium, and no one knew what was wrong, except the Wise
Women; and at last, when it seemed that things had got so bad that they
could not be worse, the Wise Women gathered together and made a
ceremony of divination with wine and blood, and when they had learnt
what had gone wrong they summoned all the people to meet at the
crossroads in the twilight, and told them of the tributes their fathers had
paid and of the anger of the Strangers. The women, who had pining

children at their breasts and others buried in the churchyard, were anxious to go back to the old ways, and the men soon agreed with them, so the Wise Women showed them what they should do with the little food and the poor crops they still had, and bit by bit things began to mend, though the tiddy folks were never as gay as they had been in old days, for what has once been spoiled is never as good as new again.[17]

Here we have fertility spirits, treated almost as godlings and bringing blight and disease where their tribute is no longer paid.

In the Highlands of Scotland a similar tribute of milk, poured onto the cupstones, used to be paid to *The Frid*[18] who were responsible for the fertility of the land. It might well be considered fair that these spirits who brought fertility to the land, should have a right to its produce. The Frid, like the Strangers, heard what was said wherever the wind blew and people were very cautious about how they spoke of them.

The Fées or Korrigans of Brittany had many points of resemblance with these fairies. They frequented the stone circles, where gifts and tributes were laid out for them. They were generally credited with being the descendants of those nine priestesses described by Pomponius Mela, who with their attendants inhabited the Isle of La Scena, where they performed strange rites and gained strange powers, were shape shifters and prophetesses. These priestesses refused conversion from the Apostles and persisted in their heathen ways. They have in consequence a great hatred of all Christian symbols and in particular of the Virgin Mary, who takes under her special protection those human infants whom the Korrigans attempt to steal.

The Korrigans, like the Small People of Cornwall, have dwindled from their original stature and are now at most two feet in height, very beautiful by the light of the moon, though their great age is apparent by daylight. Because they are eager to reinforce their dwindling stock the Korrigans make every effort to steal mortal babies and allure mortal men to be their lovers. They are not often described as dancing, but they sing most exquisitely and draw young men to them by their music as they sit by fountains combing their pale, shining golden hair, generally with a sumptuous banquet spread out in front of them illuminated by a shining cup, so bright in the moonshine that it gives light to the whole scene. The Fairy Melusine, whose story I have already given, seems to partake of the nature of these Korrigans.

Sinister as these spirits are they are not described as wholly evil, and often give gifts and help to the heroes of fairy tales, as for instance in *Protégée des Korrigans* which is to be found in *Contes et Légendes de Bretagne* by François Cadic, whose notes and comments on his tales are most illuminating.[19]

The qualities which the Korrigans demand of their human protégés are those generally admired by the fairies. All Good Fairies love humans to be free, open and generous in their dealings. A hospitable nature is perhaps the chief qualification for winning fairy favour, and truth in word and deed is esteemed. Gentle, courteous manners are important and readiness to do a kindness. Everyone will remember fairy tales in which good fortune follows a gift of food to a beggar, while those who churlishly refuse it are punished with failure and often death. Fairies like people who give a straightforward answer to a straightforward question, but on the other hand they much dislike babblers, particularly those who betray fairy secrets, and inquisitive people who peep and pry or break rudely into a fairy assembly without invitation. The widespread story of 'The Two Humps' shows how fiercely the unmannerly intrusion upon a fairy revel can be resented. Fairy gifts are given in secret and to tell of them is to lose them. Even to give explicit thanks is against etiquette, though appreciation may be shown. Fairies who, generally speaking, live on thefts from human beings, are furiously angry if a mortal man steals from them, and pursue him to the death if they can catch him. 'All that's yours is mine and all that's mine is my own' would seem to be the motto of most of them. Many fairies are tricksy and delight in playing jokes on mortals, but when the joke turns against them they do not usually take it in good part. Many a farm has lost the services of its Brownie because of a practical joke played by a farm lad or a servant girl. In fact the fairies' practice matches so little with their precept, that one might be tempted to say that they are almost human.

There are, however, some exceptions to be made to the general conception of these ethically mixed fairies. The first in point of time are those described by Giraldus Cambrensis as having been visited in childhood by a Monk Elidurus who retained a clear memory of his experiences. It is almost a story of a lost Paradise. The full narrative is to be found in Giraldus Cambrensis' *Itinerary through Wales,* translated from the medieval Latin—Giraldus' journey through Wales was in 1188—by R. C. Hoare.

A short time before our days, a circumstance worthy of note occurred in these parts, which Elidurus, a priest, most strenuously affirmed had befallen himself. When he was a youth of twelve years,—since, as Solomon says, 'The root of learning is bitter, although the fruit is sweet,'—and was following his literary pursuits, in order to avoid the discipline and frequent stripes inflicted on him by his preceptor, he ran away, and concealed himself under the hollow bank of a river; and, after fasting in that situation for two days, two little men of pygmy stature appeared to him, saying, 'If you will come with us, we will lead you into a country full of delights and sports.' Assenting and rising up, he followed his guides through a path, at first subterraneous and dark, into a most beautiful country, adorned with rivers and meadows, woods and plains, but obscure, and not illuminated with the full light of the sun. All the days were cloudy, and the nights extremely dark, on account of the absence of the moon and stars. The boy was brought before the king, and introduced to him in the presence of the court; when, having 'examined him for a long time, he delivered him to his son, who was then a boy. These men were of the smallest stature, but very well proportioned for their size. They were all fair-haired, with luxuriant hair falling over their shoulders, like that of women. They had horses proportioned to themselves, of the size of greyhounds. They neither ate flesh nor fish, but lived on a milk diet, made up into messes with saffron. They never took an oath, for they detested nothing so much as lies. As often as they returned from our upper hemisphere, they reprobated our ambition, infidelities, and inconstancies. They had no religious worship, being only, as it seems, strict lovers and reverers of truth.

The boy frequently returned to our hemisphere, sometimes by the way he had first gone, sometimes by another; at first in company with others, and afterwards alone, and confided his secret only to his mother, declaring to her the manners, nature, and state of that people. Being desired by her to bring a present of gold, with which that region abounded, he stole, while at play with the king's son, the golden ball with which he used to divert himself, and brought it to his mother in great haste; and when he reached the door of his father's house, but not unpursued, and was entering it in a great hurry, his foot stumbled on the threshold, and, falling down into the room where his mother was sitting, the two Pygmies seized the ball, which had dropped from his hand, and departed, spitting at and deriding the boy. On recovering from his fall, confounded with shame, and execrating the evil counsel of his mother, he returned by the usual track to the subterraneous road, but found no appearance of any passage, though he searched for it on the banks of the river for nearly the space of a year. Having been brought back by his friends and mother, and restored to his right way of thinking and his literary pursuits, he attained in process of time the rank of priesthood. Whenever David the Second, bishop of St. David's, talked to him in his advanced state of life concerning this event, he could never relate the particulars without shedding tears.[20]

The behaviour of these little people seems to be free from the usual fairy faults. Elidor was invited into Fairyland but not detained there. He could come and go at pleasure. It seems that there was no theft of human food—the milk which formed their diet would come from goats, which are the cattle of the Tylwyth Teg. They made the child welcome to the fairy court and an equal playmate with the Prince. When the little men pursued him they took back the golden ball, but their only punishment was to debar him from a return to their country since they could no longer desire his company after he had committeed a crime of the kind which they particularly detested.

The only fault that one could charge them with was self-righteousness, which could be excused in them since they had no religion to teach them humility.

The other example of an impeccable race of fairies comes also from Wales, though the record of it is of a later date. In the Bristol Channel there was supposed to be an invisible island, like the Isle of Cephalonia in the legends of Brittany and Mannanan's Kingdom, the Isle of Man. Rhys in his *Celtic Folklore* and Ruth Tongue in *Folklore of Somerset* both refer to rumours of 'The Green Land of Enchantment', which was sometimes said to rise out of the sea occasionally and then disappear again. John Rhys, in *Celtic Folklore*, Vol. I, quotes from the Pembroke County Guardian of 1896 an experience reported by a Captain Jones which bears on this belief:

That once when trending up the Channel, and passing Grassholm Island, in what he had always known as deep water, he was surprised to see to windward of him a large tract of land covered with a beautiful green meadow. It was not, however, *above water*, but just a few feet *below*, say two or three, so that the grass waved and swam about as the ripple flowed over it, in a most delightful way to the eye, so that as watched it made one feel quite drowsy. 'You know', he continued, 'I have heard old people say there is a floating island off there, that sometimes rises to the surface, or nearly, and when nobody expects it comes up again for a while. How it may be, I do not know, but that is what they say.'[21]

Professor Rhys is inclined to agree with suggestions made to him by various people that this part of the coast is particularly liable to mirages—the *Fata Morgana*, and that the traditions of the *Plant Rhys Dwfen* and their invisible island may have sprung up from the same cause.

It was said that there was a piece of land between Cemmes in Pembrokeshire and Aberdaron in Lleyn which was invisible to ordinary eyes, and this was the home of *Plant Rhys Dwfen*, that is 'The Family of Rhys the Deep-Minded'. This was a race of fairies, handsome but a little below mortal size, who had lived in the Land of Rhys for uncounted generations. It was their custom to frequent the market at Cardigan and to pay very high prices for their goods, so that the market was sold out early and prices were raised for the local housewives. They were honest in all their dealings and appreciated honesty in the merchants. One man, Gruffyd ab Einon, was a particular favourite, and was once invited to visit them on their island. He was mysteriously escorted there, and found a land filled with treasures from all over the world, for the Rhysians were great traders. Before going home he was loaded with gifts, and, as he was taking leave of them he asked them how they managed to keep their land safe from invasion and plundering for so many centuries. 'For surely,' he said, 'one of your number might prove unfaithful and betray you in spite of the virtue of the herbs which form your safety.'

'Oh' said his shrewd old guide, 'Traitors can no more live on our soil than venomous serpents can flourish in Ireland.'

He went on to explain their immunity.

'Rhys, the father of our race, bade us, even to the most distant descendant, honour our parents and ancestors; love our own wives without looking at those of our neighbours; and do our best for our children and grandchildren. And he said that if we did so, no one of us would ever prove unfaithful to another, nor become what you call a traitor. The latter is a wholly imaginary character among us; strange pictures are drawn of him with his feet like those of an ass, with a vest of snakes in his bosom, with a head like the devil's, with hands somewhat like a man's, while one of them holds a large knife, and the family lies dead around his figure. Goodbye!'

At that abrupt ending Gruffyd looked around, and found himself at his own door. After this he and the Rhysians remained great friends and Gruffyd prospered in all he did. After his death, however, a more grasping race of farmers sprang up, the Rhysians did not come to market at Cardigan, and it was thought that they went to Fishguard or Haverfordwest.[22]

The account of their steady, domestic habit of life seems to have no trace of fairy wantonness about it, but they had certain supernatural powers and properties; they were never seen on the way to market, for instance, but suddenly became visible when they reached it, and there is a strange legend of a fairy sod on the mainland where the magical plants that gave invisibility to the island also grew. Anyone standing squarely upon it could see the Green Land of Enchantment and all that was happening on it, but if he stepped off the whole vision faded and it was not easy for him to find his way back to the sod. One might say also that the fixed following of one rule of life imposed by a distant ancestor was more natural to the fairies than to humanity. Mortal men commonly slide back from early ideals, while the fairies are fixed unchanging even in their changefulness.

Between themselves however, the fairies generally maintained a high standard of morality. It is true that not many of them are so scrupulous as the Plant Rhys Dwfen, about marital fidelity. Drayton's Pigwiggen[23] may well have had his origin in Folk tradition. Such stories as 'Knurre-Murre', mentioned in Chapter 4 suggested that there is a traditional precedent for the plot of 'Nymphidia'.

These aberrations seem to be leniently regarded, for fairy amorousness is notorious, and most of the technically 'Good Fairies' are fertility spirits; but when it comes to breaches of honesty and fairies stealing from fairies the code is severe. We have an excellent example of this given in Jessie Saxby's *Shetland Traditional Lore*.

There was said to be a boy sometimes seen wandering about the mires o'Vaalafiel, the Sma' Waters, and the burn which meanders from Helyawater to the Loch of Watley.

Whenever the boy was seen he was clad in grey and weeping sadly. His history, which I got from a woman belonging to Uyeasound, who called it 'Gude's truth,' is here given as nearly as I can remember.

The Trows are not honest. They will klikk [steal] anything they can find. But they never, never tak aught frae one o' themselves. No! that wad be the worst faut o' any! They are aubar [very greedy and eager] to get silver, and a boy o' their ain stole a silver spoon frae a Kongl-Trow. He was banished frae Trowland on the moment and condemned to wander for ever among the lonesome places o' the Isle. But once a year—on Yule Day—he was allowed to veesit Trowland for a peerie start; but a' he got was egg-shells to crack atween his teeth, followed by a lunder upon his lugs, and a wallop over his back. So he wanders wanless, poor object! But so it Maun be for dat's their law![24]

Stern penalties were exacted for the breach of any fairy law, as for instance in the case of Fenoderee in the Manx legend who was given his hairy shape and banished from Fairyland till the Day of Judgement because he had fallen in love with a mortal girl and had danced with her instead of attending the solemn Autumn Festival to which all Trolls were summoned. If this seems unnecessarily severe it must be remembered that the kindness of the fairies was often capricious and that little mercy mingled with their justice. We are dealing with a pendulous people, trembling on the verge of annihilation, whose mirth is often hollow and whose beauty is precarious and glamorous. From such no great compassion can be expected.

CHAPTER 13 – FAIRY SPORTS

'T IS WELL KNOWN,' said Grant Stewart at the beginning of Chapter 4 of his *Popular Superstitions of the Highlands of Scotland*, 'that the fairies are a sociable people, passionately given to festive amusement and jocund hilarity. Hence, it seldom happens that they cohabit in pairs, like most other species, but rove about in bands, each band having a stated habitation or residence, to which they resort as occasion suggests.'[1]

He goes on to tell of the revelry, music and dancing within the fairy *shians*, and gives a couple of stories which I have already quoted in Chapter 1.

In speaking of the fairies, Stewart is clearly meaning the Trooping Fairies of Middle Earth, although he has included the *Roane* or Seal People among the fallen angels who, according to Highland traditions, were the original fairies. The solitary and evil spirits, like the Kelpie, the Spunkie and Nuckelavee, he rates as devils rather than as fairies. The Brownie and other helpful spirits he considers to be some kin of the fairies, but he does not include them in the general tribe of The Good People.

With these exceptions it is true that the fairies as a whole seem to be gregarious. Those little groups of homely fairies, such as the family of Skillywidden or those who ask for human help to mend their peds or peels, possibly join the general troops on festive occasions, attend markets or rades or dances, and would so be listed among the Trooping Fairies.

The Fairy Rades, solemn or festive processional riding, are customary among all the Trooping Fairies, large and small, sinister or beautiful.

I have already quoted in Chapter 3 Cromek's account of an old woman's description of a Fairy Rade recollected from her girlhood, which was composed of small, beautiful and merry fairies. It was on the Eve of Roodmass and probably a ritual ride, but was festive and merry, to the accompaniment of whistles hanging from the horses' manes. The fairies either did not notice that they were being watched, or did not resent the unpremeditated intrusion. No ill fortune followed it. It was one of the most delightful of all the accounts of the Fairy Rade.

This miniature may be set beside the Rade of the Heroic Fairies, the *Tuatha dé Danann*, describe with equal delight by Lady Wilde in her chapter on the Fairy horses of Ireland.[2]

A splendid sight was the cavalcade of the Tuatha-dé-Danann knights. Seven-score steeds, each with a jewel on his forehead like a star, and seven-score horsemen, all the sons of kings, in their green mantles fringed with gold, and golden helmets on their heads, and golden greaves on their limbs, and each knight having in his hand a golden spear.

These pleasant rides were traditionally important ceremonials among the fairies, as we can judge by the Manx legend about the Fenoderee, who was given his shaggy form and exiled from the company of the fairies until Doomsday because he had danced with a mortal girl instead of attending the Harvest Moon Rade.

There is a brief account of a rather more sinister Fairy Rade in one of the Scottish Witch Trials, that of Bessie Dunlop in 1576 which is preserved in Pitcairn's *Ancient Trials*.[3]

INTERROGAT, Gif evir sche had spokin with him at ane loich and wattir-syde? Answerit, Nevir save anis that sche had gane afield with hir husband to Leith, for hame bringing of mele, and ganging afield to teddir his naig at Restalrig-loch, quhair their came ane companye of ryderis by, that maid sic ane dynn as heavin and erd had gane togidder: and incontinent, thai rade in to the loich, with mony hiddous rumbill. Bot Thom tauld, It was the gude wichtis that were rydand in Middil-zerd.

This suggests a more grotesque and formidable rade that reported by Cromek, or Lady Wilde's noble procession of knights, something nearer to that which I quoted from Montgomery in Chapter 3. Possibly Walter Scott had 'The Flouting of Polwart' in mind when he composed Urgan's description of the Fairy Rade in 'Alice Brand', the ballad sung by Allan Bain to cheer Ellen Douglas in *The Lady of the Lake*.

> 'Tis merry, 'tis merry, in Fairy-land,
>   When fairy birds are singing,
> When the court doth ride by their monarch's side,
>   With bit and bridle ringing:
>
> And gaily shines the Fairy-land
>   But all is glistening show,
> Like the idle gleam that December's beam
>   Can dart on ice and snow.
>
> And fading, like that varied gleam,
>   Is our inconstant shape,
> Who now like knight and lady seem,
>   And now like dwarf and ape.[4]

We have seen, however, how strong the tradition of fairy glamour was from the earliest times, and how the fairy ointment revealed the true grotesquerie of Fairyland to many midwives from medieval times onward, who were coopted into fairy dwellings to aid in their difficult births. It is plain that Scott was on the highroad of tradition here.

Perhaps the most famous sport of the fairies is that of dancing. Even the solitary wicked fairies danced, like Whuppity Stoorie, who twirled and danced in the evil joy of their heart, singing,

> 'Little kens oor gud-wife at hame
> That Whuppity Stoorie is my name!'[5]

And the Trooping Fairies, good and bad, danced almost compulsively.

In Ireland it was thought that the fairies and the dead were very close to each other. Finvara, one of the fairy kings, was also King of the Dead, and it was thought to be very dangerous to be out after nightfall on Hallows Eve and for a month after it, till the end of November.

Lady Wilde has a short, grim story 'The Dance of the Dead' which illustrates this belief and the part which dancing plays even in the grisly revels held by the fairies and the dead.

It is especially dangerous to be out on the last night of November, for it is the closing scene of the revels—the last night when the dead have leave to dance on the hill with the fairies, and after that they must all go back to their graves and lie in the chill, cold earth without music or wine till the next November comes round, when they all spring up again in their shrouds and rush out into the moonlight with mad laughter.

One November night, a woman of Shark Island, coming home late at the hour of the dead, grew tired and sat down to rest, when presently a young man came up and talked to her.

'Wait a bit,' he said, 'and you will see the most beautiful dancing you ever looked on there by the side of the hill.'

And she looked at him steadily. He was very pale and seemed sad.

'Why are you so sad?' she asked, 'and as pale as if you were dead?'

'Look well at me,' he answered. 'Do you not know me?'

'Yes. I know you now,' she said. 'You are young Brien that was drowned last year when out fishing. What are you here for?'

'Look,' he said, 'at the side of the hill and you will see why I am here.'

And she looked, and saw a great company dancing to sweet music; and amongst them were all the dead who had died as long as she could remember—men, women, and children, all in white, and their faces were pale as the moonlight.

'Now,' said the young man, 'run for your life; for if once the fairies bring you into the dance you will never be able to leave them any more.'

But while they were talking, the fairies came up and danced round her in a circle, joining their hands. And she fell to the ground in a faint, and knew no more till she woke up in the morning in her own bed at home. And they all saw that her face was pale as the dead, and they knew that she had got the fairy-stroke. So the herb-doctor was sent for, and every measure tried to save her, but without avail, for just as the moon rose that night, soft, low music was heard round the house, and when they looked at the woman she was dead.[6]

It was death to dance with these fairies, but there are others who are merrier and more wholesome.

Thoms quotes a reminiscence ascribed to John Aubrey, which is certainly very much in his style though it is not to be found in his published works. The fairies here are the traditional small fairies of England, and they did no harm to the bewildered Mr Hart except to pinch him in the real fairy manner.

In the year 1633–34 [says Aubrey] soon after I had entered into my grammar, at the Latin schoole of Yatton-Keynel [near Chippenham, Wilts] our curate, Mr. Hart, was annoy'd one night by these elves, or fayeries. Comming over the downs, it being neere darke, and approaching one of the faiery dances, as the common people call them in these parts, viz. the greene circles made by those sprites on the grasse, he all at once saw an innumerable quantitie of pigmies, or very small people, dancing rounde and rounde, and singing and making all manner of small odd noyses. He, being very greatly amaz'd, and yet not being able, as he sayes, to run away from them, being, as he supposes, kept there in a kinde of enchantment, they no sooner perceave him but they surround him on all sides, and what betwixte feare and amazement he fell down, scarcely knowing what he did; and thereupon these little creatures pinch'd him all over, and made a quick humming noyse all the tyme; but at length they left him, and when the sun rose he found himself exactly in the midst of one of these faiery dances. This relation I had from him myselfe, a few days after he was so tormented; but when I and my bed-fellow Stump, wente soon afterwards, at night time, to the dances on the downes, we sawe none of the elves or faieries. But, indeed, it is saide they seldom appeare to any persons who go to seeke for them.[7]

This account, with the 'small odd noises', the punishment of the spy by pinching, the wordless humming and the fairy ring, is strongly characteristic of the English fairy beliefs of that period. If Mr Hart invented the incident he was well acquainted with the fairy traditions of the country people.

An adventure with some rather ominous fairies is to be found in *Folk*

Tales and Fairy Lore by MacDougall and Calder.[8] Here the threatened human is protected by a fairy who haunts his own farm. As a rule it is the Fear Dearig who is helpful to the human entrapped by the fairies. The Fear Dearig is generally one of the recently dead. In this tale the Red-Headed Fairy is the one who suggests that they should carry away Donald Post.

Many years ago Donald Post carried letters between Ballachulish and Fort William. A part of the road he had to travel was pretty lonely and uncanny, and it had the name of being full of fairies and other bogies.

On a Hallow-e'en, Donald, after getting his business over, was returning to Corrie Chaorachain where he was staying. A good while before he reached the house, what did he see before him but a dozen fairies dancing and leaping hither and thither across the road. As soon as they noticed him coming, one of them, a slender, red-headed fairy, cried, 'We will take Donald Post with us.' But another, a fine fellow, replied: 'We will not take Donald Post with us, for he is the poor post of our own farm.' Donald then happened to look up the hill above him, and what did he behold on the green plain on the summit but a large troop of fairies wheeling and dancing like the merry-dancers. The troop on the high road also noticed them, and instantly one of them cried: 'Let us leave this,' and in the twinkling of an eye they were on the summit of the hill with the other troop.

Donald did not wait to see the end of the merry-making, but kept on his way and got home in safety. After that night he never saw the fairies; but on certain evenings of the year he used to hear the murmur of their voices in the place where he once beheld them.

In the Highlands of Scotland there were some fairies who could be watched by humans without inflicting any penalty at all. The Celtic love of beauty is apparent in the description of these fairies, and since all the fairy lore was stamped upon by the Puritan ministers as heathenish, a strong anti-clerical bias is apparent in their adherents. This account was taken down by Alexander Carmichael in 1877, from Angus MacLeod of Harris, and was translated by him into English as an addition to Evans Wentz's researches into fairy lore. Almost the same account had been given in 1865 by Ann Macneil of Barra, who showed the same strong anti-clerical bias.

Angus Macleod begins with a touchingly nostagic account of his own childhood.

That is as I heard when a hairy little fellow upon the knee of my mother. My mother was full of stories and songs of music and chanting. My two ears never heard musical fingers more preferable for me to hear than the chanting of my mother. If there were quarrels among children, as there were, and as there will be, my beloved mother would set us to dance there and then. She herself or one of the other crofter women of the townland would sing to us the mouth-music. We would dance there till we were seven times tired. A stream of sweat would be falling from us before we stopped—hairful little lasses and stumpy little fellows. These are scattered to-day! Scattered to-day over the wide world! The people of those times were full of music and dancing, stories and traditions. The clerics have extinguished these. May ill befall them! And what have the clerics put in their place? Beliefs about creeds, and disputations about denominations and churches! May lateness be their lot! It is they who have put the cross round the heads and the entanglements round the feet of the people. The people of the Gaeldom of to-day are anear perishing for lack of the famous feats of their fathers. The black clerics have suppressed every noble custom among the people of the Gaeldom—precious customs that will never return, no never again return.

He then goes on to retell an experience related by his mother of her vision of the fairies dancing, perhaps one of the most poetic ever related. I have never seen a man fairy nor a woman fairy, but my mother saw a troop of them. She herself and the other maidens of the townland were once out upon the summer sheiling (grazing). They were milking the cows, in the evening gloaming, when they observed a flock of fairies reeling and setting upon the green plain in front of the knoll. And, oh King! But it was they the fairies themselves that had the right to the dancing, and not the children of men! Bell-helmets of blue silk covered their heads, and garments of green satin covered their bodies, and sandals of yellow membrane covered their feet. Their heavy brown hair was streaming down their waist, and its lustre was of the fair golden sun of summer. Their skin was as white as the swan of the wave, and their voice was as melodious as the mavis of the wood, and they themselves were as beauteous of feature and as lithe of form as a picture, while their step was as light and stately and their minds as sportive as the little red hind of the hill. The damsel children of the sheiling-fold never saw sight but them, no never sight but them, never aught so beautiful.

There is not a wave of prosperity upon the fairies of the knoll, no, not a wave. There is no growth nor increase, no death nor withering upon the fairies. Seed unfortunate they! They went away from the Paradise with the One of the Great Pride. When the Father commanded the doors closed down and up, the intermediate fairies had no alternative but to leap into the holes of the earth, where they are, and where they will be.

This is what I heard upon the knee of my beloved mother. Blessings be with her ever evermore![9]

From the sixteenth century onwards there has been a strong and continual combat between the inherent sense of beauty natural to Celtic Highlanders, a sense successfully Christianised by Columban missionaries with the sanctification of each household action, as we can see in the Gallic chants for smooring the fire and cleansing the hearth, and the Puritan urge to clean the Faith from the vestiges of every heathen cult and practice. We see the same division evident in Scandinavia, where the water spirits so earnestly desire salvation, and sometimes the minister's verdict against them is contradicted by the flowering of the dry staff that he had thrust into the ground.

The fairies in Angus Macleod's description seem to have danced unselfconsciously, not desiring to entice mortals nor to preserve their own privacy, but there were many supernaturals who are believed to be present themselves to mortals to entice and entrap them into Fairyland. In these Islands the most alluring are those of Ireland, particularly the tribe who are under Finvara, the King of the Dead, and I have already given several examples of his overpowering desire for human reinforcement. The trait is often apparent among Fairies of all nations.

The Danish Elves or Huldre-folk are amongst the notable seductresses. The men are squat and grotesque, with wide mouths, and their breath spreads pestilence. The Elf Maidens look very beautiful in the moonlight, in soft white dresses, with their moon-bright hair hanging around them. They sing beautifully too, and the sound of their voices allures men to them, as they dance with exquisite, soft grace in front of the elder thickets or in knolls built to make dancing rooms, but they always keep their faces towards their partners and whatever figures they dance there is no twirling or spinning in them. This should put any man on his guard, for it is well known that the elle-folk have hollow backs, and that from behind they look like a lightning-struck tree trunk, hollow and blasted. So if the spectator is not bemused with the music and movement he should say, 'Turn round, fair maid, and let me see your back'. Then the Elf Maid will either vanish or turn round, and the bespelled man will be disenchanted; but if he is too bemused to think he will yield to the invitation. One herd-boy who joined the dance with an Elle Maid was found dead by the mound next morning. She had danced him to death. Another, a little boy, was alive when he was found, but never afterwards grew an inch, another was caught up and rescued by a ploughman; but all who have been under the Elf-Maiden's spell yearn all their lives to return to her.[10]

Among the fairies there are, as we have seen, beautiful dancers and there are dangerously seductive ones. There are a few who are grotesque, like the Trows of Shetland. The Trows are a kind of dwindled version of the Scandinavian Trolls, not giants, nor as malevolent as the Trolls, but small, grotesque creatures, tremendous thieves of human babies, of young bridegrooms and of beautiful girls. They have one trait which links them remotely with the giant Trolls: the Trolls must be in hiding before daybreak, if the beams of the sun strike them they turn to stone for ever. The Trows of the Scottish Islands are also allergic to sunshine, but they do not turn into stone, they are unable to regain their underground homes, but peer and mutter, running helplessly from place to place until sunset releases them. The Trows are gay but grotesque dancers, but have entirely their own technique. In the Shetland phrase 'they henk', and so are often called 'The Henkies'. Jessie M. E. Saxby, in her *Shetland Traditional Lore*, has a pathetic story of a little Trow woman who had been peering wistfully into a human dance room till she could bear her exclusion no longer and she suddenly burst into the dance room in enormous hops, squatting down on the floor as young girls used to play at 'cockeldy bread', her hands tightly held between the thighs and calves of her legs like a trussed fowl. With her long breasts bobbing and her wild hair flying she bounded up and down waiting for a partner to claim her. She looked so frightful that every man drew back. When she saw that no one would dance with her, she began to whirl round and round, screeching:

> Hey! co Cuttie; and 'ho!' co Cuttie;
> 'An' wha'ill dance wi' me?' co Cuttie.
> Sho luked aboot an' saw naebody;
> 'Sae I'll henk awa mesel', 'co Cuttie.'

And she henked on while the rest of the company watched in terror or suppressed amusement, until she was breathless, when she vanished. Poor Cuttie! But perhaps the men were wise not to accept the dangerous invitation to dance with a fairy. One rarely escapes from such an experience without some deathly injury.[11]

Though their dancing was grotesque, their dance music was beautiful. Some of the most famous of the Highland dance tunes were learned by listening outside the fairy hills. In Shetland the most famous is The Trowie Reel learned by old Fiddler known to John Spence as he rested outside the Fairy Hill of Gulla Hammar.[12]

The heroic, Trooping Fairies engage in all the sports that were popular with the medieval chivalry. One of the chief of these is hunting. The fairy

ladies go hunting as well as the fairy men, but generally in separate troops.
In the medieval poem on the theme of Orpheus and Eurydice, *King Orfeo
and Queine Meroudys,* Orfeo after his long and almost hopeless wanderings
to find the entrance to the underworld dominions at length comes near the
gateway and begins to see Fairy Rades and hunting expeditions. The
knights and the ladies ride separately.

> Than myt he se hym beside,
> In an hote undryne-tyde,
> The King off fary and all his route
> Come ryding bym all a-boute,
> With dynne, cry and with blowyng,
> And with hundes berkyng.
> Bot no dere ne bert thei nome.[13]

Next he saw a warlike foray, and shortly after came a bevy of ladies
hawking, with more success than the knights hunted.

> Anone he lokyd hym be-syde,
> And saye syxty ladés on palferays ryde,
> Gentyll and gay as bryd on ryse,
> Not a man among them y-wyse,
> Bot every lady a faukon bere,
> And rydene on huntyng be a rivere.
> Off game thei found well gode haunte,
> Suannys, herons and courmerante,
> And the faucons forth fleyng,
> And the foulys fro the water rysing;
> Every faucone hys pray slowz,
> Then sate the king Orfeo and leuz,
> And seyd, 'This is gode game,
> Thyder I wyll be Godes name,
> Sych game I was wont forto se'.[14]

At this point he sees his own lady, Queen Meroudys, among the bevy,
and they look at each other silently. His lady weeps at seeing him so lean
and wretched and naked, and the ladies wheel about and take her away
with them. But he straps his harp to his back and follows them afoot, and
so he comes to the underworld where the dead are imprisoned. In the
middle of a bright green vale rose a towered palace of gold, enamelled in
bright colours and set with precious stones, but there were grim sights all
round the walls, men who had been killed in battle or beheaded or
strangled in their sleep or treacherously murdered as they sat at meat.

And yet in this place there was great delight in music and song. King Orfeo knocked boldly at the gate and asked for admittance as a harper. The Fairy King was amazed to see him.

> 'What arte thou
> That hether arte i-come now?
> I, no' nowe that is wyth me,
> Never zit sent after thee;
> Never seth that my reyne began,
> Fond I never none so herdy man
> That hyder durst to us wend,
> But iff I wold after hym send.'[15]

In return Orfeo claimed the right and duty of all harpers to play before lords in Hall. He sat down before the King, took out his harp and tuned it, then began to play. At his first note the King of Fairies sat like a stone to listen, and from all over the palace men hurried in and flung themselves at Orfeo's feet, for in that tragic place there was nothing so potent as music. So Orfeo won back his queen, and took her safely home to Thrasseyens. Another account of Fairy Ladies hunting is to be found in The Maidens, a tale reproduced among the Gaelic stories collected by MacDougall and Calder.[16]

There once lived in Callart a gentleman who was a very famous deer-hunter. He had a greyhound the equal of which was not then to be found in Lochaber; but, like his master, he was growing old and losing his speed.

One day in autumn the gentleman, followed by his old greyhound, ascended the hill above Kinloch More to chase the deer. He reached the corries they used to frequent; but though he saw herd after herd of them all day long, he never got near enough to shoot an arrow, or to slip the dog after them. At length, when the sun was going down in the west, he came upon a fine full-grown stag all by himself, and he slipped the dog in pursuit of him. The dog stretched away with all his might, and at first was gaining on the stag; but as soon as the stag laid his antlers over his shoulders, and lifted his nostrils in the air, the dog began to fall behind, and soon lost sight of him altogether.

Wearied and vexed, the gentleman sat down on a green hillock in a deep glen between two lofty mountains. He was not long there when two maidens of fairest form and mien stood before him, one of them holding a noble dog in a leash. The other was the first to speak, and she said: 'You are tired, hunter of the deer,' said she, 'and vexed because the old dog has allowed the big stag to escape.' 'I am tired, indeed, and grieved that the grey dog's best days have passed,' answered the hunter. 'Courage, and take this dog with you,' said the second maiden, 'and there is not a four-footed creature on the face of the earth, from the little hare to the full-grown antlered stag, but he will catch and bring to you.' 'What is his name?' asked the hunter. She replied that it was Brodum. He took the leash out of her hand, and thanked her for the dog. He then bade farewell to herself and her companion, and went away home.

As soon as he rose the next day, he brought every one in the house out with him, and after turning his face towards the two mountains between which he had seen the maidens, he said: 'Do you see yonder two mountains opposite you? From henceforth remember that you are to call them the Maidens,' and that is what they are called to this present day.

The dog followed the gentleman as long as he lived. Never was a leather strap placed on a better dog. Whatever he was asked to do he did, and no creature he was sent after but he caught. And there was no man living, he would follow, or answer save his master.

When his master died, he lost heart. He followed the funeral as far as the ravine between Callart and the next farm; but he stopped there, and descended the ravine, where he was seen entering a cave, out of which he never returned. His name is preserved in the names of these two places; for they are still called Brodum's Ravine and Brodum's Cave.

Among the fascinating notes attached to the poems recorded and translated in Carmichael's *Carmina Gadelica* is one on the *cu-sith*, the fairy dog of the Spirit World. The huntsmen are described as the *Sluagh*, but these are not the evil, death-dealing host of the Unforgiven Dead, but a brighter troop on their way towards the *Tir na h-oige*, the Land of the Ever-Young, where the bright heroic fairies live.

When Clanranald resided at Nunton, in Benbecula, two men were tending calves one night in a building known as 'an tigh fada,' the long house. They sat talking of many things before the brightly burning fire, when suddenly two strange dogs rushed into and right round the house, to the consternation of the men and the terror of the calves. The dogs were leashed together on a leash of silver bespangled with gold and brilliant stones and sparkled in the bright moonbeams and the light of the fire. A voice was heard in the air without calling:

Slender-fay, slender-fay!

Mountain-traveller, mountain-traveller!

Black-fairy, black-fairy!

Lucky treasure, lucky-treasure!

Grey-hound, grey-hound!
Seek-beyond, seek-beyond!

When the dogs were thus recalled they rushed out, the men following as soon as they had recovered their scattered wits. And there in the bright blue sky they beheld a multitudinous host of spirits, with hounds on leash and hawks on hand. The air was filled with music like the tinkling of innumerable silver bells, mingled with the voices of the 'sluagh', hosts, calling to their hounds. The men were so astonished that they could only remember a few of the names they heard.

These were the spirits of the departed on a hunting expedition, travelling westwards, beyond the 'Isle of the nuns,' beyond the 'Isle of the monks,' beyond the Isle of 'Hirt', beyond the Isle of 'Rockal,' and away and away towards 'Tir fo thuinn,' the Land under waves; 'Tir na h-oige', the land of youth; and 'Tir na h-aoise', the Land of age, beneath the great western sea.

Fortune follow them and luck of game—and oh, King of the sun, and of the moon, and of the bright effulgent stars! it was they who put fear and fright, and more than enough, on the men and the calves of Clanranald.[17]

The Manx fairies were huntsmen, as Waldron recorded in his *Description of The Isle of Man*. He has a story of a young sailor, returned from a long voyage, who determined to go ashore at once, though it was after dark, and spend the night with his sister at Kirk-Merlugh. He had some miles to go from Douglas but it was a fine moonlight night with a sharp frost, and he could see the footway well. As he crossed the steep hill between Douglas and Kirk-Merlugh he heard the noise of horsemen, the cry of a huntsman, and the finest horn blowing he had ever heard. He wondered that huntsmen should be riding at night and in that frost, but presently the hunt swept past him, he could see them as clearly as by day. There were thirteen of them, all dressed in green and gallantly mounted. He was much pleased by the sight and tried to follow them, but they were too swift for him; however they crossed his path once or twice and he heard the sound of the horn for several miles. He got to his sister's at last and described the strange hunt to her. She clapped her hands with joy and relief. 'Dear brother,' she said, 'those were the *fairies* and it is well that you are safe home and they did not take you away with them.'[18]

In the chapter on Fairy Powers I have dwelt on the fairy habit of flying in a swarm to spend the night in revelry in human wine cellars. In their own hollow hills the fairies are entertained with music, as indeed it is their accompaniment everywhere, and the Celtic fairies at any rate occupy themselves with 'tables', or chess like the Celtic human kings. Chess was considered part of the essential training of kings in the art of war and kingship. It will be remembered that in the Legend of Midir and Etain, Etain was won from her human husband, Eodhaid, in a game of chess.

Lady Wilde, in one of her stories, says that the fairies are too artistic and graceful to enjoy the crude game of hurling, and will do all in their power to prevent even humans playing it, but there are many tales of fairy hurling matches and the human mortal each side had to take with it to lend power to the game. Even Lady Wilde tells one story to that effect without seeming to notice that she has contradicted herself.[19] A strange tale of Douglas Hyde's, 'Paudyeen O'Kelly and the Weasel', gives a very good example of this fairy hurling, and of the faction fights which were part of the favourite sports of the Irish fairies. The tale begins with the ghost of an old hag and her two enchanted sons, but it goes on to an almost complete sketch of fairy revelry.

There was a man named Paudyeen O'Kelly who lived near Tuam in the County of Galway. He was wanting to go the market to sell a sturk he had, and he set off in the bright moonlight. He had not gone three miles when a great rain came on and he went to seek shelter in a big house he saw at a little distance. The door was open and a good fire was burning, so he sat down to dry himself and was half dozing when he saw a weasel come up to the hearth, drop something on the hearthstone and dart away. Paudyeen saw that it was a gold guinea she had dropped. She came and went until there was a great pile of guineas on the hearth. At last when she went out again Paudyeen gathered up the gold, put it in his pocket and went off. He had not gone far when he heard the weasel screaming behind him, and she came up with him and made for his throat. He defended himself with his stick until two men came up who were going to the fair too, and one of them had a dog which drove the weasel into a hole in the wall. Paudyeen went on to the fair, and with some of the weasel's money he bought himself a horse and rode back on it. But the weasel was waiting for him and went for the horse's throat, and Paudyeen had a narrow escape with his life; but the men and the dog were behind him and drove off the weasel again. So Paudyeen got home, put the horse in the cow-byre and went to bed. In the morning he got up early and went to feed the horse. He met the weasel coming out of the byre covered with blood. She had killed the horse, two milk-cows and two calves. Paudyeen had a good dog whom he set on the weasel, but she got away from it. Paudyeen kept an eye on her, however, and saw her creep into a little hut near the Lake. He gave the dog a shake and let it in at the door. It began to bark and he followed it. There was no weasel to be seen but an old hag in one corner.

'Where's the weasel?' said Paudyeen. 'There's no weasel,' said she, 'only myself and I'm destroyed with a plague of sickness, and you'll catch it off me if you stay here.' While she was speaking the dog kept moving in on her, and now he leapt and caught her by the throat. She screamed out 'Make him loose me, Paudyeen O'Kelly, and I'll make a rich man of you.' He made the dog loose his hold, and said: 'Why did you kill my horse and cattle?'

'And why did you take my gold that I've been five hundred year gathering in the hidden places of the earth?'

'I thought it was a weasel you were. I wouldn't be taking it from a woman,' said Paudyeen. 'And if you've been five hundred years on this earth it is time for you to be leaving it.'

'I committed a great crime in my youth,' said the hag, 'and now I'm soon to be quit of my sufferings, if you pay twenty pounds for a hundred and three-score masses for me.'

'Where's the money?' said Paudyeen.

Then the hag told him that there was a pot of gold near the well and how to find it. When he lifted the flagstone over the pot, a black dog who was guarding it would come out. He was one of her sons, but he would do Paudyeen no harm. He must count out twenty pounds for the masses but the rest he could spend himself, and she advised him to buy the house he had first seen her in; he would get it at an easy price, for it had the name of being haunted. 'You'll find my other son in the cellar,' she said, 'but he'll do you no harm; he'll be a good friend to you. Now in a month's time I shall be free to go,' she continued, 'and when you find I am dead put a coal under this house, and burn me, and do all as I said.' Paudyeen made sure of her name, and they parted.

That night Paudyeen dug up the pot, and as he lifted the flagstone a big black dog dashed out and away, with Paudyeen's dog after it. He set aside the gold for the masses and he hid the rest in the cow-byre. He said nothing to anyone of all that had happened, but he stocked up with cattle, and in a short while he bought the big house from the man who owned it, and the surrounding land, and went to take possession.

So far we have had a story more of magic and witches than of fairy lore; but the hag's second son is rather after the type of a cluricaun than a black dog, and the rest of the story follows the fairy lore pattern.

The day on the morrow Paudyeen went to the gentleman, gave him the money, and got possession of the house and land; and the gentleman left him the furniture and everything that was in the house, in with the bargain.

Paudyeen remained in the house that night, and when darkness came he went down to the cellar, and he saw a little man with his legs spread on a barrel.

'God save you, honest man,' says he to Paudyeen.

'The same to you,' says Paudyeen.

'Don't be afraid of me at all,' says the little man. 'I'll be a friend to you, if you are able to keep a secret.'

'I am able indeed; I kept your mother's secret, and I'll keep yours as well.'

'May-be you're thirsty?' says the little man.

'I'm not free from it,' said Paudyeen.

The little man put a hand in his bosom and drew out a gold goblet. He gave it to Paudyeen, and said: 'Draw wine out of the barrel under me.'

Paudyeen drew the full up of the goblet, and handed it to the little man, 'Drink yourself first,' says he. Paudyeen drank, drew another goblet, and handed it to the little man, and he drank it.

'Fill up and drink again,' said the little man. 'I have a mind to be merry to-night.'

The pair of them sat there drinking until they were half drunk. Then the little man gave a leap down to the floor, and said to Paudyeen:

'Don't you like music?'

'I do surely,' says Paudyeen, 'and I'm a good dancer, too.'

'Lift up the big flag over there in the corner and you'll get my pipes from under it.'

Paudyeen lifted the flag, got the pipes, and gave them to the little man. He squeezed the pipes on him, and began playing melodious music. Paudyeen began dancing till he was tired. Then they had another drink, and the little man said:

'Do as my mother told you, and I'll show you great riches. You can bring your wife in here, but don't tell her that I'm here, and she won't see me. Any time at all that ale or wine are wanting, come here and draw. Farewell now; go to sleep, and come again to me to-morrow night.'

Paudyeen went to bed, and it wasn't long till he fell asleep.

On the morning of the day on the morrow, Paudyeen went home, and brought his wife and children to the big house, and they were comfortable. That night Paudyeen went down to the cellar; the little man welcomed him and asked him did he wish to dance?

'Not till I get a drink,' said Paudyeen.

'Drink your 'nough,' said the little man; 'that barrel will never be empty as long as you live.'

Paudyeen drank the full of the goblet, and gave a drink to the little man. The little man said to him;

'I am going to Doon-na-shee (the fortress of the fairies) to-night, to play music for the good-people, and if you come with me you'll see fine fun. I'll give you a horse that you never saw the like of him before.'

'I'll go with you, and welcome,' said Paudyeen; 'but what excuse will I make to my wife?'

'I'll bring you away from her side without her knowing it, when you are both asleep together, and I'll bring you back to her the same way,' said the little man.

'I'm obedient,' says Paudyeen; 'we'll have another drink before I leave you.'

He drank drink after drink, till he was half drunk, and he went to bed with his wife.

When he awoke he found himself riding on a besom near Doon-na-shee, and the little man riding on another besom by his side. When they came as far as the green hill of the Doon, the little man said a couple of words that Paudyeen did not understand. The green hill opened, and the pair went into a fine chamber.

Paudyeen never saw before a gathering like that which was in the Doon. The whole place was full up of little people, men and women, young and old. They all welcomed little Donal—that was the name of the piper—and Paudyeen O'Kelly. The king and queen of the fairies came up to them, and said:

'We are all going on a visit to-night to Cnoc Matha, to the high king and queen of our people.'

They all rose up and went out. There were horses ready for each one of them and the coash-t'ya bower for the king and queen. The king and queen got into the coach, each man leaped on his own horse, and be certain that Paudyeen was not behind. The piper went out before them and began playing them music, and then off and away with them. It was not long till they came to Cnoc Matha. The hill opened and the king of the fairy host passed in.

Finvara and Nuala were there, the arch-king and queen of the fairy host of Connacht, and thousands of little persons. Finvara came up and said:

'We are going to play a hurling match to-night against the fairy host of Munster, and unless we beat them our fame is gone for ever. The match is to be fought out on Moytura, under Slieve Belgadaun.'

The Connacht host cried out: 'We are all ready and we have no doubt but we'll beat them.'

'Out with ye all,' cried the high king; 'the men of the hill of Nephin will be on the ground before us.'

They all went out, and little Donal and twelve pipers more before them, playing melodious music. When they came to Moytura, the fairy host of Munster and the fairy men of the hill of Nephin were there before them. Now, it is necessary for the fairy host to have two live men beside them when they are fighting or at a hurling-match, and that was the reason that little Donal took Paddy O'Kelly with him. There was a man they called 'Yellow Stongirya", with the fairy host of Munster, from Ennis, in the County Clare.

It was not long till the two hosts took sides; the ball was thrown up between them, and the fun began in earnest. They were hurling away, and the pipers playing music, until Paudyeen O'Kelly saw the host of Munster getting the strong hand, and he began helping the fairy host of Connacht. The Stongirya came up and he made at Paudyeen O'Kelly, but Paudyeen turned him head over heels. From hurling the two hosts began at fighting, but it was not long until the host of Connacht beat the other host. Then the host of Munster made flying beetles of themselves, and they began eating every green thing that they came up to. They were destroying the country before them until they came as far as Cong. Then there rose up thousands of doves out of the hole, and they swallowed down the beetles. That hole has no other name until this day but Pull-na-gullam, the dove's hole.

When the fairy host of Connacht won their battle, they came back to Cnoc Matha joyous enough, and the king Finvara gave Paudyeen O'Kelly a purse of gold, and the little piper brought him home, and put him into bed beside his wife, and left him sleeping there.

A month went by after that without anything worth mentioning, until one night Paudyeen went down to the cellar, and the little man said to him; 'My mother is dead; burn the house over her.'

'It is true for you,' said Paudyeen. 'She told me that she hadn't but a month to be on the world, and the month was up yesterday.'

On the morning of the next day Paudyeen went to the hut and he found the hag dead. He put a coal under the hut and burned it. He came home and told the little man that the hut was burnt. The little man gave him a purse and said to him: 'This purse will never be empty as long as you are alive. Now, you will never see me more; but have a loving remembrance of the weasel. She was the beginning and the prime cause of your riches.' Then he went away and Paudyeen never saw him again.

Paudyeen O'Kelly and his wife lived for years after this in the large house, and when he died he left great wealth behind him, and a large family to spend it.

There now is the story for you, from the first word to the last, as I heard it from my grandmother.

We have nearly all the aspects of fairy revelry in this story: the drinking together in a cellar, the dancing and fairy piping, the visit to a fairy hill, the fairy ride through the air on broomsticks with the pipers going before, the hurling match with a human helper on each side to lend strength, and the faction fight which is one of the hobbies of Irish fairies. Yet these fairies were undubitably the dead, with Finvara as their King.

As we have traced the course of the fairy beliefs through various times and regions we have found that the dead take a great place among them, though Nature spirits creep in from time to time, such as the Scandinavian elves and the little English flower fairies, creatures of a different nature from our own; and we have glimpses of such lost divinities as Manannan Son of Lir, Black Annis, the Cailleach Bheur, and the spirits of rivers, lakes and the sea, of trees and mountains. In the Celtic traditional theology the places of these are taken by the fallen angels. St Augustine suggested that it was these that made themselves into the heathen gods, Milton used this hypothesis to give individuality to his devils in *Paradise Lost*, and the intelligent Celtic Highlanders adopted it. The fairy beliefs, however, are not a single thread but a twisted cord, and it is a fascinating occupation to follow the separate strands.

NOTES AND REFERENCES ∿∿∿∿∿

1   The Supernatural Passage of Time in Fairyland (*pages 11–26*)

1   Hartland, E. S., *The Science of Fairy Tales*, London, 1891, pp. 196–234.
2   Longfellow, H. W., *Poetical Works*, O.U.P., 1893, 'The Golden Legend II', pp. 466–8.
3   Thorpe, B., *Northern Mythology*, 3 vols., London, 1851–2.
4   *The Mabinogion, Stories from the Ancient Books of Wales*. Translated by Gwyn and Thomas Jones, Everyman Library 1963. The book owes its title to Lady Charlotte Guest, the first translator (1849).
5   Dulac, Edmund, *Dulac's Fairy Book, Fairy Tales of the Allied Nations*, 1916. pp. 145–57.
6   Seki, K. & Adams, R., *Folktales of Japan*, (Folktales of the World series) London and Chicago, 1963. pp. 111–4.
7   Map, Walter (circa 1160–1210) was one of the notable characters of the 12th century. He was a close friend of Geoffrey of Monmouth. A churchman, but a man of affairs. His *De Nugis Curialium* (Of Courtiers' Trifles) contains some of the earliest recorded fairy traditions, and Geoffrey of Monmouth acknowledges a debt to him for the Arthurian legends contained in his *British History*, (Trans. by G. A. Giles, Bohn Library, 1848).
8   Branston, Brian, *The Lost Gods of England*, London, 1957, p. 89.
9   Croker, Crofton, *Fairy Legends and Traditions of the South of Ireland*, 3 vols., London, 1826–28. Vol. III, pp. 274–80.
10   Sikes, Wirt, *British Goblins*, London, 1880, pp. 75–8.
11   Stewart, W. Grant, *Popular Superstitions of the Highlanders of Scotland*, 1823. Reprinted Ward and Lock, London, 1970, pp. 91–7.
12   ibid. pp. 98–102.
13   There are many sources of the Oisin legendary material. Two which give access to early manuscripts are Eugene O'Curry's *Lectures on the Manuscript Materials of Ancient Irish History*, Dublin, 1878, and Standish O'Grady's *Silva Gadelica*, London, 1892. Lady Gregory gives a very readable account of the Finn stories from these sources and from oral tradition, 1910.
14   See *The Voyage of Bran*, Alfred Nutt, 2 vols., 1894 and 97; also Augusta Gregory's *Gods and Fighting Men*, 1910, Chapter 10.
15   H. C. Coote, 'The Neo-Latin Fay', *Folk-Lore Record II*, 1879, pp. 12–15.
16   Irving, Washington, 'Rip Van Winkle', *The Sketch Book*, 1819 and Everyman Library, pp. 26–44.
17   Pitcairn, R. L., *Ancient Criminal Tales of Scotland*, Edinburgh, 1833. Vol. III, Part II, pp. 602–16.
18   Tongue, R. L., *Forgotten Tales of English Counties*, London, 1970, p. 53.

2   The Origins of Fairy Beliefs and Beliefs about Fairy Origins (*pages 27–38*)

1   *Hereditas, Essays and Studies presented to Professor Séamus Ó Duilearga*. Edited by B. O. Amqvist, Dublin, 1975. Reidar Christiansen, 'Some Notes on the Fairies and Fairy Faith', pp. 95–111.

2   ibid. p. 102.

3   ibid. pp. 103–4.

4   Wentz, Evans, *Fairy Faith in Celtic Countries*, Oxford, 1911, p. 62.

5   ibid. p. 68.

6   ibid. pp. 84–5.

7   Kirk, Robert, *The Secret Commonwealth*, edited by Stewart Sanderson, The Folklore Society, Mistletoe Series, 1976, p. 57.

8   Campbell, J. F., *Popular Tales of the West Highlands*, II, p. 75. 'The Bible Reader and the Fairy Lady'.

9   Wilde, F. S., *Ancient Legends, Mystic Charms and Superstitions of Ireland*, London, 1887, 2 vols. Examples to be found are in Vol. I, 143, 'Kathleen', 145, 'November Eve', 149, 'The Dance of the Dead'.

10   Wentz, Evans, *The Fairy Faith in Celtic Countries*. The Evidence of John Boglin, pp. 32–3.

11   ibid. pp. 33–4.

12   ibid. Footnote p. 108.

13   ibid. p. 172, *The Nature of Piskies*.

14   An example of a goddess-like fairy in Brittany is the description of the fairy of Lanascol, 'Groach Lanascol', by Professor Anatole le Braz of Rennes University in reply to questions by Evans Wentz (pp.187–8). On one occasion when Lanascol was put up for sale by its owner the company were outbidden by an invisible voice which proclaimed it to be la Groc'h Lanascol. An Arthurian Fée, Vivien, was believed to be the protectress of the forest people in the youth of Professor le Braz. This was in the ancient enchanted forest of Brocéliande, now called Paimpont.

15   Campbell, J. F., *Popular Tales of the West Highlands*, II, pp. 52–4.

16   ibid. Vol. I, Introduction CXV.

17   ibid. Vol. IV, p. 44.

18   Rhys, John, *Celtic Folk-Lore: Welsh and Manx*, Oxford, 1901, p. 455.

19   Wood-Martin, W. C., *Traces of the Elder Faiths of Ireland*, 2 vols., London, 1902. The development of the elder faiths of Ireland into the later fairy beliefs is particularly studied in Chapter IX of volume I and Chapter I of volume II.

20   Ellis Davidson, H. R., *Scandinavian Mythology*, London, 1967, p. 117.

21   Larousse *Encyclopedia of Mythology*, London, 1959, p. 187.

22   Spence, Lewis, *British Fairy Origins*, London, 1946.

23   Bottrell, William, *Traditions and Hearthside Stories of West Cornwall*, 3 vols. Penzance, 1870–80, Vol. II, pp. 95–102.

3   The Trooping Fairies (*pages 39–51*)

1   Burne, C. S. and Jackson, G. F. *Shropshire Folk-Lore*, London, 1883, pp. 25–32. Here we have the best account of the Legend of Wild Eric and his Fairy Wife as well as the tradition of Wild Eric's Rade preserved among the 19th century Shropshire miners, as well as a comparison with other Wild Hunts.

2   Stories of Welsh Lake Maidens in Chapter I of *Celtic Folk-Lore*, John Rhys, Oxford, 1901, and of The Seal Maidens in *County Folk-Lore III*, Black, F.L.S., 1901.

3   'Nix Nought Nothing', or 'Nicht Nocht Northing' was first published by Andrew Lang in Folk-Lore I. It is still in oral tradition. 'The Green Man of Knowledge' was recorded and published by Dr Hamish Henderson of The School of Scottish Studies, Edinburgh. The Wizard's daughter, the heroine, is a swan maiden in this version.

4   Croker, T. Crofton, *Fairy Legends and Traditions of the South of Ireland*, 2nd edition, 1826, Vol. I, p. 18.

5   Keightley, T. *Fairy Mythology*, London, 1900 (Bohn), p. 461, 'Pepito el Corcovado'.

6   ibid. p. 438. 'The Dance and Song of the Korred'.

7   Montgomery, Alexander, *Poems*, Scottish Text Society, Supplementary Volume, Edinburgh, 1910, p. 151.

8   Child, F. J., *The English and Scottish Popular Ballads*, 5 vols., New York, 1957 (first edition 1882) p. 313.

9   Cromek, R. H., *Remains of Nithsdale and Galloway Song*, London, 1810, pp. 298–9.

10   Hunt, R., *Popular Romances of the West of England*, London, 1931. 'The Fairy Revels on the Gump of St Just', pp. 98–101.

11   Keightley, T., *Fairy Mythology*, p. 305.

12   An example already cited is 'November Eve' in Lady Wilde's *Ancient Legends of Ireland*, Vol. I, pp. 145–8.

13   Bovet, R., *Pandemonium, or the Devil's Cloyster*, London, 1684, pp. 208–9.

14   Tongue, R. L., *Somerset Folklore*, County Folklore, Vol. VIII, F.L.S., London, 1965. pp. 112–13.

15   ibid. p. 112.

16   Hazlitt, W. Carew, *Fairy Tales and Legends Illustrating Shakespeare*, London, 1875. 'The Romance of King Orfeo', pp. 82–100.

17   Hunt, R., *Popular Romances of the West of England*. 'The Piskies in the Cellar', pp. 88–90.

18   Leather, E. M., *Herefordshire Folklore*, Hereford, 1912, pp. 176–7, 'The Boy and the Fairies'.

19   Scott, Walter, *Minstrelsy of the Scottish Border*, Edinburgh, 1932, 4 vols. Vol. II, p. 378.

20   'Discourse on Devils'. Appended to the 1665 edition of Reginald Scot's *Discoverie of Witchcraft*, by an unknown hand. Book II, cap. IV, p. 51.

21   Yeats, W. B., *Fairy and Folk-Tales of the Irish Peasantry*. Walter Scott Publishing Company, London. 'Jamie Freel and the Young Lady', pp. 52–9.
22   Chaucer, Geoffrey, Complete Works, O.U.P., 'The Tale of the Wyf of Bath', p. 576.
23   Miller, Hugh, *The Old Red Sandstone*, Edinburgh, 1841, footnote pp. 214–15.
24   Tongue, R. L., *Somerset Folklore*, County Folklore VIII, 'Withypool Ding Dongs' p. 117.
25   Thorpe, B. *Yule-Tide Stories*, Bohn's Library, pp. 355–9.

4   House Spirits (*pages 53–65*)

 1   M.S. B.M. Harleian 6482.
 2   King James VI (of Scotland) I (of England). *Daemonologie*, Edinburgh, 1591, p. 65.
 3   ibid. p. 74.
 4   Ritson, Joseph, *Fairy Tales*, London, 1831, p. 16.
 5   Larousse *Encyclopedia of Mythology*, London, 1959. The Penates, The Lar, p. 232.
 6   An entry about 'Puddlefoot' is to be found in *A Dictionary of Fairies* by Katharine Briggs. It is a traditional story of the road between Pitlochry and Dunkeld. So potent is a name over a fairy that even an improvised nickname given by a drunken man to a Brownie had the power to dispel it.
 7   Peacock, M. G. W., *Folk-Lore* III, 1891, pp. 74–91. Note—Also Rhys, John, *Celtic Folk-Lore*, I, p. 322, for a comment on Miss Peacock's note.
 8   Warner, William, *Albion's England (A Continuance)*, 1606, Book 14, Chapter 91, p. 368.
 9   Kennedy, Patrick, *Legendary Fictions of the Irish Celts*, London, 1891, 'The Kildare Pooka', pp. 296–7.
10   Keightley, T., *Fairy Mythology*, 1900, pp. 296–7.
11   Wright, E. M., *Rustic Speech and Folklore*, O.U.P., 1913, p. 209.
12   Keightley, T., *Fairy Mythology*, 1900, pp. 402–4. From Train's *Account of the Isle of Man*.
13   Broome, Dora, *Fairy Tales from the Isle of Man*, Puffin Books, pp. 24–8.
14   Keightley, T., *Fairy Mythology*, pp. 240–54. From Grimm Deutsche Sagen, I, pp. 103 seq.
15   ibid. p. 256–7.
16   ibid. pp. 257–8.
17   *Grimm's Fairy Tales*. Translated by Margaret Hunt and James Stern, London, 1948, No. 39, pp. 197–8.
18   Henderson, George, *Popular Rhymes of Berwickshire*, Newcastle, 1856, pp. 65–6.
19   Rhys, John, *Celtic Folk-Lore*, Oxford, 1901, pp. 593–6.
20   Keightley, T., *Fairy Mythology*, pp. 141–3.
21   ibid. p. 147. Quoting from Afzelius *Sage Häfdar*, II, p. 169.

22 Atkinson, J. C., *Forty Years in a Moorland Parish*, London, 1908, pp. 54–7

5 Nature Fairies (*pages 66–80*)

1 Kirk, R., *The Secret Commonwealth*, F.L.S., 1976, p. 61. On page 68 the seer asserts that the fairies' airy bodies were made of their alms deeds when alive.
2 Richardson, M.A., *The Local Historian's Table-Book*, III, p. 239, Newcastle-on-Tyne, 1846.
3 Kennedy, P., *Legendary Fictions of the Irish Celts*, pp. 114–6.
4 Mackenzie, D. A., *Scottsih Folk-Lore and Folk-Life*, London, 1935, pp. 156–75.
5 Surtees, *History of Durham*, Memoir prefixed to Vol. IV. Newcastle, 1890.
6 The Brown Man is mentioned in Leyden's ballad 'The Court of Keeldar', Scott's Border Minstrelsy, Vol. IV, p. 261. In the introduction to it Scott calls The Brown Man a Duergar.
7 Shakespeare, *A Midsummer Night's Dream* (1600) Act II, i. 11 81–117.
8 Henderson, W., *Notes on the Folk-Lore of the Northern Counties of England and the Border*, 2nd edition, F.L.S., 1879, pp. 265–6.
9 ibid. p. 65.
10 Douglas, George, *Scottish Fairy and Folk Tales*, Scott Publishing Library, London, pp. 147–9.
11 Chappell, W., *Popular Music of the Olden Time*, London n.d. II, p. 742. The song was collected in 1840. In this version the last line runs: 'For want of a life-belt they all went down.'
12 Chambers, R., *Popular Rhymes of Scotland*, Edinburgh, 1870, p. 332.
13 Cromek, R. H., *Remains of Galloway and Nithsdale Song*, London, 1810. Quoted by R. Chambers in *Popular Rhymes of Scotland*, p. 331.
14 Chambers, R., *Popular Rhymes of Scotland*, p. 331.
15 Hunt, R., *Popular Romances of the West of England*, London, 1830, pp. 152–5.
16 Bottrell, William, *The Traditions and Hearthside Stories of West Cornwall*, 3 vols., Penzance, 1870–80, Vol. I.
17 Keightley, T., *Fairy Mythology*, p. 149.
18 ibid. p. 150.
19 ibid. p. 259.
20 ibid. pp. 259–60.
21 ibid. pp. 465–6 (Gervase of Tilbury *Otia Imperialia* III, Hamburg, 1856).
22 ibid. p. 479. Also 'The Legend of Melusine' 480–2 from *L'Histoire de Mélusine, Tirée des Chroniques de Poitou*, Paris, 1698.
23 Potter, Beatrix, *The Fairy Caravan*, U.S.A., Philadelphia, 1929, Chapters XV and XVI.
24 Tongue, R. L., *Somerset Folklore*, F.L.S., 1964, p. 26.
25 Tolkien, R. R., *The Fellowship of the Ring*, London, 1954, pp. 127–31.
26 Andersen, Hans Christian, *Fairy Tales*, illustrated by Arthur Rackham, London, 1932, pp. 175–84. This is a literary rather than a folk-tale and is not found in many Andersen collections. It is founded on a folk-name for the elder.

27   Evans, A. J., 'The Rollright Stones', *The Folk-Lore Journal*, 1895. See also Briggs, *The Folklore of the Cotswolds*, London, 1974, pp. 13–15.

28   Gutch and Peacock, *County Folk-Lore V: Lincolnshire*, F.L.S., 1908, pp. 20–1.

29   Keightley, T., *Fairy Mythology*, p. 93.

30   Craigie, William, *Scandinavian Folk-Lore*, London, 1896, p. 171.

31   ibid. pp. 173–4.

32   Grimm, Jacob, *Teutonic Mythology*, translated by J. S. Stallybrass, 4 vols., London, 1888, Vol. III, p. 929.

33   Nuckelavee. Douglas G., *Scottish Fairy and Folk Tales*, London n.d., pp. 160–5. Quoted from Traill Dennison, *The Scottish Antiquary*.

34   Wilde, F. S., *Ancient Legends of Ireland*, London, 1887, Vol. I, pp. 178–9.

35   Douglas, G., *Scottish Fairy and Folk Tales*, London n.d. p. 153. Quoted from *Folk-Lore and Legends, Scotland*, by W. W. Gibbings, 1889, pp. 86–8.

36   *The Mabinogion*, translated by Gwyn Jones and Thomas Jones, Everyman Library, 1963 'Manawyden Son of Lir'. The episode of the mouse is found on pp. 49–54.

37   Christiansen, Reidar Th., *The Migratory Legends*, Helsinki, 1958, p. 91. Type 5070.

38   Craigie, W., *Scandinavian Folk-Lore*, London, 1896, 'A Birth among the Bergfolk' pp. 98–100.

39   Keightley, T., *Fairy Mythology*, pp. 120–1. From Thiele.

40   Briggs, K. M., *A Dictionary of British Folk-Tales in the English Language*, London, 1970, Vol. I, p. 565.

41   Gregory, A., *Gods and Fighting Men*, London, 1910, Part II, chapter iv, 'Oisin's Mother' 174–8. In this book Lady Gregory retells the ancient legends of Ireland which have been copied and recopied and which are now supposed to date at least from the third century. The Oisin stories are part of the Fenian cycle.

42   Bottrell, William, *Traditions and Hearthside Stories of West Cornwall*, Penzance, 1870–80, Vol. II, pp. 95–102.

6   Fairy Habitations (*pages 81–91*)

1   Tongue, R. L., *Somerset Folklore, County Folklore VIII*, F.L.S., 1965, pp. 93–4.

2   Yeats, W. B., *Fairy and Folk Tales of the Irish Peasantry*, Walter Scott Publishing Company, London, pp. 61–79.

3   Tongue, R. L., *Forgotten Folk-Tales of the English Counties*, London, 1970, pp. 24–6.

4   *Gervase of Tilbury*, reported by T. Keightley in *Fairy Mythology*, pp. 465–7. The Dracs commonly frequented the Rhône Valley.

5   *The Crodh Mara* of the Highlands and the *Taroo Ushtey* of the Isle of Man are the water cattle of Scotland—less dangerous than the water horses. See J. G. Campbell's *Superstitions of the Highlands and Islands of Scotland*, p. 216, and John Rhys' *Celtic Folk-Lore*, 284–5. In Chapter I of the same book there

is an account of the water cattle of Wales who formed the dowry of the fairy wives.

6 Broome, Dora, *Fairy Tales from the Isle of Man*, Puffin Books, pp. 9–12, 'The Magic Legs'.

7 Rhys, John, *Celtic Folk-Lore: Welsh and Manx*, pp. 158–62.

8 Tongue, R. L., *Somerset Folklore*, F.L.S., p. 110.

9 Agricola, Georgius, (1490–1555) *De Animantibus Subterranis*, Basle, 1621.

10 Hales, John, *The Golden Remains of the Ever-Memorable Mr. Hales*, London, 1673, p. 34.

11 A good brief article by Daniel Phillips on Paracelsus' development of the Neo-Platonist's doctrine of the Elements is to be found in *Man, Myth and Magic*, Vol. II, pp. 801–3.

12 Hunt, R., *Popular Romances of the West of England*, p. 346–8.

13 Wright, E. M., *Rustic Speech and Folk-Lore*, O.U.P., 1913, p. 199.

14 Hunt, R., ed. cit. pp. 98–101.

15 Keightley, T., *Fairy Mythology*, pp. 281–8.

16 Hunt, R., ed. cit. pp. 120–6.

17 Child, F. J., *The English and Scottish Popular Ballads*, New York, 1957, Vol. I, pp. 317–54. The Romance is to be found in Carew Hazlitt's *Fairy Tales, Legends and Romances Illustrating Shakespeare*, London, 1875.

18 The *teind* or tithe to Hell which is also mentioned in 'The Ballad of Young Tam Lin' expresses the theological view of the fairy origins, in which the fairies are regarded as fallen angels.

19 The story of Thomas Rymour's recall to Fairyland is found in Scott's *Minstrelsy of the Scottish Border*, Vol. IV, p. 83. He appears as a counsellor of the Fairies in the story of 'The Tacksman of Auchriachan' (Keightley pp. 390–1) and in 'The Two Fiddlers' (ibid. pp. 387–8).

20 Bowker, James, *Goblin Tales of Lancashire*, London, 1883, pp. 73–6.

21 Scott, Walter, *Minstrelsy of the Scottish Border*, Vol. II, pp. 359–80.

22 Arnold, Matthew, *Poems*, O.U.P., 1909, p. 83.

23 Stewart, W. Grant, *The Popular Superstitions of the Highlanders of Scotland*, pp. 65–71.

24 Gregory, Augusta, *Gods and Fighting Men*, London, 1910, p. 54.

25 Kirk, R., *The Secret Common-wealth*, edited by Stewart Sanderson, F.L.S., 1976, p. 54.

26 ibid. p. 53.

27 Gould, S. Baring, *Lives of the Saints*, 16 vols., Edinburgh, 1914, Vol. XVI, pp. 223–4.

28 Stewart, F. Grant, *The Popular Superstitions and Festive Amusements of the Highlanders of Scotland*, pp. 127–34.

29 An example is to be found in Crofton Croker's *Fairy Legends of the South of Ireland*, pp. 250–63, but this journey of Daniel O'Rourke is not supposed to be more than a drunken dream.

30   Allingham, W., *Selected Poems from the Works of William Allingham*, London, 1912. 'The Fairies', p. 40.

7   Fairy Midwives and Fairy Changelings (*pages 93–103*)

1   Keightley quotes from *Otia Imperialis* by Gervase of Tilbury (12th century) *Fairy Mythology*, p. 466.
2   Bottrell, William, *Traditions and Hearthside Stories of West Cornwall* (3 vols.) 1870–80.
3   Kennedy, Patrick, *Legendary Fictions of the Irish Celts*, London, 1841, pp. 96–9.
4   ibid. pp. 105–9 'The Fairy Cure'.
5   Rhys, John, *Celtic Folk-Lore*, O.U.P., 1901, pp. 212–13.
6   Keightley, T., *Fairy Mythology*, pp. 123–3.
7   Ó Súilleabhain, Seán, *Folktales of Ireland*, Chicago and Great Britain, 1966, 'The Fairy Frog', pp. 169–71.
8   *The English Chronicles of Ralph of Coggeshall*, Rolls Series 66, 1857, p. 170.
9   Grimm, Jacob. *Teutonic Mythology*, translated by J. S. Stallybrass, London, 1882, Vol. II, p. 486.
10   Keightley, T., *Fairy Mythology*, p. 126, f.n.
11   Briggs, K. M., *A Dictionary of British Folk-Tales*, Part B, Vol. I, p. 290.
12   Campbell, J. F., *Popular Tales of the West Highlands*, Vol. II, pp. 57–60.
13   Wilde, F. S., *The Ancient Legends of Ireland*, Vol. II, pp. 147–52.

8   Captives in Fairyland (*pages 104–117*)

1   Stewart, W. Grant, *The Popular Superstitions and Festive Amusements of the Highlanders of Scotland*, pp. 116–121.
2   Keightley, T., *Fairy Mythology*, London, 1900, pp. 391–2.
3   Kirk, R., *The Secret Commonwealth*, F.L.S., 1976, p. 51.
4   Yeats, W. B., *Fairy and Folk-Tales of the Irish Peasantry*, pp. 52–5.
5   Croker, T. Crofton, *Fairy Legends and Traditions of the South of Ireland*, London, 1826 (2nd edition) pp. 159–74.
6   Cromek, R. H., *Remains of Galloway and Nithsdale Song*, London, 1810, p. 305.
7   Curtin, Jeremiah, *Tales of the Fairies*, London, 1895, pp. 23–8.
8   Scott, Walter, *Minstrelsy of the Scottish Border* (1st edition 1801) reprinted Edinburgh, 1932. Vol. II 'Introduction to the Tale of Tamlane' p. 370.
9   Craigie, W. A., *Scandinavian Folk-Lore*, Paisley, 1896, pp. 150–1.
10   Scott, Walter, Letters on Demonology and Witch-craft, London, 1884, pp. 138–9.
11   Child, F. J., *English and Scottish Popular Ballads*, New York, 1957, Vol. I. No. 39a, pp. 335–58.
12   Scott, Walter, *Minstrelsy of the Scottish Border*, ed. cit. Vol. II, pp. 372–5.
13   Hazlitt, W. C., *Fairy Tales and Romances Illustrating Shakespeare*, London, 1875, f.n. 'Romance of King Orfeo' pp. 82–100.

14 Craigie, W. A., *Scandinavian Folk-Lore*, ed. cit. pp. 103–4.
15 Simpkins, J. E., County Folk-Lore VII, F.L.S., 1914, p. 316.

9 Powers Exercised by the Fairies (*pages 118–131*)

1 Stewart, W. Grant, *The Popular Superstitions and Festive Amusements of the Highlanders of Scotland*, Edinburgh, 1823, pp. 125–7.
2 Kirk, R., *The Secret Commonwealth*, F.L.S., 1976, p. 50.
3 Stewart, W. Grant, ub. supra. pp. 123–4.
4 Keightley, T., *Fairy Mythology*, pp. 305–6.
5 Since one four-leafed clover clears the sight from fairy glamour, it seems reasonable to suggest that ointment made from four-leafed clovers would have special potency, though it would be difficult to obtain enough. A recipe to give fairy sight to mortals is to be found in Bodleian M.S. Ashmole 1406.
6 *The Denham Tracts*, F.L.S., 1892, Vol. II, p. 142.
7 Sikes, Wirt, *British Goblins*, London, 1880, pp. 22–3.
8 Douglas, G., *Scottish Fairy and Folk Tales*, Scott Publishing Library, pp. 146–7.
9 Thoms, W. J., *Three Notelets on Shakespeare*, London, 1865, p. 78.
10 Tongue, R. L., *Somerset Folk-Lore*, County Folklore, 1965, pp. 115–16.
11 Hunt, R., *Popular Romances of the West of England*, London, 1930, pp. 98–101.
12 ibid. p. 81.
13 Keightley, T., *Fairy Mythology*, The Isle of Rügen, pp. 174–8.
14 Jacobs, J., *More English Fairy Tales*, London, 1894, p. 50.
15 Briggs, K. M., *The Fairies in Tradition and Literature*, London, 1967, pp. 138–9.
16 Curtin, J., *Tales of the Fairies*, London, 1895, pp. 6–17.
17 Stewart, W. Grant, *Popular Superstitions and Festive Amusements of the Highlanders of Scotland*, ed. cit. pp. 127–34.
18 Henderson, W., *Folk-Lore of the Northern Counties*, F.L S., 1st edition, 1866. Tales contributed to the Appendix by S. Baring Gould, No. 5, pp. 321–2.
19 MacManus, D. A., *The Middle Kingdom*, London, 1959, see pp. 62–3 (Cutting a fairy tree) pp. 103–5, (Building on fairy paths).
20 Warner, W., *Albion's England, A Continuance*, London, 1906, Book XIV, Chap. 91, p. 368.
21 Shetland Folk-Book III, Lerwick, 1957, p. 3.
22 See Crofton Croker *Fairy Legends of the South of Ireland*, ed. cit. 'Master and Man.'
23 Scott, W., *Minstrelsy of the Scottish Border*, ed. cit. II, p. 366–7.
24 Simpkins, J. E., County Folk-Lore VII, pp. 316–17.
25 Scott, W., *Minstrelsy of the Scottish Border*, ed. cit. pp. 367–8.
26 Henderson, George, *The Popular Rhymes, Sayings and Proverbs of the County of Berwick*. Newcastle-on-Tyne, 1856, pp. 68–9.
27 Simpkins, J. E. County Folk-Lore VII, ed. cit. Clackmannanshire, pp. 311–13.

10   Fairy Dealings with Mortals (*pages 133–140*)

1   Wentz, Evans, *The Fairy Faith in Celtic Countries*, Oxford, 1911, p. 46.
2   Scattered references are to be found in books on fairy lore and in fairy legends. For instance, Patrick Graham, who was Minister of Aberfoyle about a hundred years after Kirk's time, speaking of the fairies, says in page 120 of *Sketches Descriptive of the Picturesque Scenery on the Southern Confines of Perthshire*, 'Being supposed always, though invisibly present, they are on all occasions spoken of with respect. In general conversation concerning them is avoided.' Evidence to the same effect is given in the footnote to p. 82 in *The Fairy Faith in Celtic Countries*, by Evans Wentz; who quotes J. F. Lynch, speaking of the fear felt by the Lough Gur peasantry of the dwarf Fer Fi, the proprietary spirit of Lough Gur. 'For the sake of an experiment I once spoke very disrespectfully of the dwarf to John Pound, an old man, and he said to me in a frightened whisper: "Whisht! he'll hear you." ' In some parts of England there used to the same fear of being overheard. A lively example is 'The Green Mist', recorded by Mrs Balfour, Folk-Lore 1891, p. 262.
3   Hartland, E. S., The Suffolk Rumpelstiltskin, County Folk-Lore I, p. 43 (Suffolk section) from 'Suffolk Notes and Queries', *Ipswich Journal* 15th January, 1878.
4   The Cornish version of Tom Tit Tot, R. Hunt's *Popular Romances of the West of England*, London, 1930. 'Duffy and the Devil', pp. 239–46.
5   The Scottish 'Rumpelstiltskin', 'Whuppity Stoorie', Chambers, R., *Popular Rhymes of Scotland*, Edinburgh, 1890, p. 76.
6   *Habetrot*, Henderson, W., *Folk-lore of the Northern Counties*, ed. cit. p. 258.
7   See Briggs, K. M., *A Dictionary of British Folk-Tales in the English Language*, London, 1970, Part A, Vol. I, p. 233.
8   Hotham, D., *The Life of Jacob Behmen*, London, 1654, Preface C 2.
9   Webster, J., *The Displaying of Supposed Witchcraft*, London, 1677, p. 301.
10   Wentz, E., *Fairy Faith in Celtic Countries*, ed. cit. p. 106.
11   Gould, S. Baring, *The Lives of the Saints*, Edinburgh, 1914, 16 vols., Vol. XVI, p. 224.
12   Mackenzie, D. A., *Scottish Folk-Lore and Folk Life*, London, 1935, p. 219.
13   Wilde, F. S., *Ancient Legends of Ireland*, 1887, Vol. II, pp. 75–7.
14   Leather, E. M., *Herefordshire Folklore*, Hereford, 1912, p. 44.
15   Wentz, Evans, *Fairy Faith in Celtic Countries*, ed. cit. p. 122.
16   ibid. pp. 127–8.
17   ibid. p. 44.

11   Fairy Patrons and Fairy Wives (*pages 141–150*)

1   See Andrew Lang's Introduction to *Perrault's Popular Tales*, Oxford, 1888.
2   Larousse's *Encyclopedia of Mythology*, London, 1959, pp. 203–9.
3   Adam de la Halle, '*Le Jeu Adam ou de la Feuillie Oeuvres Complètes du Trouvère Adam de la Halle*, Paris, 1872.

4   Bourchier, *The Boke of Duke Huon of Bordeaux* done into English by Sir John Bourchier, Lord Berners. Early English Text Society, London, 1883–7, Vol. I. The most interesting passages are included in Carew Hazlitt's *Fairy Legends and Romances*, pp. 139–72.

5   Malory, *The Works of Sir Thomas Malory*, edited by E. Vinaver, O.U.P., 1947, p. 10.

6   Weston, Jessie L. *The Legend of Sir Lancelot du Lac*, London, 1901.

7   Paton, Lucy A. *Sir Lancelot of the Lake*. A French prose romance of the thirteenth century. London, 1929. See also *Lanzelet* Ulrich von Zatzikhoven. Translated from the Middle High German by Kenneth G. T. Webster, annotated by R. S. Loomis. New York, 1951.

8   Paton, Lucy., ed. cit. pp. 72–3.

9   Keightley, T., *Fairy Mythology* pp. 480–5.

10 Burne, C., and Jackson, G., *Shropshire Folk-Lore*, London 1883, pp. 33–4.

11 Bonnechose, Émile de, *Bertrand du Guesclin*, London and Paris, 1896, pp. 33–4.

12 Keightley, T., *Fairy Mythology*, ed. cit. pp. 480–5.

13 ibid. pp. 485–6.

14 ibid. pp. 458–9.

15 ibid. p. 485.

16 Hartland, E. S., *The Science of Fairy Tales*, London, 1891, pp. 253–332.

17 Hazlitt, W. C., *Fairy Tales and Romances Illustrating Shakespeare*, London, 1875. 'The Romance of Sir. Launval, pp. 47–79.

12   Fairy Morality (*pages 151–161*)

1   Carmichael, A., *Carmina Gadelica*, Edinburgh, 1928, Vol. II, p. 357.

2   ibid. loc. cit. pp. 357–8.

3   Map, Walter., *De Nugis Curialium*, trans. and edited by Tupper and Ogle, London, 1924, p. 322–3. Notes to pp. 15 to 18. Reference to Ordericus Vitalis (*Ecclesiastical History*).

4   A story very like the English 'Dando and his Dogs' is to be found in 'Jon the Hunter'. It can be found in Craigie's *Scandinavian Folk-Lore*, pp. 22–3. Jon is connected with Odin, who is the chief Wild Huntsman of Scandinavia, and chases the little wood-wives and elf-women. See Craigie, pp. 24–5.

5   Christiansen, R. T., *Folktales of Norway*, Folktales of the World, Chicago, 1964, pp. 53–4.

6   ibid. Introduction pp. XXXII–XXXIII.

7   ibid. pp. 75–6.

8   Wilde, F. S., *Ancient Legends of Ireland*, London, 1887, Vol. I, pp. 115–18.

9   A good example of them is to be found in 'The Enchanted Cave of Keshcorran', S. H., O'Grady, *Silva Gadelica*, London, 1892, Vol. II, pp. 343–7.

10 Billson, C. J., *County Folk-Lore I, Part 3, Leicestershire*, London, 1895, pp. 4–9.

11   *Russian Fairy Tales*, collected by Aleksandr Afanas'ev, translated by Norbert Guterman, New York, 1973. 'Baba Yaga', p. 194–5.
12   Douglas, G., *Scottish Fairy and Folk Tales*, Scott Publishing Library, pp. 160–3.
13   Henderson, W., Folk-Lore of the Northern Counties, F.L.S., 1879, pp. 253–5.
14   Grice, F., *Folk Tales of the North Country*, London, 1944, pp. 130–3.
15   Keightley, T., *Fairy Mythology*, 'The Fairies' Nurse', pp. 353–4. Quoted from Cromek. A similar legend is cited in Graham's *Picturesque Sketches from Perthshire*.
16   Wilde, F. S., *Ancient Legends of Ireland*, ed. cit. Vol. I, pp. 136–9.
17   Balfour, M. C. 'Legends of the Cars'. Folk-Lore II, 1891. 'The Strangers' Share', p. 278.
18   Mackenzie, D. A., *Scottish Folk-Lore and Folk Life*, Glasgow, 1935, p. 244.
19   Cadic, François, *Contes et Légendes de Bretagne*, Paris, 1922, pp. 77–85.
20   Giraldus Cambrensis, *The Itinerary Through Wales*. Trans. by R. C. Hoare, Bohn Library, 1863, pp. 390–1.
21   Rhys, John. *Celtic Folk-Lore*, 2 vols., Oxford, 1901, pp. 171–2.
22   ibid. pp. 158–60.
23   Pigwiggen, the fairy knight—the Queen's lover—in 'Nymphidia', the poem about miniature fairies by Michael Drayton.
24   Saxby, Jessie. *Shetland Traditional Lore*, Norwood Editions, 1974, p. 149.

13   Fairy Sports (*pages 162–180*)

1   Stuart, W. Grant, *The Popular Superstitions and Festive Amusements of the Highlanders of Scotland*, 1822. Ward Lock Reprints 1970, p. 90.
2   Wilde, F. S., *The Ancient Legends of Ireland*, London, 1887, 2 vols. Vol. I, pp. 178–9.
3   Pitcairn, R. H., *Ancient Trials in Scotland*, Edinburgh, 1833, Vol. I, Pt. II. pp. 161–3.
4   Scott, Walter, *Poetical Works*, Edinburgh, n.d. pp. 299–300.
5   Chambers, R., *Popular Rhymes of Scotland*, Edinburgh, 1870, pp. 72–3.
6   Wilde, F. S., *The Ancient Legends of Ireland*, ed. cit. I, pp. 149–50.
7   Thoms, W. J., *Three Notelets on Shakespeare*, London, 1865. pp. 90–1.
8   Macdougall, J. and Calder, G., *Folk Tales and Fairy Lore*, Edinburgh, 1910. 'The Fairies of Corrie Chaorachain', p. 126.
9   Wentz, Evans., *The Fairy Faith in Celtic Countries*, ed. cit. pp. 115–16.
10   Craigie, W., *Scandinavian Folk-Lore*, Paisley, 1896, pp. 175–7.
11   Saxby, J., *Shetland Traditional Lore*. Norwood Editions, 1974, pp. 116–17. There are several versions of this story.
12   Spence, John, *Shetland Folk-Lore*. Lerwick, 1899, pp. 151–2.
13   Hazlitt, W. Carew., *Legends and Romances Illustrating Shakespeare*. ed. cit. 'Romance of King Orfeo', p. 91.

14   ibid. p. 92.
15   ibid. p. 95.
16   Macdougall and Calder, *Fairy Tales and Fairy Lore*, ed. cit. 'The Maidens', pp. 285–7.
17   Carmichael, Alexander., *Carmina Gadelica*, ed. cit. Vol. II, pp. 266–7.
18   Keightley, T., *Fairy Mythology*, ed. cit. pp. 401–2.
19   Wilde, F. S., *The Ancient Legends of Ireland*, ed. cit. 'The Hurling Match.' pp. 215–16. Contrast with 'The Fairy Spy', pp. 222–3, where the fairies are seen having a hurling match of their own.
20   Hyde, Douglas, *Beside the Fire*, London, 1890, pp. 73–91.

GLOSSARY OF FAIRIES ⌇⌇⌇⌇⌇⌇⌇⌇

Aengus. One of the Tuatha de Danann or god-fairies of Ireland. Wentz 301.

Berg People or Hill-Men. (Denmark). These spirits belong to the race of the trolls. They are not essentially malicious and often live on terms of friendship with their human neighbours. Keightley 118.

Bogie Beast. Universal in England. A mischievous goblin.

Brown Man of the Muirs. A guardian of wild life, hostile to man. Henderson 281.

Brownie. The best known of the domestic spirits (hobgoblins). Chiefly in the North of England and Lowlands of Scotland. William Henderson, Robert Chambers etc.

Bucca. Cornish. There are Bucca Dhu, the Black Bucca, and Bucca Gwidder, the White Bucca. Margaret Courtney, Sikes 165.

Bwbachod. The Welsh Brownie People. Friendly and industrious, but they dislike dissenters and teetotallers. A story in Sikes 31. Rhys 81.

Bwca. The Welsh Boggart or Brownie. Rhys 596.

Bwca'r Trwyn. Brownie who became a Boggart. Rhys 594–7.

Bwcca. Cornish. Mine Spirit Bogie. Bottrell. A song of the Bwcca can be found in *Old Cornish*, Vol. I:
'Tommy Trevarrow, Tommy Trevarrow,
We'll send thee bad luck tomorrow.
Thou old curmudgeon, to eat all thy baggan,
And not leave a didjan for Bucca.'

Cailleach Bheur. The Blue Hag of the Highlands. Campbell, J. F., MacKenzie.

Cauld Lad of Hilton (Cauld Lad of Gileland). Henderson. A Brownie, haunting Hilton Castle, who is definitely described as a ghost, and yet was laid as Brownies are always laid by the present of a green cloak and a hood. Quoted by Keightley.

Cluricaun. An Irish fairy, nearly allied to a lepracaun, though Keightley gives a story of one who is very near to the ordinary hobgoblin type. Keightley 369.

Corrigan. Brittany. See **Korrigan.**

Cu Sith (The Fairy Dog). Highland. This is a great dog, as large as a bullock and with a dark green coat. Nearly related to the English Black Dog. See Carmichael's note on the Cu Sith.

Dando and his Dogs. Wild Hunt Story. Hunt, Hartland.

Daniel O'Donoghue. King of the Fairies of Connaught. Curtin 6.

Daoine O'Sidhe. (Ireland). The heroic fairies of Ireland. Very like the Highland Sleeth Ma. Yeats and Lady Wilde.

Deeny Shee. The popular pronunciation of Daoine O'Sidhe.

Devils Dandy Dogs. Cornwall. A black pack, fire-breathing, and with fiery eyes, whom the Devil leads over lonely moors on tempestuous nights. They will tear any living man to pieces, but they can be kept off by the power of prayer. Hunt.

Dracs. French Medieval Fairies who haunted the River Rhône. Described by Gervase of Tilbury. Keightley 465.

Dwarf. Or Trolls. Scandinavian and German. Black, Brown, White. See Keightley.

Elf. Originally Anglo-Saxon for Fairies. Later applied in England to small fairies, retained in Scotland for some time for all fairies. Scandinavian—The Elves or Elle people. Elfname—Scots name for Fairyland. See Keightley for Scandinavian Elves.

Fairy. General name for the whole race. Originally Fé erie, enchantment from Fées. Originally Fay from Fatae, the Fates.

Fear Dearc. (The Red Man). A spirit known in Munster whose visits give good luck to a farm. He is described as a little man, about two and a half feet in height, dressed in a scarlet sugar loaf hat and a long scarlet coat, with long grey hair and a wrinkled face. He would come in and ask to warm himself by the fire. It was very unlucky to refuse to let him in. Keightley.

Fées. The French Fairy Ladies.

Fenoderee (or Phynoderee). The Manx Brownie. Waldron, Gill, S. Morrison, etc.

Finvara (Fin Bheara). The King of the Connaught Fairies. A King of the Dead. Lady Wilde, Wentz 42.

Fir Bolgs. Ireland. Primitive Fairies conquered by the Tuatha de Danann. Wentz 32.

Fir Darrig (Fear Dearg). Irish. Crofton Croker.

Friar Rush. Will o' the Wisp. Chapbook.

Frid. The Fridean. Supernatural beings that dwell under rocks to whom offerings of milk and bread used to be made. Mackenzie 244.

Ganconer (Gancanagh). Irish. The love-talker. A fairy who appears in lonesome valleys with a pipe in his mouth and makes love to young maidens, who pine and die for love of him. They occasionally appear in troops. Yeats, *Fairy and Folk Tales of the Irish*.

Gathornes. Cornish mine spirits.

Gentry, The. The polite Irish name for Fairies, equivalent to the People of Peace, for it is not lucky to call them fairies.

Giants. Creatures in roughly human form of monstrous size. Generally ogres but occasionally gentle and friendly. See Hunt.

Gnomes. The earth spirits among the Neo-Platonic elementals, but also to be found in folk-lore, even in these islands. Evans Wentz, 242, for gnomes in Ireland seen by a percipient.

Goblins. Mischievous or evil spirits, generally small and grotesque in appearance.

Godda, the Fairy Wife of Wild Edric. A very early example of the Fairy Wife who imposes a taboo on her husband which is infringed. See Burne and Jackson, *Shropshire Folklore*.

Good Neighbours. The euphemistic name for the Fairies in the Scottish Lowlands.

Good People. General euphemism for the Fairies.

Green Children. A medieval story given in Ralph of Coggeshall's Chronicle. Keightley.

Gwarwyn-A-Throt. A Welsh name of a fairy of the Tom Tit Tot type. Rhys.

Gwragedd Annwn. Nature Spirits. Sikes 34. The Water Maidens who live below the Welsh Lakes. Beautiful and not dangerous like the mermaids and nixies. They have often wedded with mortals.

Gwyn Ap Nudd. The Welsh King of the Fairies. Sikes 6. Wentz 319–20.

Hedley Kow. A kind of Bogey Beast who haunted the village of Hedley. *Northumberland Folk Lore*, F.L.S., 17.

Heinzelmann German. Little domestic kobolds who worked in troops. They left Cologne because they were watched at their work. Keightley 257.

Hob or Hobthrust. A Yorkshire and Durham Brownie, particularly good at curing whooping cough. Henderson 264.

Hobbedy's Lantern. Midlands. A name for Will o' the Wisp or Hob-Lantern. E. M. Wright 200.

Hobgoblin. A friendly and helpful spirit, occasionally mischievous. The Puritans used the word for 'Goblin'.

Host, The, see **Sluagh.**

Howlaa. Manx. A spirit who wails on the shore before storms. *A Vocabulary of the Anglo-Manx Dialect.* A. W. More and Sophia Morrison.

Huldu Folk. Scandinavian. An alternative name for the Scandinavian Elves, or Elle-Folk. It means 'The Hidden People' and derives from the legend about the origin of the Elle-Folk. Craigie, *Scandinavian Folk-Lore*, 142 seq.

Hunky Punk. Somerset-Devon Border. Will o' the Wisp. "One leg and a light and lead you into the bogs". Miss Tongue, Four members of Dulverton W.I.

Hyldemoder. The Elder Tree Mother. Scandinavia.

Jenny Burnt-Tail. One name for Will o' the Wisp. Cornish.

Joan the Wad. Cornwall. Variant of Will o' the Wisp. J. Couch *History of Polperro*, (1871), 144. Holloway *General Dictionary of Pronunciations*, 1839. Kittredge, *The Friar's Lantern.*

'Jack o' Lantern, Joan the Wad,
Who tickled the maid and made her mad,
Guide me home, the weather's bad.'

Kelpie. Scottish. A malignant water spirit, which is generally in the form of a horse, but which can take the form of a handsome young man. A kelpie's chief delight is to induce mortals to mount on its back, and plunge with them into deep water, where it devours them.

King Godemar of Voldmar. A kobold or house-spirit who haunted the house of Neveling von Hardenberg in the fifteenth century. Keightley 258.

Kit-with-the-Canstick. Will o' the Wisp in Scot and Harsnet.

Knocker see **Bucca.** Cornwall. Mine spirits. Said to be ghosts of the Jews who worked there. Hunt.

Knurre Murre. Scandinavia. Nickname of an individual old Troll. Keightley.

Kobold. German house-spirits, of which the most famous was Hinzelmann. Keightley 256 seq.

Korrigan. There is some uncertainty about these Breton spirits. Some distinguish them from the Korreds and trace them from the priestesses of the Isle of Sena described by Pomponius Mela, some identify them with the Korreds, the dwarfs. Keightley 421–2. F. Cadic, *Contes et Legendes de Bretagne*, identifies them with Korreds.

Lady of the Lake. The Fairy Lady who carried the infant Lancelot into her lake and who was greatly concerned with the fortunes of King Arthur in the late Arthurian Romances.

Lake Maidens or Gwragedd Annwn. Welsh.

Land pirits. Scandinavian. Craigie, *Scandinavian Mythology*.

Lepracaun, Irish. The Fairy Shoemaker; solitary; a miser. See Yeats *Fairy and FVOLK Tales of the Irish Peasantry*, pp. 80–83.

Lil Fellas, the Crowd, the Mob, Themselves. Manx euphemisms for the Fairies. W. Gill, *Second Manx Scrap-Book*, 217

Lutin , or Gobelins. These are the House Fairies of Normandy. They ride horses and plait up their tails. They are very fond of children.

Malekin. Malekin was a spirit who haunted the Castle of Dagworthy in Suffolk and who was described by the twelfth century chronicler, Ralph of Coggeshall. She claimed to be a human child stolen by the fairies, and still hoped to regain her freedom.

Manannan, Son of Lir, The god of the Sea, was the deity of the Isle of Man. He occurs in the Irish Heroic Legends. See *The Voyage of Bran* (Nutt).

Meg Mullach. Meg Mullach, or Hairy Meg. A female Highland Brownie. Maug Vuluchd was the name of another very like her who haunted a Highland household with a male Brownie, called Brownie-Clod. Mentioned by John Aubrey.

Melusine. The serpent-fairy of France, the ancestress of the Lords of Lusignon. Keightley 480.

Mermaid. A sea fairy, half woman, half fish. Generally a sinister and murderous character, but occasionally wise and benevolent with great medical knowledge. Chambers, Hunt.

Merman. The male form of Mermaid. Often uglier and rougher in the British Isles, but a more sympathetic character in the Scandinavian tradition.

Merrows. Ireland. The Merrows are the Irish mer-people. Like the Roane they live in dry land under the sea, and need an enchantment to make them able to pass through the water. The female Merrows are beautiful, but the males are very ugly, though friendly. See 'Soul Cages', Crofton Croker.

Midhir. Irish. The Fairy husband of Etain. Lady Gregory, Evans Wentz 374–5.

Morgan La Fée. The Fairy enchantress of Arthurian legend. Originally a sea fairy. Wentz 311.

Moss Women. Small Scandinavian fairies pursued by Odin. Keightley.

Neckan or Neck. A Scandinavian river spirit. Plays sweetly upon a harp. Anxiously concerned about his soul. Keightley, Craigie.

Niamh of the Golden Locks. The Fairy bride of Oisin, the son of Fion, who took him with her to the Land of Tir Nan Og.

Nisses. The Scandinavian Brownies. Keightley 139–46.

Nixies. German water spirits. Keightley 259–61.

Nuala. Ireland. Finvarra's Fairy Queen. See Wentz 28.

Nuckelavee. A horrible monster who

came out of the sea, half man and half horse, with a breath like pestilence and no skin on its body. The only security from it was that it could not pass fresh running water. *The Scottish Fairy and Folk Tales*.

Nuggies. Shetland water kelpies. *County Folk-Lore, Orkney and Shetland*.

Nykur or Water Horse. Scandinavian, Craigie 233.

Oakmen. English wood spirits. Often hostile to men, though sympathetic to wild life. Ruth Tongue, *Forgotten Folk Tales of English Counties*.

Oberon. The King of the Fairies according to Shakespeare, *Huon of Bordeaux* and some popular traditions, possibly founded on Huon of Bordeaux. Auberon or Oberycorn, names of familiar spirits in late medieval times.

Old Lady of the Elder Tree. See Hans Andersen, 'Elder Flower Mother', *Lincolnshire Folk Lore*. 21.

Oonagh. Ireland. Finvarra's Fairy Queen (according to Lady Wilde). See also NUALA.

Oriande, la Fée. The good Fairy of a fifteenth century Romance, summarized by Keightley in *Fairy Mythology*.

Padfoot. Yorkshire, Lancashire. A Yorkshire version of the bogy beast. Generally described as the size of a donkey, black, shaggy and with fiery eyes. It follows people along dark roads at night. It can however take any shape, and often appears as a white dog. It gains its name from the sound of its feet, padding along beside the traveller in the darkness. Sometimes the rattling of a chain is heard too. Like the black dog it must not be spoken to or touched. It generally portends disaster. Henderson, 273.

Pechs, Pechts, or **Picts.** Scottish mound fairies, dwarfish and red-haired like the Pixies of Somerset. L. Spence, MacRitchie, etc.

Peg O'Nell. Lancashire. The spirit of the Ribble. Said to be the ghost of a servant girl from Waddow Hall who was drowned in the Ribble: but like other river spirits she demands a human life every seven years.

Peg Powler. The spirit of the Tees. Long green hair; insatiable for human life. The frothy foam on the higher reaches of the Tees is called 'Peg Powler's Suds'. Henderson 265–6.

People of Peace. One of the Highland names for Fairies. Of the same nature as the Good Neighbours of the Lowlands and the Borrowing Fairies of Worcestershire. A characteristic story is given in Campbell's *Tales of the West Highlands*, II, 52. The Woman of Peace and the Kettle. The woman of the house had to say as the kettle was taken:

'A smith is able to make cold iron but with coal.

The due of a kettle is bones and to bring it back again whole.'

This rhyme secured the return of the kettle.

Phooka or Pouka. The Irish Puck. Crofton Croker; Lady Wilde.

Picktree Brag. This is a Durham version of the bogy beast. It appears in various forms, sometimes as a horse, sometimes like a calf, sometimes as a 'dick-ass' and sometimes as a naked man without a head. It plays all the usual tricks of the bogey beast.

Pinket. The Worcestershire name for Will o' the Wisp. Jabez Allies.

Piskies. The Cornish metathesis of Pixies.

Pixies or Pisgies. The Devonshire and Cornish Fairies. Mentioned in section II, Trooping Fairies. Hunt, Mrs Bray, Bottrell. The white moths that come out in twilight are called Pisgies in Cornwall and regarded by some as fairies, by some as departed souls. In parts of Cornwall too they say that Pixies are the spirits of unbaptised children.

Plant Rhys Dwfen. Welsh. A race of fairies, (perhaps half-human), on whose land there are some plants growing that make it invisible. They came to market in Cardigan, and raised the prices of the corn and goods. This invisible land is full of treasures. They are generally very honest, but have been known to change some babies. Rhys.

Portunes. English. Very small trooping fairies who visit houses at night and roast frogs at the human fires. Puckish stories told of them. Gervase of Tilbury.

Pressina. Fairy wife of King Elimas of Albania, and mother of Melusine. Her story is told by Gervase of Tilbury. An early example of the broken taboo imposed by the Fairy Wife. See Keightley.

Puck. A half domestic fairy, something between a Brownie and a Will o' the Wisp. Shakespeare's Puck gives a good representation of his type. The names Robin Goodfellow, Robin Hood and Hobgoblin seem to be indiscriminately applied to the same character. Suffolk Folk-Lore, F.L.S. Proverb 'To laugh like Robin Goodfellow'.

Pwcca. The Welsh Puck is much like the same character in England and Ireland. He likes his nightly bowl of milk, but does not seem as a rule to work for it as the Bwbachod do. He is especially fond of misleading night wanderers.

Roane or Highland Merman. These Mermen are distinguished from others by travelling through the sea in the form of seals. In the depths of the sea caves they come again to air. There and on the land they cast off their seal skins, but their seal skins are necessary to carry them through the water. The Roane are peculiarly mild and unrevengeful fairies of deep domestic affections, as the stories of The Fishermen and the Merman, and of The Seal Catcher's Adventure show. The Shetlanders called the Roane 'Sea Trows', but their character is substantially the same. *Scottish Fairy and Folk Tales*, Alice Stewart's Tale, etc.

Robin Goodfellow. English. This is one of the Elizabethan names for Puck, but whether it had existed long or had been invented by the unknown author of the Merry Jests of Robin Goodfellow, published about 1584, it is now difficult to decide. Robin Goodfellow in this book is said to be the child of a marriage between a mortal and a fairy. All the regular fairy activities were ascribed to him. He turned himself into a horse and dropped his rider into water, he worked for a farm servant but was laid by a present of clothes, he misled travellers as a Willy Wisp. Reginald Scot gives much the same account of him and so does Burton. *Suffolk Folk Lore*. F.L.S. County Folk-Lore, I.

Sadbh. Irish. Fion's fairy wife, stolen from him by the Dark Wizard. The mother of

Oisin. Lady Gregory. *Gods and Fighting Men.*

Seely Court. Seely stands for Blessed. The malignant fairies were sometimes called the Unseely Court. J. M. Macpherson, 100, The Fairy Knots, The Miller's Fairy.

Shellycoat. A mischievous bogle, dressed in water weeds and shells, whose chinking tells who he is. Like the Dunnie and Brag and Pixies, he delights in misleading night wanderers. He specially haunts the old houses of Gorrinberry in Liddesdale.

Shock. Suffolk F.L. 91.

Shoopiltee. Isle of Man. Sea Horse. This appears like a pretty little pony. Its aim is to persuade a human being to mount it and then carry him into the sea. Keightley 171.

Short Hoggers of Whittinghame. An un-named child, very near to a Pixie or Brownie.

Sidh. The general Celtic name for the fairies.

Skillywidden. The name of a little fairy boy found sleeping and carried home by a farmer in Treridge. Quoted by Hunt.

Sluagh. Highland. The Host. The Host of the Dead. These are the evil fairies of Scotland. L. Spence, *Fairy Tradition*, Evans Wentz 108.

Small People. Cornish. One name for the diminishing fairies. The best account of them given by Bottrell in 'The Fairy Dwelling on Selena Moor'.

Spriggans. Cornwall. Some say the Spriggans are the ghosts of the Giants. They haunt old ruins and cromlechs and standing stones, and guard their buried treasure. They are grotesque in shape with the power of swelling from small into monstrous size. For all commotions and disturbances in the air, mysterious destruction of buildings and cattle, loss of children and the substitution of changelings, the Spriggans may be blamed. Hunt, Bottrell.

Spunkies. Scottish Will o' the Wisp. Kittredge, Henderson.

Strangers. The encompassing fairies believed in by the Fenmen, who exacted tributed and punished negligence. Described by Mrs Balfour in 'Legends of the Lincolnshire Cars', *Folk-Lore Record*, II.

Swan Maidens. Fairy maidens who can be

transformed to swans by a feathered garment whose loss forces them to remain in human form, as the Seal Maidens cannot take to the sea without their skins. See Hartland, *Science of Fairy Tales*.

Tarans. Primitive beliefs in the North West of Scotland. The spirits of unbaptised infants are called Tarans in the North East of Scotland (Short Hoggers of Whittinghame).

Terrytop. Cornwall. The Tom-Tit-Tot of the Cornish drolls. Bottrell, Hunt.

Thomas the Rhymer. Thomas of Ercildoune, who was carried off into Fairyland by the Fairy Queen. Child, Popular Ballads.

Tiphaine. The wife of Bertrand du Guesclin, popularly supposed to be a Fée.

Tom Tit Tot. The English Rumpelstiltskin. Quoted originally from an old number of the Ipswich Journal. He is described as a black thing with a long tail, and sometimes as an impet. Suffolk Folk Lore. Tom Tit, a Tot, or a Tot-grid is a Lincolnshire name for a hobgoblin.

Tomte. The Swedish Brownie, or Nis. Small, laborious and well-disposed, but easily driven away. Keightley 139.

Trolls. Scandinavian. Dwarfs, grotesque and often mischievous, or Giants (sometimes many headed). Wicked: turn to stone if they are caught by daylight.

Trows. Shetland. Trows appear in Shetland and other places with a Scandinavian ancestry. In *Scottish Fairy and Folk Tales* the Shetland Story of Thomas and Willie gives some idea of the appearance and habits of the Trows.

True Thomas. One name for Thomas Rhymour, Thomas the Rhymer. See *Child's Ballads*.

Trwtyn-Tratyn. The Welsh Tom-Tit-Tot. Rhys, *Celtic Folk Lore*.

Tryamor. The Fairy wife of Sir Launval. See W. Carew Hazlitt, *Fairy Legends and Romances Illustrating Shakespeare*.

Tuatha De Danann. People of the Goddess Danu. Lewis Spence, Lady Wilde, etc.

Tylwyth Teg. Wales. 'The Fair Family'. The ordinary fairies of Wales, given to the fairy tricks of child-stealing etc. Sikes 83.

Urchins. Urchin, the popular name for hedgehogs, was used in the sixteenth century and earlier for a rather pixie-like fairy. Reginald Scot mentions it in his list of fairies, and so does Shakespeare and Jonson, but it is not, so far as I know, used currently for any fairy in any dialect.

Urisk or Uruisg. Highland. A kind of rough Brownie. Half-human, half-goat, very lucky to have about the house, who herded the cattle and did the work about a farm. He haunted lonely waterfalls, but would often crave human company, and follow terrified travellers at night, without doing them any harm, however. The Urisks lived solitary in recesses of the hills, but would meet at stated times for solemn assemblies. A corrie near Loch Katrine was their favourite meeting place. Mackenzie.

Wag-at-the-Wa'. A Scottish Border Spirit. This spirit though domestic and friendly to the family was much dreaded in the Border country and it was considered unchancy to swing the pot-hook hanging from the chimney when it was empty, for it was an invitation to the Wag-at-the-Wa' to sit there. Henderson 257.

Water Cattle. Crodh Mara in the Highlands. Sometimes given to human favourites. Harmless and valuable. Water Bulls sometimes mate with mortal cattle and greatly improve the breed. The Water Bull can give good protection against the Water Horse. J. F. Campbell, *Popular Tales of the West Highlands*.

Water Horse, see Each Uisge. Kelpie, Shoopiltee in Shetland, Tangie in the Orkneys, Neagle or Nuggle in Orkney and Shetlandl The Glashtin in the Isle of Man was equally sinister.

Waterman. Germany. One of the Nixies. Keightley 259–61.

Whuppity Stoorie. The Scottish Rumpelstiltskin. Henderson.

Wild Huntsman. The Leader of the Wild Hunt. Given various names, or sometimes the Devil, sometimes Odin, sometimes Jon or Dando.

Will o' the Wisp. Commonest name of the Ignis Fatuus, etc.

Wood Fairy. Scandinavian. A sinister character to meet, though occasionally propitious. Craigie, *Scandinavian Folk Lore*, 171.

Woodwives. Scandinavian. Harmless wood spirits, hunted by Odin.

Yallery Brown. The name of a small impet, fairy, something of the type of Tom-Tit-Tot, so malignant that it was dangerous to earn even his gratitude. Jacobs, *More English Fairy Stories.*

Yarthkins. Lincolnshire. Earth spirits. Malevolent if denied their due. Mrs Balfour, *Legends of the Lincolnshire Cars.*

BOOK LIST

Aarne, Antti and Thompson, Stith, *The Types of the Folktale*, Second Revision, Helsinki, 1961

Adam De La Hall, *Le Jeu d'Adam—Oeuvres Completes du Trouvere*, Paris, 1872

Agricola, G. (1490–1555), *De Animautibus Subterraneis*, Basle, 1621

Allingham, W. *Poems for the Children*, 'The Fairies'

Arndt, (quoted by T. Keightley), *Märchen und Jugenderinnerungen*, 1818

Arnold, M. 'The Forsaken Merman'

Atkinson, J. C. *Forty Years in a Moorland Parish*

Balfour, Mrs 'Legends of the Cars', *Folk-Lore*, II, 1891

Bourchiers, J. Lord Berners, *The Boke of Duke Huon of Bordeaux* done into English by Sir John Bourchier, Early English Text Society 1883–7

Bottrell, W. *Traditions and Hearthside Stories of West Cornwall*, Three Series, Penzance, 1870–90

Bovet, R. *Pandaemonium, or The Devil' Cloyster*, London, 1684

Bowker, J. *Goblin Tales of Lancashire*, London, 1883

Branston, B. *The Lost Gods of England*, London, 1957

Briggs, K. M. *A Dictionary of British Folk-Tales in the English Language*, 4 vols, London, 1970–71

Broome, D. *Fairy Tales from the Isle of Man*, 1951

Burne and Jackson, *Shropshire Folk-Lore*, London, 1883

Campbell, J. F. *Popular Tales of the West Highlands*, London, 1890–93

Campbell, J. G. *Superstitions of the Highlands and Islands of Scotland*, Glasgow, 1900

Carmichael, A. *Carmina Gadelica*, 4 vols., Edinburgh, 1928

Chaucer, G. 'Wife of Bath's Tale', Works O.U.P.

Child, F. J. *The English and Scottish Popular Ballads*, 5 vols., New York, 1957

Christiansen, Reidar, *Migratory Legends,—Folktales of Norway,—*'Some Notes on Fairies and the Fairy Faith' *Hereditas*, Dublin, 1975

Coote, H. C. 'The Neo-Latin Fay', Folk-Lore Record II

Craigie, W. A. *Scandinavian Folk-Lore*, London, 1896

Croker, T. Crofton, *Fairy Legends and Traditions of the South of Ireland*, 3 vols., London, 1825–8

Cromek, R. H. *Remains of Nithsdale and Galloway Song*, London, 1810

Curtin J. *Tales of the Irish Fairies*, 1895

Davidson, H. Ellis, *Scandinavian Mythology*, London, 1967

Denham Tracts, edited by J. Hardy, 2 vols., F.L.S. 1892

Douglas, G. *Scottish Fairy and Folk-Tales*, Walter Scott Publishing Company, London and Felling-on-Tyne

Dulac, E. *The Allies Fairy Book*, London, 1916, 'Urashima Taroo'

Evans, A. J. The Rollright Stones, *Folk-Lore Journal*, 1895

Gervase of Tilbury, *Otia Imperialia*, Hanover, 1856

Gibbings, W. W. *Folk Lore: Scotland*

Giraldus, Cambrensis, *The Itinerary through Wales*, Translated by Sir Richard Colt Hoare, London, 1863

Gould, S. Baring, *Lives of the Saints*, 16 vols., Edinburgh, 1914

Gregory, Augusta, *Gods and Fighting Men*, London, 1910

Grimms Fairy Tales, Translated by Margaret Hunt and J. Stern, London, 1948

Grimm, W. *Teutonic Mythology*, Translated by J. Stallybrass, 4 vols.

Gutch and Peacock, *County Folk-Lore V. Lincolnshire*, 1908

Hales, A. *The Golden Remains of the Ever-Memorable Mr. Hales*

Hartland, E. S. *The Science of Fairy Tales*, London, 1891

Hazlitt, W. Carew, *Fairy Tales, Legends and Romances Illustrating Shakespeare*, London, 1875

Henderson, G. *Popular Rhymes, Sayings and Proverbs of the County of Berwickshire*

Henderson, Hamish, 'Finger Lock'. Recorded from Walter Johnson. Archives of School of Scottish Studies.—'Johnnie in the Cradle'. Recorded by Hamish Henderson from Andrew Stewart. School of Scottish Studies.

Henderson, W. *Notes on the Folk-Lore of the Northern Counties*, 2nd edition, F.L.S. London, 1879

Hotham, Durant, Preface to the *Life of Jacob Behman*, London, 1654

Hunt, R. *Popular Romances of the West of England*, London, 1930

Hyde, D. *Beside the Fire*, London, 1890

Irving, I. Washington, *Rip Van Winkle*

Jacobs, Joseph, *English Fairy Tales*, London, 1890

James I, *Daemonologie, in Forme of a Dialogue*, Edinburgh, 1597

Joyce, P. W. *Old Celtic Romances*, 2nd Edition, London, 1894

Keightley, Thomas, *The Fairy Mythology, Illustrative of the Romance and Superstition of Various Countries*, Bohn Library, 1850

Kennedy, P. Legendary fictions of the Irish Celts; collected and narrated by P. Kennedy, 2nd Edition, London, 1891

Kirk, Robert, *The Secret Commonwealth of Elves, Fauns, and Fairies*, Edited by Stewart Sanderson, F.L.S.

Larousse, *Encyclopedia of Mythology*, Hamlyn Press 1959

Leather, E. M. *The Folk-Lore of Herefordshire*, London, 1912

Longfellow, Henry Wadsworth, 'The Golden Legend', *Poetical Works*, O.U.P., 1893

Mabinogion, The, Translated from the *White Book of Rhydderch*, and the *Rod Book of Hergest*, by Gwyn Jones and Thomas Jones, London, 1948 and Everyman Library, 1963

Macdougall and Calder, *Folk Tales and Fairy Lore*, London, 1910

Mackenzie, D. A. *Scottish Folk Lore and Folk Life*, London, 1935

MacManus, D. A. *The Middle Kingdom*, London, 1959

MacRitchie, David, *The Testimony of Tradition*, London, 1890—*Fians, Fairies and Picts*, London, 1893

M.S. British Museum, Harleian 6482

Map, Walter, *Nugis Curialium*, Translated by Frederick Tupper and Marbury Bladen Ogle, London, 1924

Miller, Hugh, *The Old Red Sandstone*, Edinburgh, 1841

Montgomery, Alexander, 'The Flouting of Polwart' Poems, Supplementary Volume, Edinburgh, 1910

Nutt, Alfred and Meyer, Kuno, *The Voyage of Bran, Son of Febal*, 2 vols., London, 1895–7

Ó Curry, E. *Lectures on the Manuscript Materials of Ancient Irish History*, Dublin, 1878
Ó Súilleabháin, Seán, *Folktales of Ireland*, (Folktales of the World), London, 1966
Otmar, *Traditions of the Harz*, (cited by E. S. Hartland in the *Science of Fairy Tales*)
Paterson, T. F. G. *Ulster Folk-Life*, 1938
Pitcairn, R. *Ancient Criminal Trials in Scotland*, Edinburgh, 1833
'Pranks of Robin Goodfellow' (often attributed to Ben Johnson), Reproduced by
    W. C. Hazlitt in *Fairy Tales, Legends and Romances Illustrating Shakespeare*,
    London, 1875
Ralph of Coggleshall, (12th Century Chronicles), Rolls Series 66, 1857
Rhys, John, *Celtic Folk-Lore, Welsh and Manx*, 2 vols., Oxford, 1901
Richardson, M. A. *The Local Historians Table-Book*, Newcastle-on-Tyne, 1846
Ritson, Joseph, *Fairy Tales*, now first collected, to which are prefixed Two Dis-
    sertations 1. On Pygmies, 2. On Fairies, London, 1831
Saxby, Jessie, *Shetland Traditional Lore*, Norwood Editions Reprint, 1974
Scot, R. *The Discovery of Witchcraft*, 1584. A Discourse on Devils and Spirits
    (Anon.) added to the 1655 Edition of *The Discovery of Witchcraft*
Scott, Walter, *The Poetical Works of Walter Scott*, Edinburgh, 1830. The Lady of the
    Lake. 'Ballad, Alice Brand.'—*Letters on Demonology and Witchcraft*, Edinburgh,
    1830—*The Minstrelsy of the Scottish Border*, ed. T. F. Henderson, 4 vols., Edin-
    burgh, 1932
Shetland Folk Book III
Sikes, Wirt, *British Goblins*, London, 1880
Simpkins, J. E. 'Folk-Lore of Clackmannanshire' *Scottish Journal of Topography*,
    1848—*Folklore of Fife, Clackmannan and Kinross, County Folk-Lore: VII*, F. L. S.
    1912
Spence, Lewis, *British Fairy Origins*, London, 1946
Stewart, W. Grant, *The Popular Superstitions of the Highlands*, 1823, Reprint Ward
    Lock 1970.
Surtees, R. *A County History of Durham*, 4 vols. Newcastle, 1816–40
Thompson, Stith, *Motif-Index of Folk Literature*, Copenhagen, 1955
Thoms, W. J. *Three Notelets on Shakespeare*, 'The Folk-Lore of Shakespeare', Lon-
    don, 1865
Thorpe, Benjamin, *Northern Mythology*, 3 vols., London, 1851–2—*Yule-Tide Stories*,
    'Toller's Neighbours', Bohn's Library, 1884
Tolkien, J. R. R. *The Fellowship of the Ring*, (Chapter 6: The Old Forest), London,
    1954
Tongue, Ruth, *Somerset Folklore*, County Folklore VIII, F. L. S. 1965—*Forgotten
    Tales of English Counties*, London, 1970
Train, J. *An Historical and Statistical Account of the Isle of Man, from the earliest times to
    the present day*, 2 vols., Douglas, 1845
Waldron, G. *A Description of the Isle of Man*, 1791, Reprinted for the Douglas Manx
    Society, 1865
Warner, William, *Albion's England*, 1602; *A Continuance*, London, 1606
Weston, Jessie L. *The Legend of Sir Lancelot du Lac*, London, 1901
Wentz, Evans, *Fairy Faith in Celtic Countries*, Oxford, 1911
Wilde, Lady, *Ancient Legends, Mystic Charms and Superstitions of Ireland*, 2 vols., Lon-
    don, 1887
Wood-Martin, W. G. *Traces of the Elder Faiths of Ireland: Pre-Christian Traditions*, 2

vols., London, 1902

Wright, E. M. *Rustic Speech and Folk-Lore*, Oxford, 1913

Yeats, W. B. *Irish Fairy and Folk Tales*, Scott Publishing Library

Zatzikhoven, Ulrich von, 'Lanzelet'. Translated, Webster, G. T., New York, 1956

INDEX OF TALE TYPES ༾༾༾༾༾

Folktales are named and classified on an international system based on their plots, devised by Antti Aarne and Stith Thompson in *The Types of the Folktale*, 1961; numbers in this system are preceded by AT. A further group of legends was classified by R. Th. Christiansen in *The Migratory Legends*, 1958, and his system was expanded by K. M. Briggs in *A Dictionary of British Folktales*, 1970–1. These numbers are preceded by ML, and the latter also followed by an asterisk. Brackets mean that the resemblance to the prototype is imperfect.

MOTIF INDEX ~~~~~~~~~~~~~~~

A motif is an element recurring within the plot of several folktales, e.g. 'cruel stepmother' (in 'Snow White', 'Cinderella', etc). These have been classified thematically in Stith Thompson's *Motif Index of Folk Literature*, 1966, and in E. Baughman's *Type and Motif Index of the Folktales of England and North America*, 1966. The numbering given below is drawn from these two books.

GENERAL INDEX

About the Author

Katharine Briggs was born in 1898, one of the three daughters of water-colorist Ernest Briggs. She studied English at Oxford, earning her Ph.D. with a thesis on folklore in seventeenth-century literature, and became a D.Litt., Oxon., in 1969. Her writings include *The Personnel of Fairyland, The Anatomy of Puck, Folktales of England, The Fairies in Tradition and Literature,* and *An Encylopedia of Fairies* and *British Folktales,* both published by Pantheon.

She has been president of the English Folklore Society, has taught and lectured in American universities, and has made friends in many parts of the world.